SON TECHNICAL INSTITUTE NORTH CAROLINA
STATE BOARD OF EDUCATION
DEPT. OF COMMUNITY COLLEGES
LIBRARIES

Library
Sampson Technical Institute

The Far Western Frontier

The Far Western Frontier

Advisory Editor
RAY A. BILLINGTON
Senior Research Associate
at the Henry E. Huntington Library
and Art Gallery

F
396
H64
1973

DRAGOON CAMPAIGNS

TO THE

ROCKY MOUNTAINS

BY A DRAGOON

[JAMES HILDRETH]

Library
Sampson Technical Institute

ARNO PRESS
A NEW YORK TIMES COMPANY
New York • 1973

Reprint Edition 1973 by Arno Press Inc.

Reprinted from a copy in The University of Illinois Library

The Far Western Frontier
ISBN for complete set: 0-405-04955-2
See last pages of this volume for titles.

Manufactured in the United States of America

Library of Congress Cataloging in Publication Data

[Hildreth, James]
    Dragoon campaigns to the Rocky Mountains.

    (The Far Western frontier)
    Reprint of the 1836 ed.
    1. United States. Army. 1st Cavalry.
2. Southwest, Old--Description and travel.
3. Indians of North America--Southwest, Old.
4. United States. Army--Military life. I. Title.
II. Series.
F396.H64 1973   976'.03   72-9449
ISBN 0-405-04977-3

DRAGOON CAMPAIGNS

TO THE

ROCKY MOUNTAINS;

BEING A HISTORY OF THE

Enlistment, Organization, and first Campaigns

OF THE REGIMENT OF

UNITED STATES DRAGOONS;

TOGETHER WITH INCIDENTS OF A SOLDIER'S LIFE, AND SKETCHES OF SCENERY AND INDIAN CHARACTER.

BY A DRAGOON.

"Though in old lands, beyond the heaving deep,
"Are tombs wherein imperial ashes sleep;
"Though feudal wrecks in solemn grandeur rise,
"Stirring the soul to lofty memories;
"Remains of long-forgotten nations rest
"Within the charnel caverns of the west;
"Beneath the verdure of our prairies lie
"The mournful relics of a world gone by;
"And guardian oaks, that whisper of the past,
"On antique mounds their darksome shadows cast."

NEW-YORK:

WILEY & LONG, No. 161 BROADWAY.

1836.

D. Fanshaw, Printer.

Entered, according to Act of Congress, in the year 1836, in the Clerk's Office of the Southern District of New-York.

TO THE

NON-COMMISSIONED OFFICERS

AND PRIVATES

OF THE REGIMENT OF

UNITED STATES DRAGOON'S,

The following Pages are inscribed,

AS A FEEBLE TRIBUTE OF RESPECT AND FOND REMEMBRANCE,

BY THEIR LATE COMPANION

AND FELLOW-SOLDIER,

THE AUTHOR.

PREFACE.

In preparing the following pages for the press, the author has culled from a large series of letters, those which contain information peculiarly connected with the subject under consideration, of course leaving out the greater portion of that kind of matter which usually fills up the pages of friendly correspondence.

Necessarily, such works must wear the appearance of roughness, from the sometimes disconnected manner in which they are thrown together; but this should rather be construed as a commendation than as a fault, because, oftentimes when an author would sit down to the task of revising such documents, for the purpose of weaving their contents into a pleasing narrative, they are apt to overstep the limits of their circumscribed boundary of truth, and soar away upon the wings of imagination, into the boundless and inviting realms of fiction.

Had the author been so disposed, he might have extended the limits of this work to the usual size of two octavo volumes; but his effort has been rather to condense than extend the records of the expedition, therefore, in selecting materials from a prolific correspondence, he has had to pick here and there a scrap, and cement them together as well as circumstances would admit. In regard to the various quotations interspersed throughout the work, he would merely say, that there were many points upon which he had neither opportunity or ability to inform himself, and consequently, his only means of supplying such deficiencies in the connection of the work as the nature of the case seemed to demand, was to resort to the pages of those authors who, by their scientific researches, had been enabled to furnish him with the required material.

At first, the manner in which to lay the incidents of the expedition before the public was a matter of serious consideration; and the reasons which led to the adoption of the present form, over that of a journal or narrative, was simply that the letters themselves would be better calculated to carry with them the impress of the truth, than if the story had been told in the smoother style of romantic narrative. A journal is too prolix, too digressive, too much mixed up with details containing no matter of interest whatever, except to the writer himself; therefore, except in some few instances, the attempt to give the details of a journey in such a form has been unfortunate.

There are many things of which he would speak in this preface in relation to his motives, both for having at all published a book, and also for having endeavored to compress the matter of which it is composed into a single volume. In the first place, when he left the army, he promised his late comrades that he would, as far as in him lay, advocate their cause, and lay some of the grievances and oppressions under which they suffer before the public; and in the following pages he has occasionally touched upon this theme, and although in some instances it may be imagined that he has written under the influence of excited feelings, yet he declares that he has written coolly and dispassionately, and exhibited the grievances of which he speaks, in by no means as bad a light as truth might allow. Had he been so disposed, he might have entered into detail of individual circumstances, and have related many a wrong that he has passed over as recorded in his private journal; and on account of the personal respect that he bears towards those concerned, has entirely omitted them. He very much regrets that he has been unable to procure a copy of an article that appeared in a St. Louis paper some two years since, relative to the treatment of the dragoons by their officers, which he believes was signed "VINDEX"—which article caused a great excitement at Jefferson Barracks, and, upon suspicion of having written which, a certain dragoon was compelled to undergo a trial before a court-martial, but was acquitted for want of evidence. The article in question was well written, and in all respects true—and he should have incorporated it into the body of this work, had he been able to procure it, for the purpose of substantiating his own account.

It will be perceived, that in the following pages are huddled together promiscuously, statistics, anecdotes, narratives, and reflections, the one as an antidote to the other. The author having indulged the hope that he might, by interspersing through his work a spice of merriment, relieve it from the perhaps tedious monotony of its necessary details.

The more immediate intention of the author was to throw together the prominent incidents of the Dragoon Campaigns, that each man engaged in the expedition might preserve the records of the scenes and actions connected therewith—and in after times, when he shall look back upon these scenes, that he may the more vividly bring back the recollection of them—and perchance when his infant boy shall lisp his predilection for a soldier's life, he may chide him to beware how he barters away his liberty to follow after the phantom of glory and renown.

To avoid the imputation of plagiarism, the

author would here take occasion to acknowledge all the different means made use of in the following compilation. In the first place, by far the greater portion of the work is the result of his own experience and observation during his term of service in the regiment of dragoons. The latter chapters are compiled from the private letters that he has constantly received since his return from his old companions, and to bring these letters more effectually into requisition, he has had recourse to the journal of Lieutenant Wheelock of dragoons, which being an official document, could be relied on as a correct detail of the circumstances attending the journey from Fort Gibson to the mountains. To the journal of the expedition performed in the years 1819-20, by the party under command of Major Long, the author of these pages has also had recourse—all the other extracts, and, indeed, these now referred to, are acknowledged in the body of the work, or in the notes prefixed thereto.

After the works that have already appeared,

treating of the vaunted regions of the far west, the author of these pages could hope to add nothing to a description that has luckily fallen into abler hands; therefore, independent of the immediate connection of his narrative, he has attempted but little to picture those scenes where nature has so richly displayed her powers of creation, and upon which fruitful theme Irving, Cooper, Paulding, Hoffman, and a host of other able and distinguished writers, have expatiated in glowing terms.

He has therefore taken, as the ground-work of his book, the incidents peculiarly connected with the formation, organization, and subsequent movements of the regiment of United States dragoons—a regiment enlisted under peculiar circumstances, and for special purposes, having enrolled in its ranks a band of young men, which, taken as a body, are an honor to their country, and an ornament to the army establishment.

To the members of the regiment—to the army generally—and to the friends and relatives of the dragoons, the details of the following pages may afford some matter of interest. Therefore, in case his book should fail to find readers among the public generally, he confidently hopes that it will not be neglected by those who should feel an interest in its welfare.

DRAGOON CAMPAIGNS.

LETTER I.

Enlistment—Commencement of Journey from Geneva—Arrival at Buffalo.

Buffalo, August 9th, 1833.

My dear Sir,

I may appear impatient to seize upon the kind offer of your friendship, in having thus soon embraced the privilege it affords me: I pray you to attribute it to my eagerness to commence a correspondence which I am well assured, will prove a source of pleasure and gratification to me; and, as I would fain believe, may in some measure be interesting to yourself, inasmuch as my letters will treat of subjects, as I anticipate, of a novel if not of a romantic character. As I am no stranger to the able productions of your pen, I rely upon being often cheered during my journeyings by its agreeable delineations. For some time yet you may not expect in my homely communications much matter of interest above the ordinary occurrences incidental to a long journey; but meanwhile, unwilling to lose the benefit of your answers, I will from time to time dedicate to you an epistle.

But to begin my news. At Geneva, immediately upon my arrival, I met with Lieut. B. and made known to him that I was now ready to enter upon the line of life for which you know I evinced an early predilection. He told me that he intended setting forward upon his journey the next morning, and accordingly that all things necessary must immediately be arranged. The ceremony of enlistment was but a momentary affair; that finished, I was what I had panted to be ever since I knew the meaning of the word—a soldier. Two or three flying visits occupied my time till evening, when we commenced the business of packing up. You cannot well imagine my eagerness to proceed: the Lieutenant often laughs at me for being in such haste to arrive at Head Quarters, but every thing that savors of military life has an indescribable charm for me, and I am sure that I shall never regret my course, your prophecy to the contrary notwithstanding. However, should I be disappointed, I can only blame my destiny; for although I am no Phrenologist, yet, if there is a word of truth in the doctrine, I have the bumps of a roving disposition most strongly developed. Joking aside, the prospect is delightful, whatever the reality may prove. The wild regions of the West, prairies, Indians, are all objects of intense interest to my romantic imagination, and should I chance to be spared to return again, after my campaigns, to the more tame regions of the East, I shall no doubt be wiser, and perhaps more willing to settle down than at present. Having so frequently traveled between your metropolis and this city of the west, and every object being so familiar as well to yourself as to me, it would be but taking up a trite theme were I to enter into any detail of my route thus far; but, as from this place forward every thing will wear the aspect of novelty, I imagine that I shall not be deficient in materials to work upon for the future. We have taken passage to Cleveland, and in all probability will again set forward to-morrow. Our point of destination is Jefferson Barracks, but Lieutenant B. being as ignorant of the best and most direct route as I am myself, and as but little regard to truth is to be paid to the information one may chance to get piecemeal from agents and contractors, (who, of course, all recommend the way whereby they themselves may be most benefited,) we shall proceed according to our own judgment.

The troop to which Lieutenant B. is attached, and to which he promises I shall be also, are on their route towards Head Quarters, having left Madison Barracks (the station on Lake Ontario, at Sackett's Harbor) last Wednesday; and as they therefore have three days advance of us, we shall hardly expect to overtake them on the road. I anticipate much pleasure from being attached to this troop. They are all "Yorkers," that is, from the western portion of our state, and therefore I shall not need to undergo any great change to become at once initiated. The Captain, too, is said to be an excellent man as well as a superior officer; so, all things considered, I shall no doubt fall into good hands. I assure you that I feel the utmost anxiety to join them; indeed I have so precipitately jumped into this scheme, that I have scarce made an inquiry in relation to it, either as to the exact object of the regiment or the duty upon which it will be employed. It was enough for me that a regiment was to be organized to "scour the prairies of the region beyond the waters of the Mississippi." That announcement carried conviction with it; and I am the victim of its influence, lead to what it may. In my next you shall have some of my future gleanings. As I shall be continually on the move, I will not request an answer to be directed to me on the route; therefore please superscribe your letters, "Jefferson Barracks."

Yours, &c.

LETTER II.

Journey continued from Buffalo to Steubenville, on the Ohio River.

Steubenville, Ohio, August, 1833.

DEAR SIR,

"Thank Heaven!" was the hearty ejaculation that I uttered upon seating myself in the parlor of the principal inn of this smoky town; and never was weary traveler more thankful for a moment's rest. It would be asking too much, to request you even to imagine so bad a road as that over which, for the last two days and nights, we have been traveling. But not to anticipate, I will return to the period of our leaving Buffalo. The morning was delightful, and the steamboat left the wharf heavily laden with freight, independent of two hundred passengers, including all sorts. After a pleasant sail of about two hours, a squall came on, which was so violent as to cause great destruction among the movables, and not less fear and uneasiness among the passengers. It continued raining violently throughout the whole afternoon and night, during which time we were tossed and buffeted about most unmercifully by the waves. At length morning appeared, but brought with it scarce a brighter prospect. The wind was still very high, although the rain had ceased. We soon came in sight of Erie, but found it impossible to land there, on account of the high sea; however, during the afternoon, after a great deal of difficulty, we came to alongside the wharf at Ashtabula. Unwilling to proceed any further by the boat, we ordered our luggage to be carried on shore, and determined to make the best of our way across the country to the Ohio river. Our better genius seemed to have directed us to this place, for a mail-coach was to be in readiness early the next morning to proceed directly on this route. A good night's rest and a hearty breakfast brought us again into traveling condition, and soon after daybreak we took the undisputed possession of the inside of the coach. The driver, with a loud crack of his whip, started off at a furious rate; and we seemed accidentally to have hit upon the very route of all others that we should rather have chosen. During the first twenty miles of our ride the road proved as level and smooth as one could wish, but afterwards commenced a series of hills and hollows, occasionally varied by a delightful strip of corduroy, as you may recollect a species of causeway is fancifully termed, which is constructed of logs closely placed together across the road, where otherwise there might be no possible way of making a substantial foundation, the nature of the soil being loose and springy. This species of turnpike is by far the most intolerable that I yet experienced. In many places the logs were decayed, and the consequence was a provoking succession of ups and downs, almost jolting us to death, and pitching us from one side of the coach to the other with an uninterrupted regularity. Owing to the sterility of the soil and the broken and hilly nature of the country, this portion of the state is but thinly populated; and as nothing of interest occurred or presented itself upon the route to divert the attention, I assure you that we were right glad to arrive at the end of a journey the most uncomfortable that can be well conceived. We passed through the town of Warren on the evening of the second day's ride, and this morning came in sight of the waters of the Ohio at Wellsville, where we arrived about sunrise. We were surprised to find the river, which at this place is quite narrow, wrapt in a thick mantle of cloud, which, as the sun arose, gradually disappeared. This phenomenon, we were informed, is not uncommon on these western waters. We had hoped to be able to take the steam boat from Wellsville, but, owing to the unusually low state of the water, boats could not proceed above Steubenville, for which place we started, after about three hours respite and a hearty meal.

What a contrast this place presents to the villages in the western region of our own state! There, every thing looks bright and new; here, a thick coat of black covers the whole town, and gives to every thing an appearance of gloom and wretchedness. This is caused by the atmosphere's being filled with dense clouds of coal smoke which issues from the chimneys of the various manufactories, all of which burn the Pittsburgh stone-coal. We called for rain-water to wash in, and that which was brought us looked more like dye stuff than any thing else to which I can compare it. This however is a town of growing importance and considerable size. The supper-bell is ringing; I will write from the Barracks immediately upon our arrival, if not again on the route.

LETTER III.

Journey continued from Steubenville to Jefferson Barracks.

Jefferson Barracks, August, 1833.

MY DEAR SIR,

After a long and tedious journey we arrived at this post. I was gratified to find among the letters that awaited my arrival, one from yourself, and I sincerely hope that it may be the precursor of a regular correspondence. In my last I gave you an account of my progress as far as Steubenville, from which place the next morning we took passage to Wheeling, one of the prettiest and most bustling little cities in this part of the country, built upon a commanding site on the west bank of the Ohio river, in the extreme corner of the State of Virginia. From this place to Columbus we were rapidly hurried along over the great Cumberland road—which, by the by, is the most splendid example of perseverance, and at the same time one of the most advantageous improvements yet undertaken in this section of the country. After a few hours' stay at this flourishing town, we again took the stage for the metropolis of the West, and found ourselves next day at a spacious hotel in the city of Cincinnati, having journeyed the whole distance from Wheeling, over a country than which no other is more lovely and interesting. This part of Ohio reminds me of the western portion of our own State, not indeed so densely settled, but exhibiting much of that appearance of freshness and enterprise so strikingly developed in the almost fairylike growth of our towns and villages. Xenia and Springfield are the most conspicuous of the many through which we passed. We remained a day or two at Cincinnati, and again varying our mode of conveyance, took passage on board a steamer bound for Louisville, Ky. owing to the very low state of the water, we were somewhat longer than usual in performing this portion of our journey. Thus far our route has furnished me with nothing worthy of special remark; but the subsequent incidents of our passage from Louisville to this place partake rather more of the romantic character. I might indeed have furnished you with a description of scenery; but it possessing no particular feature of interest, I concluded that the bare mention of such details would scarcely serve to interest you; and besides, of late years this route has become so great a thoroughfare, that any remarks which I might make would only be a work of supererogation. At Louisville we met Lieut. Colonel Kearney, who informed us that Captain Summer's troop had embarked on board the steamer Helen Mar about a week before. This you may remember is the troop to which I anticipated being attached. At another time I would have taken much pleasure in noticing more minutely the various scenes through which we passed; but my mind has been continually occupied in the anticipation of our prospective campaign, and every thing, except affairs of a military nature, appear tame to me. I think even now, as I write, that I can see you smile at my enthusiasm, and shake your head doubtingly at my anticipations ever being realized; but variety has ever been my watchword through life, and, even should an occasional dark cloud obscure the brighter prospect for a season, it serves to render its return the more cheering. Once more shifting our baggage, we became the incumbents of a spacious cabin of one of the splendid steamers which ply between the various ports of this noble stream, and about four o'clock the same afternoon, recommenced our journey down the Ohio. This we imagined would be our last change of the sort; but it proved otherwise, as the sequel will show. The first twenty miles of our route was performed without interruption; but coming suddenly in contact with a sand-bar, our boat was "brought up," to use a cant phrase, "all standing;" and so unexpected was the shock, that a thousand vague conjectures were in an instant formed as to the cause, before we became acquainted with the fact. After we had all hastened upon deck, and the ears of the captain had been assailed with an hundred inquiries as to the matter, we began to think of a remedy. It was soon discovered that we were fairly grounded upon a sand-bar, and so firmly bedded, that our utmost efforts to disengage the boat seemed fruitless.

" What's to be done ?" inquired the passengers.

" We must try to work her into channel, or we must wait for a rise," replied the captain.

" *Wait for a rise!*" exclaimed the passengers one and all, and a kind of sympathetic sigh went through the whole of them.

"However," said the captain, "we must first try and get her into the channel."

And accordingly, suiting the action to the word, he jumped overboard, and was soon followed by both crew and passengers, who, after repeated efforts by rocking the boat from side to side, at length got her afloat; and, after working her into deeper water, we again got on board and proceeded on our way; and, without having experienced any serious obstruction during the afternoon, "*turned in*" soon after tea, in hopes to wake in the morning and find ourselves well advanced upon our journey; but alas, we awoke to a most provoking disappointment, for we were but three miles further than when we lay down, having again, during the night, grounded upon another bar, from which, after long and repeated attempts, we found it impossible to get her off: therefore the only way to get along comfortably was to play the part of the philosopher and trust to Providence. Morning passed away, the bell rang for dinner, but we had no appetites, vexation seemed to have eradicated every other feeling. After dinner, almost all the passengers, for the purpose of more effectually killing time, went to sleep. I however went on deck, and, with my segar in my mouth, and taking up the whole of three chairs, determined to make the best of a bad bargain; and thus sat, puffing away care, for the greater part of two hours, as patiently (at all events, in appearance) as Job himself could have behaved in like circumstances. This river, which winds itself along in most fantastic curves and angles, exposed, at the peculiar point at which we lay, a view of the stream for several miles in either direction; and as I sat in the comfortable attitude which I before hinted, something like a boat in appearance glided round the point of land, which before had hid it from my view, and slowly sailed towards us. Taking advantage of the first opportunity that presented itself, I immediately awakened Lieut. B. and urged him to take passage on board of her, whatever she might prove to be. Accordingly our baggage was got in readiness, and we hailed her as she was gliding by us in all the pristine glory that these lumbrous conveyances seemed to enjoy before the usurpation of their territory was effected by the introduction of steamers, for she turned out to be a "broad-horn," as this species of craft is euphonically called. It put me in mind of the pictures I had seen of Noah's ark more than any thing of recent invention. Willing, however, to take the advantage of even the unpromising accommodations which she might afford, we stood but little upon appearances.

She sent her yawl alongside; and in half an hour we were again on our way down the river. The next thing to be done was to lay in something to eat during the voyage; and accordingly appointing one of our company "steward," he with the yawl went on shore and laid in a fine supply of bacon hams and hard biscuit, to say nothing of the peaches and melons, which he said the fellow "hove in for greens." Thus supplied, and having with the means of proceeding on our journey recovered our spirits, we once more began to be cheerful; and the remainder of the day passed off more pleasantly. But alas, how the sweet and bitter things of this world are mingled together! bedtime came, but no bed was there.

"*Heigh-ho!*" said the Lieutenant, as he threw his cloke across the flour barrels, and taking a little keg of ten-pennies for a pillow, resigned himself to the keeping of the drowsy god.

"*Heigh-ho!*" thought I too, when, after having searched the hold of the boat from stem to stern for my own cloke to do likewise, at length found one half of it stowed snugly away under one of my fellow-passengers, who, in a strife for it with his neighbor, had between them rent it in twain, and were each enjoying themselves upon the severed portions of it. Leaving them to their sleepy enjoyment, I climbed up on deck, and, picking for the *softest plank*, stretched myself upon it and soon fell asleep.

We remained for three days on board of the broadhorn, and having moved along so smoothly, almost entirely forgot the vexations that we had experienced in consequence of the sand-bars; but being overhauled by another steamer bound down stream, and drawing, as the captain assured us on his honor, less water than any other boat on the river, we thought best again to shift our quarters, hoping thereby to make more rapid progress. Again moving our luggage on board the steamer, we bade adieu to our good friends the captain and crew of the broad-horn, who were as clever a set of fellows as ever pushed a sweep against the tide. However, our change proved to be of no avail in the end; for although we met with no obstructions on the first day and night, yet the next morning bringing us to that part of the river opposite the mouth of the Cumberland, our boat grounded on the bar which is also distinguished by that name. And here we remained despite all our efforts to the contrary, and might have remained until the fall freshet, had no vessel come to our assistance; but on the morning of the next day, as we were at breakfast, our ears were saluted by the sound of a familiar voice, which screamed out, "Hollo there, stranger!" springing to the deck, to our great joy we saw the identical broadhorn which had before so opportunely come to our assistance, with her good natured captain standing on deck.

"I say, stranger, didn't I say that old 'Slow and Easy' was a sure thing in the end?" said he exultingly—" How are you, *Leftenant*?" "How are you, old friend?" answered Lieutenant B.

" Why, better off, I reckon, than that 'ere steamer; why, she's as fast *sot* as the old sycamore root; *prehaps* you'd like to try the old 'Slow and Easy' again."

Overjoyed at the idea of going ahead again, even at the snail-pace rate that the broad-horn proceeded, he signified his wish to do so, and in a few moments we again became the occupiers of our old quarters on board the broad-horn, determined not again to be induced upon any account to leave her until she should arrive at the mouth of the river.

The Ohio is a noble stream, differing from the other large rivers of this country both in the swiftness of its current, width of its bed and character of its channel. The obstruction to its navigation, as has before been hinted, is caused by the sand-bars in a stage of low water, together with snags, sawyers and rapids. During a middle or high stage these obstructions entirely disappear; and the only difficulty then to be encountered is an accelerated current. The navigation of this river may be relied on from about the middle of February to the end of June, and again the water is increased by a fall freshet, which usually takes place in October or November. The scenery of its banks is neither striking nor peculiarly tame; many places might be favorably noticed, but the description would be familiar to all, as of late years this route has become a thoroughfare to the whole world of country on the south as well as to the west and north.

Once more relieved from the monotony of lying upon a sand-bar, we were now sailing down that portion of the Ohio which glides between the shores of Kentucky upon one side, and Illinois and Indiana on the other. The good natured captain of the broad horn tried to do every thing that lay in his power to render our quarters on board of his boat as comfortable as possible; he was one of that facetious kind of fellows that this portion of the country abounds in, a thorough-bred Kentuckian, full of *chin music*, as the species of loquacity which he possessed is termed here, that is, he never found himself in want of words, but, on the contrary, an argument, or perchance a song, if the occasion admitted of it, all came within the limit of his powers. In fact, the man saw our impatience, and truly he did much to alleviate it. Another character, however, of this motley crew, is worthy of remark. He was a man somewhat above the middle stature, and of a sunburned complexion, but with a set of features that denoted a more than ordinary man; a noble and projecting forehead, and a Roman nose, gave a prominency to his appearance that one could not help but observe; but there was a wildness of expression about his eye which told that reason had partially resigned her empire over his mind. He cheerfully and steadily performed his duty, which was to take his turn at the oars or sweeps by which our boat was propelled. His beard had been neglected for several weeks, and, from its uncouth appearance, made the contrast between it and his noble features the more striking.

After evening had closed upon us, and our lumbrous vessel heavily groped her way through the waters, I went upon deck, and found the man that I have been describing, who had just before been relieved from his oar, lying upon his back, and gazing intently upon the moon as she shone brightly in her full orbed splendor; and although I seated myself close beside him, he neither moved nor appeared to notice me; at length he broke out into an apostrophe to the queen of night, and for a long time continued in a wild and almost sublime strain of Ossian-like poetry, till apparently recovering from the thraldom of lunacy, he ceased, and raising himself from his reclining posture, sat beside me for some time silent ; at length I drew him into a conversation, and allowing him to follow the bent of his own mind, he turned the topic upon England and her internal policy ; he discoursed with a fluency and familiarity that proved his acquaintance with the subject, and as he expatiated in glowing terms upon the characters that for ages past had figured upon the soil of Britain, his oratory became vehement and impressive. I gazed upon him with astonishment, and wondered how one so apparently moulded for greatness could have fallen so low. I dared not ask his name, lest I should betray a curiosity which in reality I felt; but at length, however, I inquired why he left England. " Because," said he, " I am a Republican."

And drawing himself up to his full height, " Yes," said he, " the son of Richard Brindly Sheridan is a Republican."

I involuntarily started. What! was he, the miserable being before me, the son of the mighty Sheridan ? I ventured to question him, but his mind had caught another channel, and was hurriedly flowing along with it; his words seemed the impulse of immediate thought, and passed from him only to give utterance to new. If it be so, thought I, nature hath freaks, and this is one of them. We parted, and I retired for the night.

The next morning we arose bright and early, and

had the gratification of hearing that we were not far from the mouth of the river, which was, of all other intelligence, the most pleasing to us, as we had now been so long upon the water, and under so many and trying vicissitudes, as to have become somewhat weary. No obstruction or event worthy of notice took place, until about two o'clock in the afternoon. All the passengers were enjoying a little nap in the hold upon the flour barrels, when I was awakened by a shout from the captain of our boat.

"Hollo there, Ben, isn't that 'ere boat ahead there the Helen Mar?"

"I reckon 'tis," replied Ben, "for she's got two white chimneys."

"Why," replied the captain, "them 'ere soldiers might have footed it faster than she's carried 'um."

The mention of soldiers naturally aroused me, and I jumped on deck. "What soldiers are you talking about, captain?" I asked. "Why, some of them 'ere Horse Dragoons that's come from York State; they've been ever since two weeks ago last Monday since they left Louisville, and there they are tight aground, and likely to be so, for all I know."

Lieut. B. now came on deck, and learning that the troop to which we were to be attached were on board the boat that lay aground about half a mile before us, ordered that our baggage should be again got in readiness to make another move; and soon after we were again settled in the yawl, and bidding adieu to the captain and crew, steered for the Helen Mar.

As we approached the shore I observed several young men (attired in what I afterward learned to be the fatigue uniform, a blue roundabout trimmed with yellow lace, white pantaloons, and forage caps) standing upon the beach, and as we landed many others approached, and immediately we found ourselves surrounded with those who were to be our future associates.

One of the number, who appeared to wear the air and carriage of an old soldier, touched his cap as he came up to me, and in a very respectful manner remarked that the Captain was on board the boat, and had sent them to see our baggage taken care of, adding, as he again touched his cap, " Lieutenant, it shall all be attended to."

Turning to him immediately, I remarked that he had mistaken my rank ; nevertheless, I was gratified at the compliment of being mistaken for the Lieutenant.

" There," said I, " is the Lieutenant ; I am only a recruit." At this, his reserve forsook him, and finding that he was not addressing an officer, he became quite familiar, and introduced me to the others around him. I in a few moments, therefore, became as an old acquaintance with them all.

My first introduction to the troop being over, I put on my laced jacket and forage cap, and having thus speedily effected my transformation, was no longer the citizen, but the youthful soldier, buoyant with expectation, and eager to enter upon a line of life that was at least new, and promised to be as pleasing as continual change of scene can make it. My companions are generally about my own age, and having been born and bred in the same State with myself, no change of habits or manners was requisite to become immediately associated with them. They were not old soldiers, or I should have received more severe handling from them; for I have now learned that when a recruit joins an old company, he has to pay pretty dearly for the inconvenience that his awkwardness occasions the rest, and, like the jokes practiced upon the youthful mariner when he first crosses the ocean, the more good naturedly he takes it the better for himself.

Now for the first time did I begin to realize that I was a soldier; for while I had been traveling with the Lieutenant,* I had received no treatment from him that reminded me of the difference of rank between us.

Two days after we had joined the company on board the Helen Mar, she was got off the sand bar, and without farther interruption we soon after arrived at the mouth of the Ohio; after a short stay here we doubled the point and began to beat up against the powerful tide of the Mississippi, and on the evening of the second day arrived at about one mile below Jefferson Barracks.

My notes would furnish me with other incidents of minor importance, but presuming that this long letter must ere this have wearied you, I conclude by requesting you would write often, and by adding in the language of Chesterfield—*Jubeo te valere.*

---

* I can truly say that, throughout my whole term of service in the army, my treatment by that gentleman was ever more of the friend than the officer—and with no greater pleasure do I note down any event of these campaigns, or aught connected with the army, than to award the title of gentleman to an officer. I shall ever respect Lieutenant Bergwin as one marked out peculiarly among his fellows as deserving of the title of gentleman as truly as he merits the name of being an excellent officer.

LETTER IV.

Remarks relative to the organization of the Regiment—Instructions from Hon. J. C. Calhoun to Major Long, in 1819—Enlistment of Rangers after the Black Hawk War—Disbanding of Rangers, and enlistment of Dragoons—-Bad arrangement in regard to clothing.

Jefferson Barracks, September, 1833.

MY DEAR SIR,

You are undoubtedly impatient to learn something concerning our organization, and I will endeavor in this letter to lay before you all in relation to it that I have myself learned. Excuse me, however, if I preface them with some remarks which may serve as an introduction to the subject.

As early as the spring of 1819 the settlement of that vast tract of territory extending between the Mississippi river and the Rocky Mountains was looked upon as an object sufficiently near at hand to warrant the fitting out of an expedition to explore it. In the preliminary notice to the records of that expedition, which in 1823 was published under the title of " Maj. Long's expedition to the Rocky Mountains," we find the object of the campaign contained in the following instructions from the Hon. J. C. Calhoun, then Secretary of War, to Major Long.

1. " You will assume the command of the expedition to explore the country between the Mississippi and the Rocky Mountains.

2. " You will first explore the Missouri and its principal branches, and in succession the Red River, Arkansas, and Mississippi above the mouth of the Missouri.

3. "The object of the expedition is to acquire as thorough and adequate knowledge as may be practicable of a portion of our country which is daily becoming more interesting, but is as yet imperfectly known; with this view you will permit nothing to escape your attention. You will ascertain the latitude and longitude of remarkable points with all possible precision. You will, if practicable, ascertain some point in the 49th parallel of latitude which separates our possessions from those of Great Britain: a knowledge of the extent of our limits will prevent collision between our trades and theirs.

4. "You will enter on your Journal every thing in relation to soil, face of the country, water courses, and productions, whether animal, vegetable, or mineral. You will conciliate the Indians by kindness and presents, and will ascertain, as far as practicable, the number and character of the various tribes, with the extent of country claimed by each.

5. "Great confidence is reposed in the acquirements and zeal of the citizens who will accompany the expedition for scientific purposes, and a confident hope is entertained that their duties will be performed in such a manner as to add both to their own reputation and that of our country." &c. &c.

Copious and interesting as the Journal of this expedition is, possessing as it does a collection of matter that evinces the faithful discharge of their duties, as well as the intimate acquaintance with those duties, on the part of the scientific gentlemen connected with the expedition, still we are told by the compiler that the work is far less extensive than was contemplated, and indeed than was specified in the foregoing orders, which however was on account of the retrenchment in all expenditures of a public nature that took place about that time; and consequently the means necessary to the prosecution of the expedition being withheld, the officers were recalled, and all farther researches abandoned. Since this expedition was concluded, however, this country has been fast settling to the west, and a large portion of what was then wilderness is now thickly inhabited.

The field over which our regiment will roam, will for the most part lie west of the Arkansas, comprising that vast wilderness of fertility extending to those piles of towering and fantastic rocks that rear their lofty heads above the clouds. A district so unknown, so wild, so vast, and so laden with interest as this, must carry with it, even in a description, a deep and strong feeling of interest, especially to us, who may within the bounds of reasonable calculation look forward to the time in our own days when the rapid increase of this country will have disrobed the prairie of its wild verdure and loveliness, and reared upon its soil the habitation of the farmer, the tradesman, and the mechanic. Description can convey no adequate idea of that region where nature seems to have wrought upon so grand a scale. where the impenetrable forest, extending over unmeasured space, echoes back in wild and solitary grandeur the accents of the still wilder notes that it listens to; where the prairie sweeps, like the wave of ocean, so far on every side that the horizon alone can bound it; where stupendous mountains rear their rock-imbedded crests to the heavens; where the wild elk and buffalo range over their native plains; and where the stately savage, the lord of his inheritance, gazes toward the horizon on either side, nor dreams that the world contains aught else than the hunting ground of his fathers, and the tribe that honors him as their chief.

What a field is here for the moralist, painter, poet, or historian ! Here, the eye never tires of roaming, for, even upon the prairie, the infinite variety of herb and flower, of every hue and aspect, affords a gratifying subject of contemplation to the casual observer as well as to the scientific botanist. Here it is that man feels the true spirit of devotion to his Creator, for all around him is calculated to impress upon his feelings a sense of his power and greatness. Standing amidst the mighty expanse that surrounds him, his mind naturally reverts to the greatness of that Being, whose word of power spoke worlds into existence, and contrasting his own comparative nothingness with the grandeur of creation, he can better appreciate the omnipotence of his Creator. There is a moral sublimity in scenes like these : calm and quiet, the mind may here roam undisturbed and gain new expansion with every exercise.

To me the reflection is a melancholy one, that ere long the time will come when this glorious region shall be changed into the crowded mart of traffic ; that the woodman's axe shall resound and reverberate through these mighty forests ; that soon the last Indian must be swept from off the land that his ancestors reigned over; and that these vivid scenes which the adventurous traveler now looks upon as fraught with a living interest, must ere long only be numbered with the things that were. But such is the march of improvement, such the rapid settlement of western America, that, if we may be allowed to judge of what will be by what has been, the subjugation of this whole western world to the renovating influence of industry and art is not far distant.

But a truce to this long digression—my anticipation has carried me over the ground more rapidly than my horse will; but to return to plain matter of fact, I will attempt to relate the causes which led to the formation of our regiment, and what may be our destination.

During the summer of 1832, Gov. Reynolds, of Illinois, ordered out 1500 mounted men, who joined the regular troops, under command of General Atkinson and Colonel Dodge, at Winnebago. After the termination of that series of Indian disturbances which ended in the capture of Black Hawk, many of these men enlisted in the different companies of mounted rangers, which Congress ordered to be raised for the more perfect defence of the frontiers bordering upon the lands of the Indians. They were to find their own horses and equipments, government supplying them only with provision. These companies occupied the greater portion of their year of enlistment in foraging, and they were discharged at the expiration of their term of service, which was but a few months since. Previous to this, the President proposed the enlisting of six companies of dragoons, of one hundred men each; which proposition coming before Congress, it was, after several amendments, at length carried, that a regiment of dragoons, consisting of ten companies, of seventy-one men each, should be organized and stationed upon the western frontier. The orders for the enlistment of this corps were issued last March, and Officers from the different regiments of infantry were appointed upon this service. Five of these companies were ordered to be organized at the Head Quarters of the regiment (which was appointed at Jefferson Barracks) this fall, and the other battalian the ensuing spring.

It was the policy of government to allow no sectional feelings towards this corps. To effect this, they appointed depots in almost every section of the Union, and when the regiment came together at the Head Quarters, nearly every State in the Union was found to have its representatives.

The immense tide of emigration to the regions of the West, and the rapidity with which the States bordering on the Mississippi were settling, had induced all that class of adventurers, who hate nothing more than society, to quit these densely populated places, and as fast as they were incommoded by their neighbors' settling so near them that they could see the smoke from their cabin chimneys curling up above the tops of the forest trees, they began to imagine that emigration was too rapidly coming upon them, and consequently they, to use their own words, "had to pull up stakes," and seek some more retired abode, amid the still deeper solitudes of the West.

Thus arose collisions and disputes between the squatters and the different tribes of Indians that inhabit, in wandering communities, this wild and luxuriant region; and thus, as has been before intimated, was this regiment of dragoons to be stationed upon the far western frontier, for the more perfect defence of the white settlers against the depredations and attacks of the Indians.

Some of the troops that had been enlisted in the neighboring states arrived at this port, which was appointed for the head-quarters of the regiment, as early as the first part of May, from which it may be seen how little time was employed in their enlistment; the orders having been published only the March preceding, and on the sixth day of the present month the last troop took up their quarters here, having been enlisted in the western part of the state of New-York, under command of Capt. E. V. Sumner and Lieut. Burgwin, to which troop your humble servant is also attached. The officers now assembled at this post, attached to the dragoon service, are Col. Dodge, Lieut. Col. Kearney, Maj. Mason, Adj. Lieut. J. Davis, belonging to the Staff; Capt. Clifton Wharton, in command of Company " A," Capt. E. V. Sumner, of Company " B," Capt. Holmes, of Company " C," Capt. Hunter, of Company " D," and First Lieut. David Perkins, of Company " E," which last troop is composed of young men from the city of New-York, Lieuts. Burgwin, Swords, Van Deveer, Lupton, Ury, Edwards, Watson, Northrop, Cooke, &c. the subaltern officers not all having as yet arrived.

To give any adequate idea of the appearance of this regiment when they were for the first time drawn up in line, would be a task of no ordinary difficulty; but if you will please to recollect the description of Jack Falstaff's ragged regiment, you may form some idea of this one.

Having been assured by the recruiting officers that their military clothing was in readiness for them at the Head Quarters, they were induced to part with or leave behind them every rag of clothing except what they might deem sufficient to serve them until their arrival there; and the result was, that as there was no clothing at all at the Barracks, the most of the dragoons soon began to grow gradually threadbare. I am not now complaining on my own account; for Capt. Sumner, as well as Lieut. Perkins, who has command of another troop, (also from our own state,) with a foresight for which they deserve great credit, provided their men with a full supply of every article of clothing necessary for their comfort as well as uniform appearance. The other three troops present rather a ragged appearance, and there has been some murmuring among them; I for one, however, am determined to put up with every thing as well as I can, and hope to be fully compensated, by the novelty and enjoyment of our prospective movements, for all minor evils.

We have no course marked out yet. I think that we shall remain in quarters here this winter. We are drilled every day in the manual, and will not receive our horses for some time to come. I have a rather laughable account of our first drill to communicate to you, but my time will not allow me to protract this scrawl any farther.

Do not fail to send me papers regularly.

Yours, &c.

LETTER V.

Breaking-in Drill—Reception of Muskets—Description of Officers.

Jefferson Barracks, September, 1833.

Dear Sir,

In my last I promised you an account of our first drill; I can do but little toward describing so ludicrous a scene; but you shall have it, as I noted, at the time, the description in my journal. It runs thus:

Having been allowed two days to recover from the languor and fatigue incidental to our journey, our company was reported for duty; and accordingly a detail was made from our ranks for guard the next day. The remainder of the company were assembled in the afternoon for drill; and now commenced a scene that yielded much to the enjoyment of those who were our seniors by only a few weeks in the service. Sergeant Roberts (the same man that I before have had occasion to notice) was the only one in the troop that knew how to put his left foot foremost; and to attempt to describe the ludicrous piece of work we made of it, would be entirely out of the question; however, we were drawn up in line, and the command was given, "*right dress!*" Every one looked at the Sergeant to see how he did it; and after a good deal of shuffling and squinting, we presented somewhat of a fair front. The orders to let the arms hang loosely, to keep the little finger straight down the seam of the pantaloons, and to turn the toes out to a proper angle, at the same time to keep the chin erected to its proper height, all followed in regular and rapid succession; and when we were thus modified according to the "Rules and Articles," we must have had the appearance of so many statues. The company thus arranged, the captain cast upon us a smile of complacency, and walked around to the rear for a more minute inspection.

" Turn your toes out more, Cooke; and you, Grantor, let your arms hang more loosely, and hold up your head," said he, when he had again taken a glance at the front.

" *Very well, that,*" said the captain, when these requisitions had been complied with, (which was the expression that he always used when any thing was done to his liking.)

Taking advantage of the hints that had been given to my companions, I screwed myself into the position that I imagined to be nearest in accordance with the prescribed rules, (a position, by the by, as uncomfortable as one may well imagine,) but for all that I did not escape being the subject of a special remark; for the captain soon after, pointing to me, asked in a stern tone of voice,

" Where's your stock, sir ?"

I replied that I had left it in the Barrack-room, at the same time wondering how he could perceive that I was without it, for my jacket collar was buttoned close up in my neck.

" Go and put it on, sir, and never again come half-dressed upon parade," was his only reply.

These little matters at length being all properly adjusted, we commenced operations, and spent full an hour and a half in marching in open files (that is, individually) across the parade ground, each one taking his turn of becoming the subject of a titter throughout the troop.

Again formed in line, the command was given:

"Attention!"—"column forward!"—"guide right!" "march!"

At the last word some put forward the right foot, others the left, some looking to one flank, some to the other, and before we had got six paces ahead, there were no two marching together.

"Halt!" cried the captain.

"Right dress!" screamed the sergeant, and once more we were got into shape.

"Try that again, and see if you cannot manage to put forward the left foot, and keep dressed on the sergeant."—"Attention!"—"column forward!"—"guide right!"—"march!"

This time all except three put forward the left foot, and we managed to keep together for some fifteen or twenty paces; when by that time our front becoming somewhat semi-circular, we again received the order to "halt!"

We repeated this manœuvre several times; but Cooke and one or two others still persisting in putting forward the right foot instead of the left; the captain lost all patience, and dismissing the rest of the troop, ordered them in the *awkward squad*, to have half an hour's extra drill.

Thus ended our first day's duty, and some of us already began to feel that we knew almost as much as the captain himself.

Time and practice, however, has corrected many of our mistakes, except poor Cooke, who never could learn to put his left foot forward. He deserted, however, the next week; and, fortunately for both himself and the service, he has not since been heard of.

Having thus mastered the breaking-in drill, we were now to commence the manual; and for the first time since we had been soldiers, was a musket placed in our hands; these however were in no way dangerous, being a lot of condemned pieces that had lain in the arsenal since the last war; and however well they answered the purpose of "shouldering arms," they were nevertheless deficient as to the " aim," and altogether refractory at the command, "fire!" for, with the exception of one or two that had been carelessly packed away loaded, and, after repeated snapping, went off, to the disquieting of the nerves of the fellows that held them, I believe none of them were capable of doing any injury.

It was really laughable to see one of these pieces brought to bear, by a sentinel, upon some luckless fellow who might chance to have wandered after dark beyond the precincts of the barracks:—"Stand!" cried the sentinel, in the peculiar accents of authority, at the same time levelling his piece, which would have been as effectual, had he really wanted to fire it, as a broomstick.

But, nevertheless, we soon learned how to handle them, and are beginning to be·exercised upon the more intricate principles of tactics, such as skirmishing, ambush fighting, and the different manœuvres that serve to show that war may be reduced to a science, and how to take advantage of circumstances.

Perhaps you would like some description of our officers. Col. Dodge is in command of the regiment, a man about say fifty, thick set, somewhat gray, a thorough backwoodsman, very fond of talking over his own exploits; he was, I believe, a militia general, and obtained the colonelcy of this regiment on account of his late exertions during the Black Hawk war on the whole a clever man, but not much of a soldier. Next in command comes Lieut. Col. Kearney. This officer has not yet, however, joined the regiment at Head Quarters. Report speaks highly of his skill in tactics. A few days after our arrival here, an errand brought me early in the morning to the Major's quarters. After I had twice knocked at the door, he called out in somewhat of a surly tone, "Come in!" whereupon I obeyed the summons, and next minute stood in the presence of Major M. He had not yet made his toilet, and sat at the breakfast table *sans culotte*, surrounded by his four favorite dogs. The apartment presented a bachelor-like appearance, and my first glance gave me no very favorable impression of its inmate. I have heard that he was a man severe to a fault, and although well esteemed by his brother officers on account of his soldiership, yet not much of a favorite with those under his command. Our company officers are generally men well selected for this service; and, as is natural, each troop think their own officers best. As for myself, I am, as Addison says, only a "*spectator*"—a looker on; and although one of the number, I often forget that I have aught else to do than to notice the movements of others. As yet, we have only known the life of a soldier in barracks, which I admit is rather monotonous; but the field and the camp are before us. My duties compel me to close.

      I remain your friend, &c.

LETTER VI.

Disappointment of Dragoons——Disaffection and Desertion—Description of Jefferson Barracks—Dragoons made to build Stables—Comments—Deserter whipped—Comments.

Jefferson Barracks, October, 1833.

DEAR SIR,

I will no longer withhold from you the fact, that there is much murmuring and disaffection in our regiment, and I must say, justly so. Desertions are becoming every day more and more numerous. I complain of nothing individually, but the treatment of this corps has been very different from any thing we had reason to expect. A few weeks since we mustered, independent of the five full troops, a detachment consisting of upwards of forty men; now there is not left the entire strength of the five troops. Five, six, and even eight, have deserted in a single night; not only privates, but corporals and sergeants.

The high commendations that were every where heard in relation to this corps, and the glowing and artful stories of those whose duty it was to enlist men for the service, induced young men to enroll themselves in this regiment, who, in point of talent, appearance and respectability, perhaps never were surpassed in the history of military affairs. Many were enlisted under the express declaration that they were to rank with the cadets at the military academy, and under the belief that they were rather to be considered as a volunteer corps, whose wants and comforts were to be attended to, and that they should not be subjected to the more severe restrictions of army discipline. Many were told, when they were entreated to enlist, that they would have nothing to do but to ride on horseback over the country, to explore the western prairies and forests, and, indeed, spend their time continually in delightful and inspiring occupations; and particularly and often was the remark made, that it would disgrace a dragoon even to speak with an infantry soldier. I only mention these things to show how so superior a band of young men could have been induced to enlist themselves as common soldiers in the illiberal army of America, where the very fact of a man's being a soldier seems to imply that he is fit for no other employment.

Widely different from their anticipations the members of this deluded regiment found themselves placed immediately upon their arrival at Head Quarters. Instead of enjoying any of the privileges and comforts that had been promised to them, they now found that they were nothing above the other portions of the army; indeed, subject to all the duties of the infantry soldier, in addition to those that peculiarly belong to the dragoon. Their barrack-rooms were neither provided with bunks, or any thing substituted for them; and the very implements in the kitchen were paid for out of the soldiers' money.

Notwithstanding these and many other grievances that might be here enumerated, the dragoons would have still submitted to their fate, and much disaffection and desertion might have been prevented among them, had the officers of this regiment treated those whom they had drawn into its ranks in such a manner as their standing and deportment merited. But, unfortunately, they had a little brief authority, and they seemed determined to use it.

On account of the non-fulfillment of contract on the part of the officers, the men soon began to grow disaffected, and during the first month several deserted. Oppression every day growing more and more insupportable, the dragoons began openly to murmur, and the guard-house was kept continually filled to overflowing. Courts-martial were in continual session; and for the most trifling neglect of duty, men were tried and sentenced either to walk the tow-path all day with a bag of shot on their shoulders, or to confinement in the guard-room.

Jefferson Barracks is peculiarly favorable to the accomplishment of the designs of those who had been forced, as it were, to desert; for, indeed, although I would not upon any account attempt to palliate the crime of desertion, yet I do here say that the deception practiced by the officers was no less a crime.

This Post is beautifully situated upon the Mississippi river, about ten miles below the city of St. Louis; the river rapidly flowing along, keeps on its course until it mingles its waters with that of the ocean, and consequently a boat in the night, without any noise or trouble, may be launched into the stream, and ere daylight gave notice of his departure, the deserter might be well under way towards New Orleans, or wherever he might choose to shape his course.

The barracks are built of hewn stone, upon a delightful bluff, and formed in shape of a hollow-square, or rather oblong; the buildings occupied by the officers are two stories high, and those by the soldiers but one, extending along on either side of the parade ground, which is handsomely graded, and from the river presents a fine appearance. The land in this vicinity is broken, and full of pitfalls, and subterraneous caverns leading to the river; the soil so poor that nothing but dwarf oaks can be seen, except in the immediate neighborhood of the barracks.

I forgot to mention in my last, that every day immediately after morning drill, the different troops were marched off, armed with shovels, pickaxes, hammers, saws, and various other implements of mechanical use, to a spot of ground in the neighborhood of the barracks, for the purpose of building stables. Now, were we in the woods, and placed in circumstances which demanded of us such labor, I should not have a word to urge against it. But something is wrong to my mind, in the affair as it stands. Most assuredly government pays for all public works, and stables for Uncle Sam's horses, attached to a military post, are certainly public buildings. Be that as it may, this regiment was not enlisted to build stables, and some of our men have signified their disrelish of the work by *not remaining to see it finished.* Some captains have ordered timber ready hewn from St. Louis, and allowed some of the dragoons extra pay (although merely a nominal sum) for their labor; but others have made their men cross the Mississippi, cut down timber and tow it to the opposite side, without the smallest compensation.

Not to be at all personal, I have wondered whether *somebody* did not make money out of this speculation. If government paid for the labor, those who performed it had no share in the profits.

The stables, however, are nearly finished; and in a few days we are to receive our horses, which we are all anxious to have.

* * * * * *
* * * * * *
* * * * * *
* * * * * *

One afternoon, while engaged in building our stables, the orderly sergeant came running to the place and gave orders to be in readiness for a full dress parade at 4 o'clock the same afternoon. Accordingly we broke off work an hour beforehand, and commenced preparations: not knowing, however, for what purpose we were to be assembled.

The bugle at the appointed hour called the whole battalion from the quarters, and a few moments after we were formed in a line across the parade ground. The orderly sergeants brought their respective troops to "right dress," and with the usual salutation, reminding their company officers that the preliminaries were completed, took their proper stations on the right of each troop. The captains in turn inspected the columns of platoons, and again wheeling to the left, brought the column into line. Next in order of inspection came the adjutant, and, commencing at the right of the line, "told off" the battalion by equal troops, the subalterns taking their stations in the rank of file-closers. The whole being now properly organized, the major received intimation from the adjutant, and took command.

Various evolutions occupied the time until about the hour of five, when were drawn up in a hollow-square, and the command given to "rest." Presently from a little distance was heard the sound of a drum and fife approaching, and it grew louder and louder, until, turning the point of the angle that before hid them from our sight, we discerned a small detachment of the guard advancing towards us, preceded by three or four musicians. In the centre of this little group was a man with his hands tied behind his back, and destitute of nearly all his upper garments. The truth now flashed upon my mind.

About ten months before, this man had been apprehended as a deserter, and sentenced to undergo the penalty usually awarded to that crime, but subsequently feigning derangement, (as was afterward learned,) he was reprieved, and had been ever since in the hospital. Unfortunately for himself, in an unguarded moment he left the ward in which he had been placed, and returned to make a visit to the sutler. Becoming rather too happy in the company of the congenial spirits that he met there, he forgot entirely his self-command, and drank deep draughts from the foaming bowl. On his return to the hospital, that asylum in which he had been sheltered from the fate that awaited him, he was accosted by the head physician, who immediately seeing his situation, demanded his excuse for leaving the grounds without permission. The soldier, too deeply inebriated to distinguish friend from foe, returned an insolent answer to the inquiry, and, upon the second interrogatory of the doctor, leveled a blow directly in his face.

That unlucky blow sealed his fate—and, as if instinctively becoming sensible of his situation, consciousness seemed in an instant to have returned. A file of the guard immediately remanded him to prison, and an arrangement was made to carry into effect his previous sentence.

Such are the facts in brief. The detachment that had brought the prisoner to the guard house, now awaited the command of the Major. Three of them were ordered to make a pyramid of muskets with fixed bayonets, and tying the hands of the unfortunate man to the top, made fast his feet to the base, first having taken off the last garment which had covered his back.

Could I have retired from the scene, I felt that I would willingly have given all that I possessed. My heart sickened—my limbs quivered with a nervous excitement, and the blood forsook my features—and whilst the prisoner evinced no apparent sign of disquiet, I trembled at every limb.

The Major now took his station in the centre of the square near the prisoner, together with the doctor, and two drummers, who were to be the intermediary ministers of justice—if indeed such cruelty can be so termed.

The signal was given, and with an instrument called familiarly a *cat-o'-nine-tails*, fifty successive lashes were laid upon the back of the wretched victim! The first six or eight, although applied with force enough to make the blood flow copiously from the lacerated wounds, brought no sign of flinching, but as the subsequent successive strokes fell upon the wounded flesh, groans, and at length piercing shrieks rent the air, and before the last blow had fallen, the unhappy man had sunk into a swoon.

After being taken down from the place of execution he was carried to the hospital, and an application of salt and water roughly applied to his wounds—after which he was again consigned to the dreary walls of the guard-house, to serve out in confinement the remainder of his enlistment.

I forbear to make any comment upon this scene—all the finer feelings of our nature shrink from the contemplation of so horrid a sight; but custom, imperious, unyielding custom, has sanctioned it, and we are constrained to be the unwilling spectators of such appalling outrages upon humanity.

Rumors are afloat that we are to be sent to the Arkansas for winter quarters. I know not yet how this will be, but am disposed to think it only a "camp story."

Please continue your favors. Postage is the most welcome item in my catalogue of expenses.

Yours, &c.

LETTER VII.

Description of Horses—First Mounted Parade—Inspection—Guard Duty—Romantic Reflections—Remarkable Appearance of the Stars.

Jefferson Barracks, Nov. 19th, 1833.

My dear Sir,

To-morrow we commence our march. As you may suppose, we have not been idle since the date of my last. We have been employed for the week past in almost continual drill. My time has indeed been so completely occupied that I have not till this moment found leisure to attempt an answer to your communication of the 12th.

I believe that as yet I have given you no description of our horses. They indeed deserve more than a passing notice. We have been in possession of them about six weeks, and by constant practice have rendered them quite familiar with military usage. Each troop have three of a different color—blacks, greys, sorrels, creams, and bays. We have not yet received our uniforms, (as they have been sent to Fort Gibson;) but even in our '*fatigues*,' we make an imposing appearance when mounted.

Our first-battalion parade on our horses took place on the morning of the 9th, on a beautiful spot of green sward, about an hundred rods in rear of the barracks. We were drilled by Major Mason, and considering the many disadvantages under which we labored, and the very little practice that we have had, we came off with much credit. The next day *(Sunday)* we were again assembled upon the same ground, and the Inspector General with his *suite* marched through our ranks, and pronounced both men, horses and equipments in excellent order. * * *
* * * * * * * * * *

All the romantic ingredient of my composition was called into action a few nights since. My name had been read in orders at retreat rol-call, for guard next day: this was the first time that I had been chosen for that duty. Accordingly, I reported myself next morning at the Adjutant's quarters. It was not, however, until my third watch that I experienced the sensations of peculiar excitement that then pervaded my frame. The spot upon which I was stationed was upon the bank of the Mississippi, over whose rippled current the full moon shone with her silvery light. I watched that bright orb as she climbed up behind the dim blue outlines of the distant hills, and cast her gentle beams through the latticed foliage. Soon she rose above the tops of the tallest trees, and majestically journeyed on her upward course. Silence reigned triumphant, save when the loud neigh of some impatient steed echoed through the air, or the autumn wind sighed through the half-naked branches

of the trees. I was alone—a soldier—a sentinel : as
I paced up and down the sentry-walk a thousand reflections crowded upon my mind; now my thoughts
would wander back over the hours of school-boy
days, and fondly dwell upon the recollection of childhood's sports and the associations of home and friends.
O what a joyous season is that of youth—happy,
careless, buoyant youth—life then indeed is sweet—
its fountains pure and gushing—its streams transparent—its tendrils elastic—its hopes, affections, joys,
all, all pure, unalloyed, unmixed with sorrows and
with griefs. Then we drink from the crystal rivulet
of life, and no dregs are mingled with the draught—
no rooted sorrows—no lingering remnants of long
blighted hopes—no memory of crushed affections
throw their dark shadows over the sunny pathway of
early youth : untrammeled with cares, unused to disappointments, the young heart, free as the air of heaven, leaps with joy at the anticipation of every change
—men then seem Gods—nature seems drest in eternal smiles—the gushing waterfall, the early matin of
the birds fall upon the ear as the delightful harmony
of sweet sounds—but more than all this, FRIENDSHIP
then seems REALITY. The heart knows naught but
confidence—envy, deceit, misfortune, sorrow, anguish, misery are unknown : smiles and caresses meet
us at every turn; and we deem that this will last.
Futile, deceptive vision! would that it might last—
would that the curtain of futurity might remain un-
furled, and life, in all the joyousness of childhood,
cling to us forever! * * * * * *
* * * * * * Then the aspirations
of the soldier would flit over me, and in turn every
hero of by-gone days would rise in imagination be-

fore me. Footsteps approached, and disturbed my reverie.

"Who goes there?"
"A Friend."
"Advance and give the countersign."
"*Kosciuszko.*"
"Pass, Friend. What's the hour?"
"On the stroke of one."

Can it be, thought I, that time has flown so rapidly? Two hours had glided by, and it had seemed but as a moment, so occupied had been my mind with bright reflections and brighter anticipations.

The relief came in a few moments, and after the usual manœuvres I returned to the guard-house, and enjoyed four hours respite in a comfortable doze.

A few nights after this a very remarkable appearance of the heavens took place. Loud conversation on the back porch of our quarters awakened me about midnight, and the unusual lightness of the sky induced me to think that there was a large fire in the neighborhood of the barracks; but upon coming into the open air I was struck with admiration at the beautifully strange aspect of the stars. It seemed as if every one of them was jumping from its sphere; lingering for a moment in the air, then darting forward, leaving in its train a glittering corruscation.

After my first moment of surprise subsided, I was induced to laugh outright at the remarks of a cowardly fellow, who read in this strange phenomenon the prophecy of some terrible event.

I remembered to have once heard of a lady in Connecticut remarkable for her ingenuity. One evening, at a ball, her dress attracted a good deal of attention, and some inquisitive being prying into the secret of it, found that the ingenious fair one had caught and imprisoned in the folds of her dress some hundred dazzling fire-bugs. This glittering of the stars called to my mind the dress of the Yankee lady.

The next morning nothing else was talked about in the barracks but the falling stars.

Two or three fine matches were made up between some of our nags, which afforded us a good day's sport the next day, and proved that we could boast of having some superior horses in the regiment.

We have had a large number of desertions take place within the last few days, and, with the exception of a very few only, they have got beyond the reach of apprehension as yet. There appears, however, to be more cheerfulness now prevailing throughout the regiment: our prospective journey has had a favourable impression upon most of the dragoons. As I before mentioned, we start to-morrow. I intend keeping a journal, and will transmit to you whatever may occur worthy of notice. Please continue to send me papers, and superscribe your communications hereafter, "Fort Gibson."

P. S. I took a little jaunt by special permission to St. Louis* the other day, and met our old friend J. D. I had no time to make observations, as my pass extended only till sundown, or, in military phraseology, "Retreat."

---

* I hope that I may be excused for making the following somewhat lengthy extract from the " *Winter in the West.*" It will, I hope, serve to supply my own omission of remarks upon this Western city. Mr. Hoffman thus speaks of this place :—

"It was too late in the evening to cross when we arrived opposite to St. Louis, and I amused myself before retiring for the night in listening to the sound of the church-bells—the first I had heard in many a month—and watching the lights as they

LETTER VIII.

Commencement of march to Fort Gibson—Supper at a Squatter's hut—Various Encampments—Scenes along the road—Description of a rolling Prairie—Description of the remains of an Indian town—A Speculator—Punishment for negligence—Crossing the Illinois River—Description of a cane-brake—Arrival at Fort Gibson—Remarks upon Soldiers—Incident in a grave yard.

Fort Gibson, Cherokee Nation,
Arkansas Territory, Dec. 1833.

My Dear Sir,

You may well imagine how thankful I was to receive your kind letter accompanying the package of

danced along the lines of the dusky city, and were reflected in the dark rolling river. We crossed in time for breakfast, and I am now tolerably established at the best hotel in the place.

" Here, the Spaniard, the Frenchman, and the American have in turn held rule, and their blood, with no slight sprinkling of that of the aborigines, now commingles in the veins of its inhabitants.

"The aspect of the town partakes of the characteristics of all its original possessors: in one section you find the broad steep-roofed stone edifices of the French, with the Spaniard's tall stuccoed dwelling raising its tiers of open corridors above them, like a once showy but half defaced galleon in a fleet of battered frigates; while another will present you only with the clipper-built brick houses of the American residents,—light as a Baltimore schooner, and pert-looking as a Connecticut smack. The town, which is situated about eighteen miles below the mouth of the Missouri, lies on two plateaux, extending along the Mississippi for some miles. The first of these steppes rises gently from the water, till, at the distance of about a hundred yards, it becomes perfectly level, and affords a fine plane for the main street of the place, which runs parallel to the river. An acclivity, rather longer and steeper, then intervenes, when the second plateau commences, and runs back a perfectly level papers. Many thanks for them; and allow me to request a frequent repetition of such favors.

I have much to say, but lack the time to express it. I will however send you the inclosed sheets, in hopes

plain, extending for miles in every direction. This plain, near the town, is covered with shrub oaks and other undergrowth; but it finally assumes the character of a naked prairie, which probably, at no very distant time, extended here to the banks of the Mississippi.

"That part of the town immediately upon the river is built, in a great measure, on a rock that lies a few feet beneath the surface of the soil; the stone excavated in digging the cellars affording a fine material for the erection of some substantial warehouses that line the wharf. The site for a great city, apart from its admirable geographical position, is one of the finest that could be found; and having been laid out of late years in modern style, with broad rectangular streets, St. Louis will, however it may increase in size, always be an airy, cheerful-looking place. But its streets command no interesting prospects, and indeed the town has nothing of scenic beauty in its position, unless viewed from beneath the boughs of the immense trees on the alluvial bottom opposite, when the whitewashed walls and gray stone parapets of the old French houses present rather a romantic appearance. The most interesting objects at St. Louis are several of those singular ancient mounds, which, commencing in the western part of the State of New-York, and reaching, as Humboldt tells us, to the interior of Mexico, have so entirely set at naught the ingenuity of the antiquary. The mounds in the north suburb of St. Louis occupy a commanding position on the Mississippi, and cover ground enough for a large body of men to encamp upon. They stand distinct from each other, generally in the form of truncated pyramids, with a perfect rectangular base. At one point four or five tumuli are so grouped together as to form nearly two sides of a square, while at another, several hundred yards off, two or more detached mounds rise singly from the plain. The summit of one of these is occupied by a public reservoir, for furnishing the town with water; the supply is forced up to that you may find interest enough in them to warrant the reading. They are the notes that I at various times took upon the road, you must therefore make

the tank by a steam-engine on the banks of the river, and subsequently distributed by pipes throughout the city. This mound, with the exception of one or two inclosed within the grounds of General Ashley, is the only one fenced from the destruction that always, sooner or later, overtakes such unproductive property, when in the suburbs of a rapidly growing city. It is a subject of surprise that, considering the want of public squares in the town, individual taste and public spirit do not unite to preserve these beautiful eminences in their exact forms, and connect them by an inclosure, with shrubbery and walks, thus forming a promenade that might be the pride of St. Louis. The prettily cultivated gardens in the environs, and the elegance and costliness of more than one private dwelling in the heart of the town, evince that neither taste nor means are wanting to suggest and carry into effect such an improvement.

"I am so little of an adept at estimating measurements, that I will not attempt to guess at the size of these mounds: they are much the largest that I have yet seen; but none of them can compare with the immense parallelogram near the Cahokia, in Illinois, which Mr. Flint describes as eight hundred yards in circumference, and ninety feet in height—one side of it alone affording a terraced garden for the monks of La Trappe, who had a monastery among the group of two hundred tumuli around.

"The population of St. Louis may be estimated at seven or eight thousand; and there are four or five churches and a noble cathedral belonging to the different religious persuasions. The inhabitants derive their wealth from the rich lead mines of their own state, and from the trade of the Upper Mississippi, the Missouri, and the Illinois. The burthensome steamboats from New-Orleans reach here at the lowest stage of the river; and here you may see river craft of every shape and form, from the thousand boatable tributaries of the Mississippi, clustering around the wharfs.

all due allowances for errors and illegibility. The pressing duties of my station will not allow me the time for further comment. My notes commence at—

Camp Burbees, November 20*th,* 1833.

This day dawned auspiciously. Our march is commenced, and our men seem in better spirits. We spent all the morning in preparation, and it was not until noon when the rear of our line passed through the postern gate of the barracks. This has been a busy day. After the labor of loading the baggage wagons and preparing of supplies, the bugle sounded the assembly-call, and each troop formed upon its respective stable ground. The several troops now underwent a thorough inspection, and after performing many preliminary evolutions and manœuvres, the signal for general assembly called us to form in regimental line upon the parade ground.

Colonel Dodge now for the first time took command and gave the order to "march."

Our cavalcade consisted of the regiment, baggage wagons and retainers, disposed in the following order: Captain Wharton's company "A" taking the right, and the wagons attached to his troop bringing up in its rear; next followed the other troops in the same order, with the exception of Captain Hunter's compa-

"In no town of the west do you find such a variety of people and character as in St. Louis; and here, in fact, only, where more than one "last of the boatmen" still lingers, have you an opportunity of studying that singular class of beings the *engages* (as they are called) of the fur trade—fellows that talk of a trip to the Rocky Mountains as you would speak of a turn on the Battery; and think as much of an Indian encounter as a city blood does of a "spree" with a watchman."

ny "D," which had been appointed for guard. The prisoners, consisting of eighteen men under sentence for desertion, and other capital offences, were made to walk hand-cuffed and chained, some with a cannon ball to the leg, flanked on either side by the rear guard. And thus commenced the Regiment of Dragoons their first march.

We proceeded but three or four miles from the Barracks the first day, and halted by a clear stream of water that glides through that sterile region of scrub oaks extending for miles round about the region of St. Louis. And now commenced a scene of novelty and excitement. Clearing away the underbrush, we pitched our white canvass tents, soon rearing an imposing encampment. Driving down our picket posts we secured our horses, and after having fed and cleaned them, began to make preparations for our own comfortable lodging and supper. Accordingly piling together large heaps of logs, we soon had many a blazing fire snapping and cracking throughout the encampment. The greater portion of the men having become tired and fatigued with the day's duty, retired, soon after tattoo, to seek repose upon the ground, under the shelter of their canvass coverings.

The encampment extended over a considerable space of ground, each troop having pitched their tents in two rows, about twenty paces apart, facing inwards, with the horses picketed in the centre of the intervening space; the tents occupied by the field-officers were in a line opposite their respective troops, six paces in rear, and the staff-officers occupying a station still six paces in rear of them.

Our blazing log heaps sent forth volumes of smoke and flame, and cast a glare of light over the whole surrounding scene, and now and then the full moon would break forth from behind the thick clouds and throw her pale light over our encampment. To a young and enthusiastic soldier this scene was one of peculiar interest, and it served to keep me from seeking repose, although I was weary and worn with fatigue and excitement; but rather preferring to indulge in a naturally romantic disposition, I remained sauntering throughout the encampment for the greater portion of the night. There was a something savoring of romance in every thing around me even the loud neighing of our horses, or the challenge of the sentinels, carried with their sound a thrilling tone of interest.

The life of a soldier differs very much from what one uninitiated would suppose it. It has its scenes of hardship and trial, but on the other hand, novelty and excitement are in the scale against them; and although the homely duties of the stable and the mess claim a portion of the soldier's time and attention, yet there are moments and hours in his life when he forgets all these, and gives way to joyousness and pleasure, and many another happy feeling that the scenes around him are calculated to give rise to.

The bright blazing logheaps had now become piles of smoking embers; the third relief had just posted the sentinels for their last watch, and still was I lingering amid this scene of novelty, regardless that the time had flown away so swiftly. Retiring to my tent, I had hardly thrown myself upon the ground, when the reveille called us to commence the duties of another day, and the encampment that a few moments before had been silent and deserted, now became speedily transformed into " the busy haunt of men."

An hour before sunrise found us upon our second day's march; and having again organized our battalion as the day before, with the exception of Capt. Wharton's Company having relieved Capt. Hunter's from the guard duty, our troop took the right of the regiment. We traveled this day about twenty miles over a portion of country somewhat improved from the day before, and passed through a long straggling log town that bears the somewhat incongruous cognomen of Manchester; and about an hour before sundown again pitched our encampment in a beautiful little valley, through which a clear stream of water winded its meandering course. The third day we made an early move, and gained several miles upon our route before the sun peered out from the horizon. The road was a tedious and toilsome one, leading over high mountains, sometimes peculiarly steep and rocky; consequently we moved along but slowly. We marched this day twenty-three miles, and brought the time to tattoo before we encamped. Nothing of special interest as yet took place upon the road. Our horses, which had been somewhat restive on the preceding nights, now became more quiet, and their guard was allowed to be diminished.

Nov. 24. Marched seventeen miles over a more level road than yesterday. Struck into a new path off of the main track, in some places so narrow that it was impossible for two horses to travel abreast. An hour before sundown struck out again upon the main path, and encamped half an hour before retreat. The weather still continued clear and favorable.

The scenery of the surrounding country was the most strikingly picturesque and romantic that I had ever seen. Mountains and valleys so richly thrown together; forests and prairies so beautifully interspersed; the elm and sycamore towered high in the air; the ledges of broken rocks emitted forth their tiny torrents, which gently meandered on their course through the tangled foliage.

It was now sunset—behind the far west hills his last rays cast up a golden halo which reflected over the surrounding scenery: gradually he declined, and the shades of twilight began to gather; the imagination might in the distant view conjure up villages, and spires, and hamlets; but reality interposing, would speedily convert them into the wild uncultured regions of native solitude.

As our regiment moved forward over the scene, it seemed like an intrusion upon its silent grandeur; any thing like civilization here would break the harmony of the scene.

An opening in the wood afforded a beautiful spot to encamp, and we pitched our tents along the margin of a clear stream that yielded us a delicious draught of nature's purest beverage.

Tattoo had sounded—most of my companions had sought repose upon the ground: a few still lingered around the camp fires. I was seated alone, raking together the decaying embers, fatigued and hungry, musingly meditating over the events of the day, when I was suddenly accosted by two of my comrades:

" Will you sup with us to-night?" asked one.

The allusion to supper roused me, but when I bethought myself for a moment of the place we were then in, I laughed at my own eagerness.

"I have ordered supper for three to-night," continued corporal Tim, in his usual strain of dryness; " will you accompany us or not?"

"Where, in the name of Heaven?" I inquired.

"Come along and I'll show you; silence now till we pass the sentry. Sh—sh——sh———."

"There, now we're safe. Now I'll explain, for I see you look rather doubtingly; and in truth a good right you have to look so," continued he, "considering the place we're in; who'd ever think of finding a dwelling amidst such a scene as this?"

"True," I answered, "some strange being indeed, if perchance any one."

"What! still doubting?" answered the corporal. "Do you see that light yonder through the trees?"

"I do."

"There we sup to-night," said Tim; "my eyes serve me a good turn now and then, and whilst you are spying out the beauties of rocky precipices, and measuring the altitude of mountains and sycamores, I keep a look out for something more palatable."

This indeed proved true, for after a few minutes walk the corporal led us to a small log cabin that we had not observed from the road; and upon entering, we found the interior to be much more comfortable than appearances indicated from without.

It may not be out of place here for a few moments to arrest the thread of our narrative, and revert to that class of people that are only to be found in the wild and unsettled regions of the west, called Squatters.

It was recorded of Daniel Boon, (whose history is familiar to every one that has ever read or heard of the early settlement of Kentucky, and indeed all the settlements to the westward of it up to the time of his death,) that he thought it high time to remove when he could no longer fell a tree, so that its top would lie within a few yards of his cabin door, thus proving his attachment to the luxury of variety, by removing as often as he had rendered his last place of abode fit to live in. Thousands of other instances may be noticed, where men of restless and enterprising dispositions have left the well-tilled farms of their ancestors and removed to settle upon the wild lands of the west; and thousands, too, have been richly rewarded for their temerity, when, unlike Daniel Boon, they remained long enough upon their new possessions to reap the reward of their labors. Old men, with their heads silvered o'er with more than sixty winters, and that now dwell west of the waters of the Mississippi, daily make inquiry of every one that they may chance to meet from any place west of them, about the state of the land, and how it would do to settle there.

This spirit of enterprise, which may be considered as one of the peculiar characteristics of this country people, may be the better appreciated by him who visits the squatter's cabin, amid the unregenerated regions of the west: he may imagine that he will find there only the half civilized being, surrounded by his wife and offspring, as uncouth and rude as himself; but indeed, although in some instances this may chance to be the case, yet how much oftener will he find the inmate of the squatter's cabin to be full as gentle and refined, often better informed, and generally by far more kind and hospitable, than the inhabitants of cities, who dwell among the luxuries, and refinements, and pleasures of civilized society. To test the truth of this, let him who doubts traverse over that yet uncultured region where the squatter seeks to dwell, far removed from the busy hum of the world; where the hardy and sun-burned father of the family plies his axe amid the forest trees through the day with cheerfulness and alacrity, and returns to his evening meal in happy mood, either spread upon the grass-plot before his door, or upon the rough table by the blazing logheap within his cabin: whilst his wife diligently sits at her loom or spinning-wheel, as happy as contentment can make her, her hardy boys may be perchance chasing the deer or buffalo over the prairies, or leveling the bee tree, or in some other way procuring food for the family support; whilst the girls, too, often as blooming as the opening rose, culture the little garden, or perform the different employments suited to their age and sex.

Often have I envied the cheerfulness, the buoyancy, the unaffected joyousness of such a family. Removed far from the world, if they enjoy not its pleasures, neither do they participate in its pains; to them the happiness of each other is their purest source of joy. The noise of aspiring mortals reaches them not; no angry strife and jarring discord surrounds them; their only sovereign is the God of nature, and they alone obey his mandates, and are subject to his power. If summer smiles upon them, the forest, the prairie, and the stream afford them an abundance both for present supply, and enough to lay up against the season when the winter shall encompass them about with ice and snow.

So far from pitying the condition of the squatter, I hold him to be by far a happier man than he who plods his way through life eternally amidst the noisy, smoky, jostling streets of a crowded city, subject to the taunts and jeers of the world, for ever embroiled in its cares, liable to its vicissitudes, with his mind continually occupied in its sordid pursuits, grasping after its honors, striving for its wealth, and, to say the least, subject to its opinions.

But to return—the squatter's cabin to which my companion had conducted me, was the home of such a happy family as I have attempted to describe; and the welcome that we received from the good mother was a warm and cordial one. After having intimated that we were absentees without leave from camp, and that our desire was to procure if possible something for supper that might be more palatable than the salt pork and hard bread rations that we began to grow tired of already, she betook herself to work in good earnest, and without delay set before us a meal that might satisfy the cravings of the most dainty palate in christendom. Sweet corn-bread, fresh from the coals, honey, cream, and venison, were the ingredients of this delicious and savory meal; and, as might reasonably be expected, we did ample justice to it.

Glancing around the apartment, I noticed the furniture of this rude dwelling, and, from many apparent vestiges of former times, I conjectured that this family was also one of that adventurous and roving character that are to be daily seen locating themselves in this region of our country; and the singular contrast that one might observe between the rude implements of husbandry and still ruder pieces of home-made furniture, and the more civilized heirlooms of other days, was peculiarly striking. About the walls of the only apartment that the dwelling contained, were displayed the antlers of the elk and the broad horns of the buffalo, together with the skins of the bear and wolf; but particularly did I notice the two portraits of the squatter and his wife that faced each other across the cabin, and amid so rude a scene they wore a far different appearance than if they had graced the drawing-room of a city residence.

When our meal had been got ready, the mother of the little group of white-headed children (the apartment boasted of more than I felt inclined to count,) took a large iron spoon filled with lard, stuck it between a crevice in the wall, and appending thereto a bit of rag, which being lighted, served us for a candle, and seating herself beside our table, she did the honors of hostess with all the attention that it was possible for us to have received.

This being the first squatter family that I had ever visited, I formed an opinion of their mode of life from the scene around me which I have not yet had reason to alter: it brought forcibly to my mind the beautiful lines of Pope:

> " Happy the man whose wish and care
> " A few paternal acres bound,
> " Content to breathe his native air
> " On his own ground," &c.

Having settled for our supper, and bought an extra loaf or two of corn-bread, we bent our steps back to camp.

The full moon now cast a lovely light over the scene; our white tents glimmered amid the forest trees, and in the distance the high hills rose fainter and fainter till lost in the shadows of night. No sound but the murmur of the rivulet broke upon the ear, save now and then the neighing of the horses as they quietly grazed around the encampment. A few of our companions still remained around the log fires.

I retired to my tent, but not to sleep; and the bugle note ere long again summoned us to enter upon the duties of another day.

Sunday, November 25th.

Up before sunrise and on the march. Cloudy all the morning, and after dinner it began to snow. We traveled seventeen miles over some barrens and oak openings: the weather becoming quite cold, we encamped about 3 o'clock P. M. Two of our men that had been apprehended as deserters, were brought into camp and placed in custody of the guard. The next day we traveled over a better road, but the country presented much the same appearance; we found some excellent streams of water along our course, and now and then a fine fat buck that one or another of our men would bring into camp, added to our supply of rations.

The route now began to grow more and more interesting as the country improved. Our next day's march led us over a beautiful undulating prairie, which, although at this time of the year it presented none of that enchanting appearance that the prairie wears during the spring season, still presented a lovely view, especially in contrast with the barren tract that we had been for several days traveling over. I lingered behind this morning, and when about six or eight miles in advance of me, the regiment, as they defiled over this lonely little prairie, looked like a spangled serpent coiling over a rich green carpet. Having obtained leave of absence for the morning, I lingered alone along the road, and, glad to be for a time freed from the strict and mechanical movements of the regiment, I remained till the bugle sounded the retreat.

We now began to find a scarcity of fodder for our horses, and hoarded our corn with more care, having but ten ears a day for each horse, and oftentimes no other feed.

Camp Delaware, December 8th.

During the three succeeding days we had a very toilsome and diversified route to travel over, and forded the streams of the big and little Piorly, and the Osage branch of the Gasconade, and clambered over several ledges of steep and rocky hills, which wearied both men and horses; and on the eighteenth day of our march, entered upon the Kickapoo prairie, which is the commencement of that immense chain of prairie land that extends in broken patches to the Rocky Mountains. This day, however, we met with one of the most interesting scenes upon our whole route.

It was drawing towards the close of the day, when at a little distance we descried a cluster of huts that we imagined might be a squatter settlement, but upon a nearer approach, found it to be the remains of a log-town long since evacuated, that had formerly been the settlement of a tribe of the Delawares, at one time one of the most powerful tribes among our aborigines, and holding a high rank among them for their prowess and courage; but now, if indeed any of the tribe remains, they have become so scattered as to have lost all recognition as a nation. The site was a beautiful one; and the associations that were connected with it, as well as the many vestiges of rude art that remained about it, invested this spot with many pleasing sources of reflection. As we entered the town, our regiment slackened their pace, and slowly rode through this now silent ruin.

A small space of cleared land encompassed the settlement, but scarce large enough to relieve it from the deep gloom of the lofty and surrounding forest of aged oaks.

Scattered along on either side of the road were the mouldering ruins of these once cheerful but now desolate dwellings. The huts were small, containing but one apartment, built of logs, many of which had become so decayed as to have fallen to the ground, and the whole was covered with a rich coat of moss. How long they had been standing we were unable to learn, but from the evident marks of antiquity which they wore, they must have been of extreme age. Many mounds now were heaped over those that have been returned to their native dust upon their own soil; and although this tribe has become extinct, still they have left behind them many vestiges of their former skill and achievements. Scattered throughout the town may still be seen standing the patriarch oaks, that serve to transmit to posterity the deeds of prowess of this warrior tribe. On the broad surface of these trees may still be seen rudely, but graphically carved, the *Tableaux* of their bloody contests. Having lingered behind the regiment, I stopped to take a more satisfactory view of these relics than could be had by merely passing through the town, and accordingly I had an opportunity the more minutely to observe some of these curious traces of Indian skill and genius.

One presented in the foreground the figure of a victorious chief, standing with one foot upon the breast of his fallen foe, while his right arm was stretched aloft grasping the fatal hatchet; the fallen savage had been disarmed, and thus being deprived of the power to resist, seemed rather willing to die than to yield. Although years have rolled away and many a rude and wintry blast has swept over the forest since the last Indian lingered around this spot, still time and the elements seemed to have had but little effect upon these almost sacred vestges; they still possess much of their original beauty, both of design and execution ; and even in the countenances of the chiefs might be traced something of the passions that pervaded their minds.

Many other groups of figures, all engaged in deadly combat, were carved in the back ground of the picture. Upon other trees were represented scenes of Indians hunting the elk and buffalo ; and the natural, although rude, delineation of the scenes which they represented would not disgrace the pencil of a more civilized age and nation.

A mere description of these rude scenes cannot convey any idea of the emotion that one feels when standing in the midst of them ; it may indeed convey some faint idea of their existence and appearance, but when upon the spot every tree and mound, and even the very whistle of the wind through the branches, seems fraught with some feeling of interest.

We encamped this night upon the top of a ridge of high land, from which situation we had a delightful and extensive view of the surrounding country.

The greater portion of our men had spent most of their money, during the first three or four days of our march, along the road, for corn-bread, honey, and other little delicacies that might be obtained, and served to give a more savory flavor to the homely rations which they received from government ; but we had one fellow among us whose pockets seemed to increase in value just in proportion as the others diminished ; bearing the formidable name of *Turpin*,*

* The name of Richard Turpin is perhaps familiar to most readers.

he was nevertheless more disposed to get gain in the manner of speculation than to emulate the example of his more adventurous namesake. Every moment that he was not actually under the eye of his officers he spent in striving to make a barter or bargain with some of his companions, whereby he was always sure to be the gainer; but one thing troubled him most sorely, and seemed to be a serious drawback to his operations, that is, it so fell out that full half of his time was spent in the guard house; and consequently, after he had managed to do all that he could to make a little out of his fellow-prisoners, his mind would pine for liberty, that he might, in some way or other, continue to gratify his favorite propensity. This fellow used to take every opportunity to get away from camp in the night, and scour the whole country round in quest of some place where he might buy articles of food, which he was always sure to offer for sale next morning; and money being a thing of less value among the greater portion of our men than something whereby to satisfy hunger, they seldom quarreled about the price, provided they could buy the article.

The twentieth day of our march gave rise to an incident for which I shall always particularly remember it. Having accidentally left my carbine standing against a tree upon our camp ground, I had mounted and proceeded several miles upon the route before it was observed that it was among the missing. Having carried them slung across our backs, we had become so used to the sensation of their being there that we could not tell, without feeling, whether they were there or not; and thus, when the gun had been handed to the Captain, I shrugged my shoulders in consciousness that mine was upon my back; but in a few moments the Captain, ordering myself to ride to the front, handed me the gun, and asked if it was mine; to my utter astonishment and confusion I found it to be so. I had been deceived by the feeling of my back, for having so long been in the habit of having the gun slung there, the sensation may, in a manner, be likened to that of one who has had a skate strapped to his foot all day, when he takes it off he cannot for an hour after help thinking it still to be there. However, I was ordered to dismount and to lead my horse in front of the regiment during the day. This turned out to be a severe punishment, for the day's travel was one of peculiar toil and hardship, and for twenty-three miles, over a hilly and rough road, I was obliged to lead my horse in penance for my negligence.

This day we crossed the boundary line between the State of Missouri and the Arkansas Territory, and traveled over some very heavy hills. In the evening some of our companies having taken a wrong road, became detached from the main body of the command, and brought the time to near eleven at night before we again assembled at our camp ground. The next morning we passed through a smart little town called Fayetteville, and encamped in the evening upon a beautiful spot about three miles distant from it. The face of the country had now become much improved, and instead of the patches of scrub oaks through which we had been traveling, we now met with heavy forests of large oaks, elms and pekaun trees, and now and then a clump of pines that retained their beautiful green appearance throughout the winter, and relieved the more sombre hue of their companions. We now urged our horses to greater exertions, and for several days averaged twenty-five miles, which, in our unprovided condition, was good traveling.

Camp Illinois, December 16th.

One, perhaps, of the most remarkable events upon our route took place last night. It was about ten o'clock, and the darkest night that I ever experienced. When we arrived at the bank of the Illinois River, our orders were to cross it and pitch our encampment upon the opposite bank; and it has ever since seemed to me to have been a miracle that this order was carried into effect without the occurrence of a single mishap. The only discernible object was the lantern upon the opposite shore that served to designate the spot to which we were to shape our course; and having nothing else to guide us, we allowed our horses to take their own course, and trust to chance for safety. The road that led to the bank of the river was upon the top of a ridge that sloped down on either side almost perpendicularly for a distance of from forty to sixty feet; unconsciously we had pursued our way along this dangerous path, which, in daylight, would (as I observed next morning) have presented somewhat of a formidable appearance; however, fortunately for us, we crossed the river in safety, swimming our horses and leaving on the opposite shore only our baggage-wagons, which we managed to get across next morning.

The most surprising part of the story is yet untold. The tops of the trees which grew below, were in some places on a level with the ridge over which we were traveling; and accidentally drawing the left curb-rein, my horse stept aside, and placing one forefoot upon a large limb which projected from the trunk in a horizontal line, actually became the occupant of the top of an old oak tree. Immediately recognizing my danger, I scarce knew what to do; but reining my horse backwards by a movement as singular as it was providential, regained a footing upon *terra firma*.

Camp Sandy, December 18th.

We remained all the next day at our encampment on the bank of the Illinois, and started the following morning before the break of day upon our march; and about four o'clock the same afternoon passed Fort Gibson, keeping on our course for about two miles, through a thick canebrake, to the bank of the Neosho or Grand River, a stream that empties into the Arkansas, near the confluence of the Verdigris; it is about eighty yards wide, with a pebbled bottom, and the water extremely clear and transparent. Fort Gibson stands upon this stream, about two miles from its mouth.

Although the name of a canebrake may be familiar to you, yet a description may not be out of place here. To the eye of a northerner, at first view, the canebrake presents a novel and delightful aspect; the one through which we now traveled, although not as extensive as many throughout the country, was still large enough to extend beyond the reach of the eye. Stretching itself along the margin of the river, it presented an apparently impenetrable breastwork of dense green. Its tall and slender stem rears itself in the air to the height of thirty or forty feet, and, towering above their heads, the massive oaks that grow to an immense size upon the rich bottom-land, seem to have been wisely placed here to protect the tender cane-stalk from the rude blasts that sweep over the forests. From the intersecting joints of the cane grow long and spiral bunches of leaves, which retain their life and greenness throughout the winter; and what more particularly rendered the first view of a canebrake interesting to us, was the striking contrast it presented to the more sterile and decayed regions through which we had passed. We found it extremely difficult to make our way through it to the spot upon which we were to pitch our encampment; the stalks were so large and close together that our horses could not move forward without breaking through by main force. As Major Long observes in the journal of his expedition, when speaking of this very spot, " Making our way with excessive toil among these gigantic *gramina*, our party might be said to resemble a company of rats traversing a sturdy field of grass. The cane stalks, after being trodden to the ground, often inflicted, in virtue of their elasticity, blows as severe as they were unexpected. It is not to be supposed that our horses alone felt the inconvenience of this sort of traveling, we ourselves received severe blows inflicted upon various parts of our bodies, and had our faces and hands scratched by the rough edges of the leaves; and oftentimes, as our attention was otherwise directed, we caught with our feet and had dragged across our shins the inflexible stalks of the green briar."

After having several times countermarched and retraced our steps through this unpleasant pathway, some misunderstanding having arisen about the spot upon which we were to pitch our tents, expresses were sent from our regiment to the fort to consult with

Col. Arbuckle in relation to the most eligible situation; and at length it was settled that we should encamp for the night upon a sand-bar that projected about half way across the Grand River; and accordingly we made our way, in the manner I have before described, through the cane to this place, which received the name of Camp Sandy; and truly I believe no dragoon of the command will ever forget the day of our arrival there; weariness and extreme fatigue were depicted upon every countenance; and now, indeed, (as we have since experienced during our stay here,) we would willingly have drained our pockets of the last copper for a morsel of bread. I never before saw so many half-starved men together; the greater portion of us had eaten scarce a mouthful since our departure from the Illinois river two days previous; our rations had become so bad that it was almost impossible to swallow them. Soon as the business of pitching our encampment and picketing our horses was over, some of us obtained permission to visit the fort, and as may be supposed, our first inquiry was for bread, which however proved to be almost as scarce an article there as among the dragoons; but we soon obtained enough to satisfy present hunger, and then began to make acquaintance with our new friends, the sixth regiment of infantry. Our welcome and reception among these men were warm hearted and cordial. Here, in such situations, and among men so circumstanced, may be found the true spirit of benevolence and charity; stationed as they are, isolated and alone, far away from the busy scenes of commerce and marts of traffic, they imbibe a natural eagerness to hear from those scenes where they had been familiar in other days; and any one that goes among them from the land of their former associations, meets with that whole-souled welcome that compensates him for a thousand hardships.

It is curious to search the countenances of the men that one meets with in the barrack-rooms of our western garrisons, and although he may read in the features of some the life of the youthful spendthrift and libertine, and often the sunken cheek and hollow eye of the intemperate, yet there are to be found there those, too, who may be marked as the peculiar victims of misfortune and sorrow; many whose bright dawn of youthful sunshine had been suddenly overshadowed by some unforeseen dark cloud, and who, with feelings too acute to bear up against adversity, have voluntarily become the inmates of the camp, hoping to find, amid its revelry and excitement, a solace for their broken and blasted hopes and anticipations.

I have already listened to the sad story of many a heart-broken soldier as he has recounted the misfortunes that led to his enlistment, and as the tear-drop has trickled down his manly cheek, my soul has sickened within me. Here, where the soothing comforts of religion might exert its salutary influence over the mind, and prepare the spirit for its upward flight, is no religion to be found. No missionary thinks of the soldier; no chaplain, no Sabbath, are there for him; but every day alike brings with it its accustomed round of duties and labors.

* * * * *

* * * * *

* * * * *

Camp Sandy, Thursday, December 20th.

"There is a little church-yard by the wave
"Of a fair river in an isle of wo;
"A pensive school-boy marked it for his grave,
"And, now an exile wandering to and fro,
"He would not change for every joy below,
"The blissful hope of mouldering there at last.
"Blow on, ye surliest winds of fortune, blow,
"He little recks it if his lot be cast
"To rest by that dear stream when all your powers are past."*

There is a certain feeling that links the hearts of men together when placed in certain situations, that the man who has never traveled beyond the precincts of his paternal dwelling cannot appreciate. But let him wend his way to some lone corner of the earth, far away from every association connected with his former life, and see how his eye will linger over some scene that reminds him of his home; how his ear will catch at any sound that speaks in familiar accents, and mark the affectionate grasp of the hand that he will bestow upon any fellow-being that he may meet, who has ever trodden the streets or breathed the air of his native land. 'Tis the exercise of this feeling of affinity that gives rise to the most joyous sensations; and he that for ever plods his way along the beaten track of life, without now and then roving from out the reach of its monotony, keeps the storehouse of his better feelings locked even from himself.

It was towards sundown that I lingered amid the graves that crowd the burial ground at Fort Gibson.

*Hymn to Nature by John M. Moore, Esq.

It is inclosed upon a little eminence that overlooks the prairie and the stream for a circuit of many a mile. Some of the mounds had stones erected at their heads, but by far the greater number bore no record of their mouldering inmates; they had died among strangers, and by strangers had they been buried. No tear-drop had been shed over their grave; no father's or brother's hand had paid the last tribute to their memory by rearing a memorial over their remains. Borne to the grave amid the pomp and panoply of a military escort, their only requiem had been the loud report of arms; but the grave makes all alike; and when the whitened bones are deserted by the flesh that encompassed them, who could tell whether they had been

"A haughty chieftain bearing sway, or lowlier, destin'd to obey?"

I noticed among the names upon the tomb-stones some that I had before known, but only one or two with whom I had ever been intimate; one was a Lieut. D——, a promising young officer, and the other a private, with whom I had formerly been a school companion. But the grave that I sought particularly to find was unmarked by any thing whereby I might distinguish it from the others around it; and after having searched in vain for several hours, I was about to return to camp, when an old man came up to me from an opposite direction, and seeing that I wore a soldier's garb, he addressed me without any hesitation, for among soldiers all are companions.

"Your choice," said the old man, after the first salutation, "of a pleasure ground is rather strange; one would hardly think of seeing a young man in a graveyard after dark, and alone."

"I am a soldier, sir," I answered.

"Nevertheless," said the old man, "I know many a man that wears the blue who would rather face an Indian in broad daylight than cross a grave-yard at night; but excuse an old man," said he, "I've been a soldier five-and-thirty years, and love the service yet. Yours is a fine regiment! noble Colonel! fine-hearted set of boys! I shook hands with most all of them to-day—but I wont disturb you."

As he was turning to go, I caught hold of his arm, and inquired if he had ever known a soldier by the name of Martin B——.

"Know Martin? Why, 'besure I did; the noblest hearted fellow in the world."

"You knew him then," said I musingly.

"Why, Martin and I were bunk-mates. Know him? Why, if he had been my own brother I could not have known him better—but," continued he, musingly, "Martin was a sad fellow—always so sober. I never remember to have seen him laugh, no, not even as much as smile, in my life. But, poor fellow, he wasn't long for this world, and he went bravely out of it."

"Do you know which is his grave?" I inquired.

"In yonder corner of the yard he lies, between Larry Davis and Jo. Smith, two fellows as much like him as two ramrods."

I thought of the old adage—"Whom the gods love die young."

The old man led me to the spot where Martin lay; a small stone bore his initials, but the tall grass had grown over it and entirely obscured it from view.

And here, thought I, lies Martin B——, but four years ago among the most joyous of earth's sons, "the observed of all observers "—but to rehearse his story here would be out of place—suffice it, that misfortune tracked his footsteps and he fell—sickened at heart, he enlisted as a common soldier, and died shortly after.

Pardon me for this melancholy strain, but indeed 'tis in consonance with my feelings. If there is aught in this long epistle that may serve to interest you, accept with it the kind remembrance of your friend.

LETTER IX.

New Camp—Stampedo—Description of Quarters in a rainy day—Evening Amusements.

Camp Jackson, Cherokee Nation, A. T.
1¼ miles west of Fort Gibson, 1834.

MY DEAR SIR,

Unusually early for this climate, the weather has set in extremely cold. Our poor horses have been suffering, as well as ourselves, for want of provender; we could only procure corn enough for about half rations, and in addition to this, endeavored to keep them alive by feeding them upon the leaves and tender stems of cane, which twice a day we cut from the brake. It forcibly reminded me of the prophecy in Shakspeare's tragedy of Macbeth, where Burnham forest is represented as being in motion, to see several hundred mounted soldiers with each a large bundle of green cane-stalks in his arms. This method, however, soon became impracticable, and was abandoned; after which it was determined that the horses should be turned into the canebrake to provide for themselves. Upon which, the next morning, each man was ordered to mount his horse with bridles only, and after riding into the midst of the canebrake, to leave them; but scarce had we reached the outer edge of the wood and crossed the little *bayou* which separated it from an open grove of elms, than the rattling of horses hoofs began to clatter more and more distinctly, and in a moment more the whole drove, headed by a powerful black leader, commenced a grand *stampedo*, and so rapidly did they advance upon us that it was with the greatest difficulty that we secured ourselves from danger by taking shelter behind the largest trees. With nostrils distended and ears set back, the foremost horse dashed by us, and after him followed the whole troop close upon his heels, and as far as the eye could discern them they kept swiftly upon their course. For several miles they kept in a body, but afterward separating, they strayed in various directions throughout the country. Small detachments of our men were now sent in quest of them and brought the greater part of them back to camp, but a number of them are still missing.

The next day after our encampment upon the sand-bar, as mentioned in my last, the regiment laid out a permanent camp ground for winter quarters in a little strip of woods skirting a fine rolling prairie. A *bayou* or small intersecting stream, furnished us with water, across which lay the canebrake that I have before described. The rainy season however had rendered this place so muddy that it was with the greatest difficulty that we could move from one place to another without constructing a pathway of logs.

We are now quartered in large barrack-rooms, built of oak shingles, situated at the outer edge of the wood, upon a high piece of ground which overlooks a wide and lovely extent of country. Each troop has one of these barrack-rooms, or rather barns; for indeed although they answer a somewhat better purpose than our tents towards keeping us from the inclemencies of the weather, still they are, in point of comfort, scarcely equal to a country barn.

During the winter our tents have been our only protection from the cold; and, as you may suppose, they afforded us but little shelter. We heaped together large piles of logs as near to them as we dared, and kept them continually lighted, and by this means endeavored to keep one side warm at a time.

The single blanket which government allowed us, was our only covering at night, and the ground on which we lay was so low and wet that we were obliged to dig trenches around the encampment to prevent it from being flooded. As to our rations, they have been poorer, if possible, than our accommodations, consisting of pork, flour, and beans; the pork rusty, the flour spoiled, and the beans of the meanest quality. I had almost entirely forgot to mention coffee, which also was a component part of our rations, and which, for aught I know, might have been good, had the quantity been sufficient to allow of a decision on the subject.

After removing to our present location, our old camp ground presented a curious appearance; here and there were left standing portions of log buildings which had been erected for store-houses and other purposes, and the chimneys and fire-places which had been appended to the officers' tents, now removed, presented the dilapidated ruins of whatever the imagination might please to conjure up.

But another scene, which would have formed no unfit subject for the pencil of Hogarth, claims to be recorded. Often, during a rainy day, our shingle barracks became the theatre of many a laughable drama; the thousand apertures in the roofs admit the water most copiously, and upon such occasions our attention cannot be entirely devoted to ourselves—movables of every description must be taken care of; and such another collection of saddles, saddle-bags, knap-sacks, and accoutrements, as are usually heaped together, cannot well be imagined.

At such times the buffalo skins, with which many of us are provided, are invaluable property, inasmuch as the owner thereof may the more reasonably expect a dry place to lie down upon when night comes, the hide being too thick and too well tanned to admit the water.

But one of the most crying evils which can befall us upon such occasions, is the additional quantity of water which pours down our wide chimneys into the open top camp-kettles, consequently rendering our solution of beans somewhat less strong than common, which, indeed, in ordinary occasions, stand but very little chance of being found fault with on that score. These, however, are but trifling inconveniences, and serve but to render the pleasanter scenes the happier for the contrast.

Oftentimes during that short period of leisure and joyousness which intervenes between retreat and tattoo, are these barrack-rooms the scene of revelry and glee. Among our number are fellows of every turn of mind and almost every species of accomplishment, which, upon such an occasion, could be brought into requisition to add to the general jollity.

One of the most conspicuous, however, of the number is Sergeant S., or, as he is more familiarly called among his companions, Long Ned, measuring six feet six in his stocking feet—a fine fellow, I assure you— and although an Englishman by birth, still Yankee enough in disposition. He was formerly a cornet in an English regiment of lancers, and afterwards effected a transfer, and received the appointment of adjutant to a regiment in the service of Don Pedro. Subsequently arriving in this country, he was solicited to join our regiment, under the express declaration that he should receive the appointment of riding master, which promise, however, as well as every other made to the members of this regiment, was forgotten as soon as made, and my friend Long Ned had to take up with the birth of orderly sergeant to the troop to which he had joined himself.

However, he made the best of a bad bargain, as many another among us was forced to, and upon such occasions as often take place in the evenings within our barrack-rooms, he adds his quota to the general amusement. Seated upon the highest bunk in the apartment, with his long legs hanging almost to the floor, may always at such times be seen Long Ned acting as master of ceremonies; around him generally are congregated a musical group of fellows, with whom Ned is always sure to join in the chorus. On the ample ground-floors, groups of Creeks, Osages, and Cherokees, from the neighboring settlements, often hold their pow-wows, and not unfrequently are they joined by a jolly set of soldiers from the fort, who, together with our own boys, join them in their dance. The Indian mode of accompaniment, which is generally effected by patting of the hands upon the knees, together with a guttural sound from the lungs, as practiced among themselves, is upon these occasions often made more complete by the addition of two or three cracked fiddles, which are the favorite instruments among our Tennessee boys. Now and then an ambitious bugler will enliven the scene by blowing a loud blast upon his favorite instrument; and upon occasions of extraordinary glee, two or three clarionets and a banjo, which complete the collection of instruments in the regiment, are brought into requisition.

Around a tallow candle, stowed away in some snug corner of the apartment, may generally be seen a card party, earnestly engaged in thumbing over a pack that can hardly be distinguished apart through the dirt that covers them; and as now and then a fellow of a pensive turn of mind retires from these more general groups of amusement, he can be seen stretched upon his bunk, seeking enjoyment from the well read pages of Robinson Crusoe, or the Life of Col. Gardner, or General Marion, which, together with three or four other books, form the whole of what may be termed the Regimental Library.

Often have I been the participant in such scenes as that which I have here attempted to describe, and so joyously too did the hours pass away, that tattoo would sound in our ears before we imagined that the evening had commenced.

P. S. Sergeant S., alias Long Ned, has been placed under arrest, upon the charge of another non-commissioned officer, for sundry misdemeanors committed in divers places. You shall have more anon—meanwhile, I remain yours, &c.

LETTER X.

Court-Martial.

Camp Jackson, Fort Gibson,
Cherokee Nation, A. T. 1834.

My Dear Sir,

I have but a moment to devote to you—the mail closes immediately. I will give you the outlines of the proceedings of the regimental court-martial in the case of my friend Long Ned, who, you may remember, was placed under arrest at the date of my last. The trial has caused some little excitement in camp, and for the want of time and material I must send you the proceedings in somewhat of a condensed form, and with but few comments.

The inclosed extracts from the minutes I hurriedly wrote down at the adjutant's tent, therefore please excuse all illegibility.

Charge and Specifications made against Sergeant S . . . ., of Company "E." U. S. Regiment Dragoons.

Charge—*Unsoldierlike conduct.*

"*Specification 1st.*—In this, that the said Sergeant S. of "E" company, did, near Camp Jackson, on or about the 25th of December, 1833, head a party of men under the assumed title of lieutenant, and seize a barrel of whiskey, and appropriate the same to the use of said party.

"*Specification 2d.*—(*Relative to an alledged misrepresentation to Captain Perkins, concerning an expression made to him by another sergeant of the same troop.*)

"*Specification 3d.*—In this, that the said Sergeant S. of "E" company, was so much intoxicated on the morning of the 26th instant, at Camp Jackson, as to be incapable of performing his duty as orderly sergeant in a proper manner.

"*Specification 4th.*—In this, that the said Sergeant S. of "E" company, did, at Camp Jackson, on or about 10th of January, 1834, use violence toward private R. of "E" company, by pulling him half way out of his tent and ordering him to clean his horse, when he the said R. was on the sick report and unable to work.

"*Specification 5th.*—In this, that said Sergeant S. of "E" company, also used similar violence toward private T. of the same troop.

"*Specification 6th.*—In this, that said Sergeant S. of "E" company, did, on or about the 26th of February, 1834, at Camp Jackson, intimate to private L. of "E" company, regiment of dragoons, what lot to draw to insure his detail as orderly.*

---

* One man was chosen each morning, from the number detailed for guard, as orderly to the colonel, which fell to the lot of the cleanest soldier of the detail. This served to excite emulation, and had an excellent effect, the duty of orderly being much lighter than that of a sentinel. In the above case, the privates to whom Sergeant S. gave the intimation which lot to draw, happened under peculiar circumstances. When two were con-

"*Specification 7th.*—In this, that the said Sergeant S. of "E" company, did, on the morning of the 10th of March, intimate to private W. in like manner, which lot he should draw to insure a like result.

"J. W. HAMILTON, *Adj't. Dragoons.*"

I will not trouble you with the list of witnesses whose names were appended to these specifications; they amount in all to thirteen, including a squatter and his wife.

This trial occupied the greater part of three days, many peculiar topics of consideration having been made the subject of discussion. In brief, Sergeant S. was the best soldier in the regiment, and it would have been impolitic to have deposed him; moreover, his knowledge of the cavalry tactics being much more thorough than any other officer, commissioned or non-commissioned, his worth was too well known to admit of a hasty condemnation in his case.

On the second day of the trial, Ned ran into my tent and begged that I would prepare a defence for him; and hurriedly giving me the heads of his arguments, I sat down to the task. After some revision, we prepared together the following defence.

" *To Major M. and the Officers composing this Court.*

"GENTLEMEN,—Unacquainted as I am with courts and the manner in which legal investigations

sidered equally worthy of the choice, resort was had to drawing lots. Privates L. and W. had but just returned from a fatiguing command, and my friend Long Ned, out of pure kindness, must have given them the wink.

are conducted in this country, it is not without a natural feeling of incapacity that I enter upon the task of preparing a defence. I will not, however, occupy much of your time, but as speedily as possible glance over the proceedings in the case, and with but few comments submit the result to you.

"The charge preferred against me admits of seven specifications.

" The first, &c.

*　　*　　*　　*　　*　　*
*　　*　　*　　*　　*　　*

"Having thus recapitulated the specifications, permit me to direct your attention to a fact which could not have escaped your observation at the time. I mean the pointedness of the evidence given by Sergeants C. and H. I do not pretend to question the veracity of these witnesses, but I wish to show that the excitement of their feelings towards me gave a coloring to their testimony against me, that materially affected its import.

" Gentlemen, you cannot but be aware of the importance that an artful representation gives to a transaction, which, when divested of its specious trappings, would fail to produce the desired effect. Sergeant C. in order of rank, would succeed me in the orderly duty, and I am not the only one who has noticed his extreme anxiety for the event of this trial. And now, gentlemen, I would not accuse him of any premeditated intention of wrong, but leave the affair to your own candid investigation. In relation to the other witness to whom I referred, I would point you to your own minutes of the evidence, and compare the erroneous statements of Sergeant H. with the calm and unbiassed testimony, upon the same point, set forth by Captain Perkins. And here, gentlemen, permit me to say, that after the flattering terms in which Lieutenant D. and other officers addressed this Court in my behalf, I more than ever feel the imbecility of any attempt, on my part, to speak in my own defence. The impressive and feeling manner in which these gentlemen gave in their opinions has bereft me of all power of bringing forward any thing in vindication of my own cause, that could so greatly conduce to my interest as the opinions so ably delivered in my behalf by these officers. I feel grateful; I feel indebted to them. Whether the issue of this trial be favorable to me or not, I shall ever cherish, with grateful remembrance, their kindness, condescension, and gentlemanly conduct towards me. Among the singular vicissitudes that time gives birth to, it may so happen that I shall chance to meet, in another walk of life, one, or perhaps all, of the gentlemen who have this day so liberally spoken in my defence; and although years may intervene, my gratitude shall still be undiminished.

" Gentlemen, I will detain you but a moment longer. When I entered the American service, it was at the earnest solicitation of several of my superior officers, and under the influence of promises which have never been fulfilled. However, I was appointed orderly sergeant of the troop to which I belonged, and in the duties of that station I have always exerted myself in striving to promote the interest of the troop and the service generally. What has been construed severity by the soldiers, I looked upon as necessary discipline; and perhaps upon reflection, now that they have become better acquainted with the soldier's duties, they will admit was intended for their good. I am aware, however, that I am an object of antipathy to many, and particularly to my accuser. Why did he not make the facts (if such he could have proved them) known at the time, and not now, after months have transpired, bring forward a list of charges, some of which are entirely false, and those which are founded in truth so grossly exaggerated as to have entirely lost their original formation? I ask why? I leave you to answer.

"By birth and education I am an Englishman, and this is 'the very head and front of my offending;' the patriotic spirits of the young Americans, with whom I have the honor to be associated, could not brook the idea of being ranked by a foreigner. They forgot that I had become virtually an American citizen, by enlisting under their country's flag. I was a stranger in a strange land. I sought for that spirit of liberality for which I had ever been taught to admire the American nation, but did I realize it? I must answer no! My nation was an odium to me, and I was considered as a disgrace to those with whom I was associated, merely because it was not my fortune to have the star-spangled banner floating over my birth-place. Reposing confidence in your proceedings, and feeling assured that this affair will be treated as it deserves, I leave the disposal cheerfully in the hands of my superior officers, composing this Court."

Such was the defence spoken by my friend Long Ned, and I have only time to add that it produced the desired effect. After a recapitulation of all the evidence, the Court decided that the greater part of the charges were disproved, and that no criminality was to be attached to those which were proved. Therefore the decision of the Court was, that Sergeant S. should return to duty in his troop, much, I assure you, to the chagrin and disappointment of several who watched the whole trial with a jealous eye.

Yours, &c.

LETTER XI.

Opening of Spring—Poaching Expedition—Gloomy Occurrence—Military Funeral.

Camp Jackson, A. T. 1834.

MY DEAR SIR,

I will not take up your time with excuses for my unusually long silence. Suffice it to say, that I have been for six weeks past on my back in the hospital, suffering from the effects of a severe wound in the leg, occasioned by a kick from a horse. I have but just now returned to quarters, and am not yet fit for duty. Spring, meanwhile, had merged from the embrace of winter; the paroquets, in large and happy flocks, whistled as they sported through the air; the prairie has laid aside its white robe, and bedecked itself in the more joyous and appropriate habiliments of spring; the oak, and elm, and sycamore begin to give token of approaching verdure, and the canebrake has put forth new sprouts, and assumed a brighter green; the sassafras and hackberry send forth their delicious fragrance, and the blossoms of the dogberry and spicewood add to the luxuriant scenery of spring. The mistletoe now no longer holds entire sway over the frostbitten verdure of its parent trunk, as in thick green bunches it shoots forth from the top branches of the oak. Winter has fled from the earth, and spring, in all the glory of a western clime, reigns triumphant over the forest and the plain. The river, now loosened from its chains of ice, flows on its gentle course. The mellow prairie in its untold variety has shot forth its myriads of blades and flowers. The thousand varied insects are swarming upon the scene; and amid the general renovation, the soldiers, too, seem to have awaked to a renewed life, and enter upon their duties with more cheerful alacrity.

We are now beginning to improve our camp ground, and resume our practice, both in target shooting as well as horse and foot tactics. Our time is occupied for the most part between guard mounting and retreat,* in various exercises, preparatory to entering upon the summer's campaign.

The encampment now presented the appearance of quite a large settlement for this country, extending over a large space of ground, and interspersed with barrack-rooms, tents, huts and wigwams.

Near to our encampment is the dwelling of an old Cherokee, named Rodger, who has grown immensely rich, and lives in the greatest affluence known to

* I would remark that guard-mounting took place at 9 o'clock in the morning, and retreat call sounded at sundown. All our movements and operations were regulated by the sound of the bugle. Reville sounding at sunrise; the Doctor's call at half an hour before breakfast, which was at 8 o'clock, and tattoo at 9 in the evening.

his rude taste; he owns a large tract of land in the neighborhood, and so many head of cattle that he cannot count them; his pigs and poultry are so numerous that, notwithstanding the frequent poaching expeditions that are directed against them, they never seem to be diminished. One day, about the first of February, three or four of us had obtained a leave of absence for the day to go a fishing, but finding that to be dull sport, we put away our rods and lines, and shouldering our muskets, trudged through the woods in quest of game, which resulted in the death of one grey squirrel. Not willing to return to camp with an empty pouch, we thought that our friend Rodger would scarce feel the loss of a roaster or two, so we wended our way in the direction most likely to meet with a party of these unoffending animals. My companions, upon this poaching expedition, were Corporal Tim, as he is familiarly called by his companions, by all odds the finest fellow in the regiment, and a bugler named Shaw, who was always up to any and every kind of sport that might be going on. Having got about half a mile from camp, we were cautiously looking out to examine whether any one might happen to be in the neighborhood, when Tim espied something, and turning to us, said "sh —sh—stop;" and leveling his piece, brought down his game. Shaw and myself getting upon the same trail, met with the like good fortune.

"Now, boys," said Tim, "we've got but a few minutes to spare, let's cover them over with brush, and after retreat come back and smuggle them into camp."

We took Tim's advice, and hid our unlawful game

under a brush-heap, and just got into camp in time to say "here" as our names were called.

As soon as it was dark enough to escape observation, we retraced our steps, and shouldering our prize, brought three fat little roasters, unobserved, into the barracks; and after we had prepared them for the spit, had no hesitation in offering a piece to our companions, under the name of "opposum," which they very nearly resemble.

An occurrence took place a few weeks since that shed a feeling of gloom over the regiment. Lieut. Bradford, a promising young officer, had been detached in command of a small party in search of some deserters. The second morning after his departure from camp, as he was preparing to take an early start upon his route, he had just finished breakfasting at an Indian hut, and his horse having been brought, he was about to mount, when he bethought himself to examine his pistols; he took one of them out of the holster, examined the priming, and returned it; then taking the other, and being likewise satisfied with it, was about to return it to its holster, when the hammer of the lock caught upon the top of the holster-pipe, and thence being drawn back and suddenly disengaged, it went off, the ball passing diagonally through the bottom of the holster-pipe, thence through his left breast, and lodged in his side; not instantly feeling the effect of the ball, he was not aware that he had been shot, until he noticed that the blood was oozing from the wound; becoming exhausted, he was carried into the Indian hut, and although treated with all the kindness that it was possible for him to receive, he expired in a few hours. Express, next morning, brought the news of his death into camp, and an order was immediately issued, directing his corpse to be sent for, and accordingly it arrived the day after. At the hour of four, the same afternoon, his remains were brought out for interment, and the scene was one of peculiar solemnity. Although we had often before been assembled for the purpose of paying the last tribute of respect to the dead, yet the peculiar circumstances of this added much to the effect upon our feelings. The body was placed in a black coffin, and shrouded with the national banner of our country. All the officers from the fort, not on duty, followed in procession, and our own regiment were mustered in their entire strength; and the sight was one of the most imposing character that may well be conceived. Not that I mean that this procession equalled, in splendor, those that upon like occasions are assembled in cities, but here every human being that could walk joined in the procession, and every heart was sorrowful, and every countenance was sad. As we passed over the space of ground that separated our camp from the burial-yard, attached to the fort, all seemed more than naturally still, and the tap of the muffled drum was the only sound that the ear might catch. Here no noisy crowd thronged the highway and jostled against the mourner; this was a sight that no idle spectator would gaze upon for a moment, then turn, and in a moment forget; for who ever looked upon a sight like this and forgot its imposing solemnity?

The grave-yard attached to Fort Gibson was situated about a mile from our encampment, and the surrounding scenery was admirably calculated to add to the solemnity of our feelings; there was none of the usual bustle and noise of the camp now to be heard the hammer of the artizan was silent, the laugh of the merry group had hushed, and even a more than natural stillness seemed to reign over the scene.

The encampment, with the now silent and deserted tent of the deceased in the midst, was turned into the house of mourning; on the one side extended an unbroken extent of prairie, bounded only by the horizon, its tall grass waving in the breeze and sparkling with daizies, and butter-cups, and roses, and the thousand of other beautiful and fragrant flowers which serve to convert the prairie into a garden, and scent the balmy air of the wilderness with a delicious fragrance; on the other side of the encampment might be seen the skirt of a deep green forest of lofty oaks, and elms, and sycamores, interspersed with the cotton-wood, the coffee-nut, and pekaun, and many other lofty trees that are only to be found west of the waters of the Mississippi. A thick under brush, intertwined with the hazel and sassafras, yielded fragrance and added beauty to the scene.

As we ascended a little eminence to the left, the eye could extend over the rich green canebrake that stretches along the margin of the Neosho, whose clear and transparent waters reflected back the objects upon its banks, and discovered its pebbled bed and thousands of finny inhabitants.

Slowly, and with measured step, this mournful procession entered within the silent inclosure that holds the mouldering remains of many a soldier, and as we rested upon our reversed arms, an aged minister, who happened by chance to be at the fort, offered up a prayer to heaven. The body was then lowered into its narrow dwelling, and as a last tribute of respect to the memory of the deceased, three loud volleys of musketry were discharged over the grave.

These scenes of military pomp have had a powerful and salutary effect upon the mind of the Indians that were staying in the neighborhood of the fort. I had forgotten to mention that immediately upon our arrival at Fort Gibson, we were met by a large number of Pawnee, Camanshe, and other representatives of still wilder tribes, that had assembled there for the purpose of holding a treaty, as they pretended, but for no other purpose in reality than to receive rations at government expense, which are allowed to the Indians when in council at our military posts.

General Leavensworth is at Fort Towson, and will be here in a few days; we shall then, probably, learn something in relation to our summer campaign. I will transmit to you the earliest intelligence in relation to our movements. Till then, I remain as ever,
Your friend, &c.

LETTER XII.

Camp Jackson, A. T. 1834.

Regimental Orders.—Remarks, &c.—Opinions upon the Academy at West Point.—Treatment of the Sick.

My Dear Sir,

The following regimental order was published to the infantry assembled at Fort Gibson, and also to the dragoons, on the 26th of April.

"*Head Quarters, Left Wing, Western Department,*
Fort Towson, April 20, 1834.

"I. In obedience to general orders, dated 12th January, 1834, Brig. Gen. Leavenworth, of the army, assumes command of the troops and the frontier mentioned in that order.

"II. Lieut. Henry Swartwout, of the 3d infantry, has been appointed aid-de-camp to the commanding general, and will be respected accordingly.

"III. In addition to the returns and reports heretofore required, commanding officers of posts and corps will transmit monthly reports of respective commands to the commanding general, at the commencement of each for the month preceding. They will also promptly send to the commanding general any information which they may possess or obtain in relation to the safety or defence of the frontier; and the commanding general invites the officers to favor him with a full, free, and liberal correspondence in relation to the situation of the Indians, the names of the tribes that reside within their command, or who visit it, for what purpose, and where—also as to the topography of the country, the best routes for roads and communications between the several posts, and generally as to all matters connected with or important to the public service.

"IV. All communications for the command will be sent to Fort Gibson until further notice.

"V. The commanding general was highly gratified with the review and inspection, yesterday, of the command of Lieut. Col. Vose. The command was in excellent order, and the highly moral condition of the troops at Fort Towson does great credit to Col.

Vose and his officers. The very fine condition of the troops at this post affords conclusive evidence of the wisdom of banishing ardent spirits from our garrisons.

"VI. The commanding officer at Fort Towson will immediately make and forward a requisition for one *caisson* for a six pounder, and one traveling forge, and for harness and equipments complete for the six pounder, and for the *caisson* and forge.

"VII. The commanding officer at Fort Towson will detach two companies of his command, and cause them to open a road, by the nearest and best route, to the mouth of the False Washita, on the Red River; the streams will be bridged or ferry boats constructed to cross them; and where boats are made, arrangements will also be made to get some of the Choctaw Indians to take charge of them. When bridges are constructed, great care will be taken to have them above inundation, if possible, and if not, they must be constructed so as not to rise or float when the water overflows them. Weekly reports will be made to the commanding general by the commanding officer of this detachment. These reports will be transmitted through the commanding officer at Fort Towson. The assistant quarter-master will furnish a horse or mule for the express between Fort Towson and this detachment.

* * * * *
* * * * *

"By order of General Leavenworth,
"H. SWARTWOUT, *A. D. C. & A. A. Adj. Gen.*"

I have inserted this order nearly at length, because I premised that it would convey an idea of the instructions therein contained, more fully than if I had clothed them in my own language, and being the first order published by General Leavenworth after having been appointed to this command, might naturally be expected to contain important matter.

Shortly after this order General Leavenworth* arrived at our camp. It was a day of gladness to every heart, for it brought with it some tidings that gave promise of entering upon our summer campaign, and getting rid of the monotony of the life that we had led through the winter.

He is a plain-looking old gentleman, tall yet graceful, though stooping under the weight of perhaps

---

* Little did I then imagine that in less than one short year his head would be laid upon its eternal pillow. Short lived indeed were the enjoyments he anticipated in his new appointment, which, to a mind like his, capable of appreciating the glorious creations of nature in the boundless forests and prairies of the far, far west, would naturally give rise to the most joyous anticipations.

Our summer campaign, which we entered upon shortly after his arrival, had but hardly commenced when our beloved commander was attacked by one of the fevers prevalent in these regions, and died while at a detached camp, surrounded by but eight or ten followers.

The imposing and gaudy pageant that followed his remains through the streets of New-York, after their disinterment, was still less imposing, with all its splendor of array and pomp, than was the little band of eight or ten that followed his body to the grave at Camp Smith. There were no spectators there—no solemn tolling of the bell—no thunder of re-echoing artillery—all was still and silent as the tomb itself; the stream of the Washita glided by the spot on one side, and the unbroken level of the prairie verged to the horizon on the other. It was his own request that his remains should be removed to his native place. This request was complied with, and the well-remembered honors with which they were every where escorted, may convey some idea of the general estimation in which he was held.

three-score winters; affable and unassuming in the society of his brother officers, mild and compassionate toward those under his command, combining most happily the dignity of the commander with the moderation and humanity of the Christian, and the modest and urbane deportment of the scholar and the gentleman; all love him, for all have access to him, and none that know him can help but love him.

As he entered our encampment and sallied from tent to tent, heartily shaking hands with many of his old friends whom he met, and bestowing a smile upon all around him, I looked upon him with peculiar sensations. He was a new inhabitant of our little lonely world, one that brought tidings from a home and country far away, and he was greeted with sounds of unaffected welcome from every lip.

The following order was published immediately upon his arrival at Fort Gibson.

"*Head Quarters, Left Wing, Western Department,*
Fort Gibson, 23d *April,* 1834.

"The troops at this post will be mustered on the last day of the present month, at 9 o'clock A. M. by the senior officer " for duty " in each corps. The dragoons and the 7th infantry will parade on the drill ground of the latter corps, near Fort Gibson, at 3 P. M. on the same day, when they will be reviewed and inspected by the commanding general. The senior officer on parade will form and command the line, and pass the troops in review in the manner prescribed in the regulations. Col. Dodge will take measures to be informed when the traders from Missouri to Santa Fe will be in readiness to commence their journey, and if they need or require an escort; and if so, the colonel will make all necessary arrangements for their escort and protection. He will send an efficient and intelligent* officer to Franklin, in Missouri, or wherever it may be necessary to obtain the information, and to make the best possible arrangements for the safety of the traders. Col. Dodge will also make an estimate of every thing that will be required by his corps to prepare them for their contemplated movement, and send it to the office of the acting assistant adjutant-general of this command as soon as possible.

"The commanding officer of the 7th infantry will cause a road to be laid out and marked by the most direct and best route, on the north side of the Arkansas river, from this post to a point opposite the mouth of the little Red River, and from thence to the north fork of the Canadian River, in as direct a course as the nature of the ground will admit, towards the mouth of the False Washita at Red River.

"He will also cause a road to be laid out and marked on the best ground and most direct course from the fort to where the route before mentioned from the little Red River will intersect the north fork of the Canadian.

"He will place a strong detachment on each of these routes, and when they shall meet they shall proceed to lay out a road in the most direct and best route from the north fork of the Canadian River to the mouth of the False Washita at Red River, or until they shall meet a detachment of third infanty heretofore ordered from Fort Towson, to make a road from Fort Towson to the mouth of the False Washita, and which detachment will be ordered to proceed from

---

* Lieut. J. H. K. Burgwin was the officer chosen for this duty.

thence in the direction of the north fork of the Canadian."

* * * * *
* * * * *

The remainder of this order related to internal matters, which would be unintelligible to you, and I have therefore omitted it.

I will merely insert one other order here, which has a more direct bearing upon the regiment of dragoons. It was published on the morning following the review and inspection mentioned in the last.

H. Q., Left Wing, W. Department, May 1, 1834.

" The commanding general was highly gratified with the appearance and performance of the troops at this post on review yesterday.

" The dragoons are in excellent order, much better than could have been reasonably expected considering the very many disadvantages which they have had to encounter during the past winter. It is evident that the officers and men have not been inattentive to their duties. The uniform is very good, as well as very soldierlike and beautiful in its appearance, and the horses appear to be very good, and all their equipments of excellent and substantial quality.

" The eyes of the whole country are upon this corps, and much is expected from it. The gratification and fulfillment of public expectation is a highly valuable prize to contend for; and if by the most ardent and strenuous exertions of every individual of the corps, it can be gained, the reward is a rich one, the esteem and gratification of the country!!

" The *personalle* of this corps is of a high and valuable quality, and the commanding general has heard with surprise and regret that *some of the enlisted men have deserted.* It is true, no doubt, that they have had hard times through the winter, as they have been without either long or short forage for their horses, and consequently compelled to guard them in a canebrake. This, it is confidently believed, will not again occur, and if it should, the enlisted men should bear in mind that it is better to suffer even DEATH than to desert; death would not disgrace their friends and relatives, and although it would distress their feelings, the pang would be far less severe and lasting than that occasioned by desertion, to all which is to be added the incalculable misery to the man himself, by knowing that he has disgraced and perjured himself, and the fear of detection and exposure must unavoidably make him a wretch and a coward for the remainder of his life. He should know also, that a conviction will debar him from being either a legal witness or a juryman in any court of justice, on account of the infamy of his crime. It is therefore to be hoped, that those who have the good fortune to be apprehended, will give such evidence of their contrition and the enormity of their crime, as to induce their gallant and worthy colonel to overlook their offence and permit them to return to duty upon their paying all the expenses of the government. If this should be done, he who should fail to serve " honestly and faithfully " the remainder of his enlistment, and should again desert his colors, would, if possible, *be doubly a villain and superlatively infamous.*

" The commanding general, as a friend to soldiers, conjures them by every thing dear to them, and as they regard either their own comfort or the comfort and happiness of their friends and relatives, to refrain from desertion as the greatest of all possible evils that can befall them."

* * * * *

" This order, or at least that portion of it that relates to desertion, will be read twice at the head of every company, and commandants of companies are required to cause it to be made known to all their men.

" By order," &c.

When this last order was read to the dragoons it brought a smile upon every countenance; but although the action was the same throughout the whole regiment, yet there were several causes that operated upon different minds to produce the same result. The expression made use of in the order, "*that some of the enlisted men have deserted*," was a powerful stimulus to produce a smile; for instead of *some*, the author of the order might have inserted the more appalling words, *over one hundred*, which, up to that date, was really the case; and no less than four men, including a sergeant and corporal, took leg-bail that very night. Another expression caused some foundation for a laugh in one's sleeve—these are the words, "*Those who have had the good fortune to be apprehended*," &c. Now, to tell the plain truth, the only good fortune that the poor fellows experienced that were so circumstanced was, that they received fifty lashes with a raw-hide upon their naked backs, after having for several months dragged a cannon ball after them chained to their legs, and then returned to their troops to serve out the remainder of their term of service, forfeiting all their pay, past and to come.

Such are some of the plain matters of fact; but I am far from attaching any blame to Gen. Leavenworth, for I believe most cordially and sincerely that his motives and intentions were of the purest and most benevolent character, and the order as published by him was proper and correct, as far as his limited knowledge of the circumstances, as in reality they existed, was calculated to effect.

There are numberless internal and external grievances and wrongs existing, in relation to the military establishment of the United States, that should receive the attention of those able to remedy and right them. The usages, the movements, the government of our army, appear to be but little known, and its advancement and prosperity but little cared for by the great mass of the people. If perchance the army becomes the topic of conversation in the domestic circle, or even at the debating club, the soldiers are spoken of as a band of outcasts and fugitives, fit for no other station or employment; and, with some small exceptions, this will not be disputed by those who are acquainted with its internal economy. The cause, too, is plain and obvious. When we reflect for a moment, how can we imagine or expect this to be otherwise; for instance, would a professional student devote his youth to toil through the tedious routine of a preparatory course of study and training for the duties of a calling, if there was an established barrier against his ever attaining to rank and distinction in the profession which he had chosen? And how, therefore, can it reasonably be expected that the respectable youth of our country will voluntarily enlist in a service that offers no hope, or inducement, or even possibility of advancement?

The regiment of the United States dragoons forms, although a small, yet a very conspicuous portion of the American army. Independent of the topographical and engineering departments of our army, its present entire strength is composed of only twelve regiments; seven of infantry, four of artillery, and one of dragoons. A force so small as this for the protection of our frontiers, although more than sufficient, should, nevertheless, be composed of a very different class of men from those that at present fill the ranks, more especially of our infantry regiments.

The Military Academy at West Point, although an institution in every way creditable to the country as well as to those intimately connected with it, is, nevertheless, more of a detriment than an advantage to our army, inasmuch as it monopolizes the right of entirely supplying the army with officers, whilst the enlisted soldier, no matter what may be his merit or his qualifications, can never hope to arrive at any thing more than the petty unthankful office of a corporal or sergeant. I believe that this arbitrary law alone exists under the republican standard of America. In Europe this is different; the enlisted soldier is not there excluded from the hope of arriving at the highest honors of the army. Were this the case in this country, the ranks of our infantry regiments would be composed of a very different material. There would then be some inducement held out to young men to enter into the service, and a spirit of emulation and laudable strife would give a zest to the military profession; instead then of enlisting every vagrant that could be got into the service, there would be, no doubt, in a short time, more young, and ardent, and aspiring competitors than would fill its limited establishment.

Such is the existing character of our army, and such, on the other hand, might be the situation of its affairs, if proper and constitutional measures were taken to effect it. But, so far from any thing being about to be adopted to better the condition of the soldier, a proposal has lately been made, through the pages of the Military Magazine, to establish a school upon the plan of the West Point Academy, for the education and training of non-commissioned officers, and from the different classes of this institution appoint them to the subordinate command of the regiments composing our army. Were this to be carried into effect, it would reduce the American army much lower in the eyes of the world than it now stands; it would be the death-blow to the hopes of the soldier, already within the power of its pernicious influence, and at once preclude all possibility of ever enlisting men of character in its ranks. The beings that would then enlist, would do so without the hope or possibility of ever becoming aught else but private soldiers during their term of enlistment. Our ranks would then be filled with a set of men lost to every thing like hope or energy, or ambition, or any of the more noble and exalted feelings that exert their powerful influence over the heart and passions of man.

I would not have dwelt upon this topic here, had the plan proposed been merely thrown out as an idle speculation, but its practicability was strongly urged; and as one that feels at least some share of interest in the advancement and prosperity of the American army, as well as every other institution in our happy country, I have denounced the proposition as one fatal to the best interests of the army.

The profession of the soldier should, as well as that of the preacher, the lawyer, or the physician, hold out to its votaries inducements worthy of their attainment, and not *unconstitutionally* debar him from arriving at the distinctions and eminence to which his qualifications and merit may peculiarly invite him.

As every monopoly is not only prejudicial to the circle of its immediate influence, but in a great degree affects the public welfare, so should the military establishment at West Point be looked upon as a monopoly, affecting the vital interests of the very class of men whose interests it was established to promote. I have ever been an admirer of that institution in its admirable management and discipline, as well as the unquestionable and eminent standing of its faculty; yet, nevertheless, from actual experience and observation, I can bear testimony to its withering influence upon our army, and am prepared to say that its pernicious tendency to keep down the ranks below the grade of what it should be, more than overbalances whatever good effects it may be calculated to promote.

Should the Military Academy at West Point furnish one-half of the army with officers, and the other portion be appointed by their merit from the ranks, it would be soon proved whether the theoretical or practical soldier made the best officer; and not only would this change be perceptible in the officers, but the intermediate grades and the ranks themselves would, in a short time, furnish a striking proof of the utility of the measure. There is one class of officers attached to the army establishment who, at least, should undergo the most strict and severe examination before they should be permitted to exercise their functions—I mean the medical staff, those in whose care is placed the too often neglected health of the soldiers. But this class of officers, in common with those around them, seem to think the life and health of the poor despised soldier of but little consequence; and as long as they can keep up an appearance of doing their duty, they care not to inquire the result.

Every morning, about twenty minutes before breakfast, or half an hour before eight, "sick call" blows, and then may be seen issuing from the different quarters a crowd of "*sick, lame, and lazy*" soldiers, as is the common phrase among them, some with arms in slings, some on crutches, and others with long faces, presenting, when arrived at the doctor's tent, as motley a group as might well be imagined. The doctor then commences calling them, one by one, as their names occur in the "sick-book" of their respective companies, and conversation to the effect of the following may be imagined to take place:

"Well, Jones, how do you feel this morning?"

"I don't see that I get much better, Doctor."

"What! No better! This is the fourth day that you have been reported sick."

The Doctor then feels his pulse, perhaps tells him to stick out his tongue, which he half the time forgets to look at, and then dismissing the patient, marks down a prescription opposite his name, and calls up the next.

"Well, Bennet, what's the matter with you?"

"I've got a scalded foot, sir."

"How did that happen?"

"The coffee-kettle upset upon it as I was making up the fire."

"You ought to take more care! This is the third time that you've complained within a month! Go to your quarters, sir!"

In this manner, not the most feeling or congenial to those who are laboring under the burden of disease, does the doctor proceed on through the whole list, marking down pretty much the same prescription in every case, no matter whether the patient be afflicted with rheumatism, mumps, fever, or fracture; in all of which cases, as well as almost every other that may occur to the soldier, calomel is the grand restorative; and little regard is paid to the quantity, whether the patient be of a weak and exhausted frame, or enjoying a hearty and robust constitution; often dose is given upon dose, without advising as to diet or aught else, until the sufferer is left to its devastating effects upon his constitution; until, too late, he becomes sensible of the inroad it has made; and although his ailment at first might have been but trifling, and very little proper advice in the first place would have restored him to health, he has now learned, by sad experience, that, through careless indifference, at least, on the part of the surgeon, his whole system has been undermined.

My own observation has been witness to a number of instances where a slight indisposition, (that might have been checked by some simple remedy,) has been protracted, by the improper and unprofessional course of treatment on the part of the surgeon, to an incurable disease. I have particularly noted several of my young companions, who, when their names were noted upon the fatal "sick-book," bore all the appearances of a sound constitution and ruddy health, gradually decline, their countenances merging from the rosy hue of healthfulness into the sallow and ghastly likeness of disease; their firm step giving way to the totter of decrepitude; their strong arms shaking with a nervous tremour; their bright eyes become sunken and dilated; and, in fact, through a course of either willful neglect, or gross mal-practice, brought down within a short period of time from the health, and buoyancy, and joyousness of youth, to a premature grave.

But I am weary of this topic. When I look around me and view the attenuated forms of many of my companions, who, but a few months since, left their happy homes in health and expectation, I cannot but feel deeply for them. My own constitution has, however, thus far withstood all the attacks of disease and privation; and having schooled my mind to bear all patiently, I live upon the anticipation of other and pleasanter scenes.

We are under marching orders, and wait only to be reinforced by the remainder of our troops, to enter upon the summer's campaign. I will perhaps write again previous to our departure. Meanwhile, I remain yours, &c.

LETTER XIII.

Company A accompanies the Traders to Santa Fe—An Adventure—Arrival of new Companies—Various Occupations—Officers instructed by a Sergeant—Reflections.

Camp Jackson, Cherokee Nation, A. T. 1834.

MY DEAR SIR,

In obedience to the instructions of General Leavenworth, Lieut. Burgwin proceeded to Franklin, and brought back word that the traders were ready to proceed on their journey over the mountains to Santa Fe, and accordingly Capt. Wharton's troop was ordered to get in readiness to escort them on their route. They left Camp Jackson on the 5th of May, and proceeded to the Red River, where they met the traders.

A few days after, company B, under command of Captain E. V. Sumner, was despatched upon a short tour into the country of the Osages, for the purpose of settling a disturbance that had taken place between the delegates from several different tribes who had committed depredations upon them whilst passing through their nation. We took several chiefs prisoners, as hostages, to insure the good behavior of the rest. Several appeared very refractory, and one chief in particular exhibited the strongest symptoms of trying to excite his tribe and the rest of the Indians to make war upon our troop when they were about to depart peacefully from the encampment. This chief became so much enraged at his being detained as a prisoner, that he stript from him his blanket and jumped into the midst of one of the blazing log-heaps that had been kindled in the different parts of the camp ground, and commenced the wild yell of desperation used by the Indians during their battles. He continued some minutes jumping and yelling amid the flames that were snapping and cracking around him, then sprung upon the earth and rolled over and over in the sand, tearing and lacerating his flesh in the most cruel and shocking manner; then again he jumped into the flames, still continuing his song of defiance.

This conduct was not perhaps so much the result of rage at his detention as a prisoner, as for the purpose of rousing the other Indians against the whites; but he failed to effect his purpose, for which he had submitted himself to such appalling and horrible tortures. At length, after having endured this scene calmly for some time, Major Mason ordered twelve soldiers to take deliberate aim at the chief, and if that did not have the effect of silencing him, to fire; but the last alternative was not resorted to, for the sight of twelve muskets directed against his breast was sufficient to make him yield; he soon became silent, and made no farther attempt to excite the other Indians.

This chief was left at the Osage lodge when our troop returned to the fort, in a most shocking and hopeless condition; his flesh was literally, in many places, burned to a crust, and the blood flowed in streams from the lacerated wounds that had been caused by rolling in that condition, on the ground.

Our troop took back to the fort with them two Pawnee squaws that had been taken prisoners by the Osages. These squaws were taken for the purpose of being carried by our regiment home to their own nation, to hold out a better inducement to that savage tribe to give up Abbey, the white man that had been taken prisoner by them during the summer of 1832 from one of the troops of mounted rangers.

Company F arrived at Camp Jackson about two weeks since, from Jefferson barracks. They were twenty-four days upon their route, and traveled over pretty much the same road that had been broken through by the first battalion the previous fall. This troop is for the most part composed of Bostonians.

Company G arrived a day or two after, and pitched their tents a little detached from the extreme left of our encampment, which has now grown into a formidable settlement, on account of this accession to our numbers. This last troop was enlisted in the state of Indiana.

More of the companies are assembled now than at any time before had been together; companies H, I, and K are expected soon to join the main body and set forward with us upon the summer campaign. Our camp is now, throughout the day, a constant scene of bustle and noise, the blacksmith shops are kept in continual operation, tailors and saddlers find constant employment, and in fact no one has time to be idle; one half the regiment are daily detailed to watch the horses whilst grazing upon the prairies, which is now the most severe duty to be performed, standing during the whole of the day exposed to the heat of a broiling sun, which during the last week has raised the mercury to from 103° to 107° in the thermometer.

Besides these occupations, the more immediate duties of the dragoons are strictly attended to. It has now become necessary to have every man and horse belonging to the regiment got into as good discipline as possible. The most egregious oversight on the part of Congress, in not providing proper instructors in horsemanship and dragoon tactics, is now most severely experienced; here is a newly recruited regiment, under marching orders to explore a wild and unknown region of country, perhaps to encounter superior numbers of an enemy whose lives have been devoted to the chase, and who are perhaps the most accomplished horsemen in the world, with but about six months training, and that under officers who know less of the manœuvres of a cavalry corps than some of the dragoons themselves.* It is rather a laughable fact,

* The accomplished and able writer of a series of letters which

and one which reflects but little credit upon the accomplished graduates of West Point, that they should be compelled to receive instruction in swordmanship from one of the enlisted members of the regiment. Such however is the case; and my friend Long Ned (with whom by this time you must have become familiar by my frequent mention of his name) regularly every afternoon exercises a class of commissioned officers in this branch of tactics, which they attempt afterward to impart to the men. They have no reason

have lately been published under the title of a "Winter in the West," has alluded to this subject in a letter dated "*Jefferson Barracks, March 8th*," in which the following remarks may be found:

"The omission of providing riding-masters and a school of practice for both horses and men, is a defect that all the care and exertions of the accomplished and energetic officers of this corps can hardly remedy. The same pains should be taken with each individual here as in "setting up" an ordinary recruit before subjecting him to company drill; and no private should be allowed to back the managed charger assigned to him before he has taken at least one regular course of lessons with the riding-master; nor should a single troop have been sent from the head quarters of the regiment before not only every squad was perfect in the drill, but every company in the regiment had manœuvred for months together. The omission of the necessary provisions in the bill reported by Congress, and the disposition of the regiment on the frontier as each company is recruited, almost forbids an approach to such a state of discipline."

The remarks of this talented writer upon the corps of dragoons in other portions of this highly entertaining work, are such as evince a spirit of candor upon his part, and are to be relied upon with the utmost exactness. In the note upon the one hundred and eleventh page of his second volume, he again alludes to the state of the regiment, which remarks are also correct. And here would I take occasion to remark, that a perusal of the volumes entitled "A Winter in the West," will amply repay the reader for his time and trouble.

however to be ashamed of their instructor, for no man in the country handles the sword with more grace and dexterity; but what I would smile at, is this reverse order of affairs—a sergeant instructing his superior officers in the very science with which, of all others, they should be most familiar. But I have already said enough about the internal policy of our army affairs to remind you that a change might be effected for the better, and the sooner such a change is made, the sooner will the ranks of our regiments be filled with better material than the *ignobile vulgus* that crowd the most of our military stations.

The hour reminds me that I must close this letter. I will merely add that we are to set out upon the summer campaign in two or three days. As I before mentioned, the three remaining troops are daily expected, and, immediately upon their arrival, we will take up the line of march for the far off regions of the west. You shall have particulars whenever I find means of transmitting them.

With respect, I remain yours, &c.

LETTER XIV.

FROM GEORGE CATLIN, ESQ.

I take the liberty of inserting in this volume the following very interesting letter from Mr. Catlin, an eminent artist who accompanied the regiment of dragoons from Fort Gibson to the Pawnee village. Mr. C. accompanied the expedition for purposes connected with his profession, and brought home with him many sketches which will doubtless gratify and delight the amateurs of the east.

Fort Gibson, A. T. 12th June, 1834.

MY DEAR SIR,

Being about to leave the civilized world again for a campaign in the Indian country, I take this opportunity to bequeath a few words to you before the moment of departure. Having sometime since obtained permission from the Secretary of War to accompany the regiment of the U. S. dragoons in their summer campaign, I reported myself at this place two months ago, where I have been waiting ever since for their organization. After the many difficulties which they have had to encounter, they have at length all assembled—the grassy plains are resounding with the trampling hoofs of the prancing war-horse, and already the hills are echoing back the notes of the spirit-stirring trumpets, which are sounding for the onset. The natives are again "to be astonished," and I shall probably again be a witness of the scene. But whether the approach of eight hundred mounted dragoons among the Camanches and Pawnees, will afford me a better subject for a picture of a gaping and astounded multitude, than did the first approach of our steamboat among the Mandans, &c. is a question yet to be solved. I am strongly inclined to think that the scene will not be less wild and spirited; and I ardently wish it, for I have become so much Indian of late, that my pencil has lost all appetite for subjects that savor of tameness. I should delight in seeing these red knights of the lance astonished, for it is then that they show their brightest hues—and I care not how badly we frighten them, provided we hurt them not, nor frighten them out of sketching distance. You will agree with me that I am going farther to get sitters, than any of my fellow artists ever did; but I take an indescribable pleasure in roaming through nature's trackless wilds, and selecting my models where I am free and unshackled by the killing restraints of society, where a painter must modestly sit and breathe away in agony the edge and soul of his inspiration, waiting for the sluggish calls of the civil. Though the toil, the privations, and expense of traveling to these remote parts of the world to get subjects for my pencil, place almost insurmountable, and sometimes painful, obstacles before me, yet am I encouraged by the continual conviction that I am practicing in the true school of the arts; and that, though I should get as poor as Lazarus, I should deem myself rich in studies for the future occupation of my life. Of this much I am certain—that among these sons of the forest, where are continually repeated the feats and gambols of the Grecian games, I have learned more of the essential parts of the art in the three last years, than I could have learned in New-York in a life-time.

The landscape scenes of these wild and beautiful regions are of themselves a rich reward for the traveler who can place them in his port-folio; and being myself the only one accompanying the dragoons for scientific purposes, there will be an additional pleasure to be derived from those pursuits. The regiment of eight hundred men, with whom I am to travel, will be an effective force, and a perfect protection against any attacks that will ever be made by Indians. It is composed principally of young men of respectable families, who would act, on all occasions, from feelings of pride and honor, in addition to those of the common soldier.

The day before yesterday the regiment of dragoons, and the 7th regiment of infantry, stationed here, were reviewed by Gen. Leavenworth, who has lately arrived at this post, superseding Col. Arbuckle in the command.

Both regiments were drawn up in battle array, in fatigue dress, and passing through a number of the manœuvres of battle, of charge and repulse, &c. presenting a novel and thrilling scene in the prairie to the thousands of Indians and others who had assembled to witness the display. The proud and manly deportment of these young men remind one forcibly of a regiment of independent volunteers; and the horses have a most beautiful appearance, from the arrangement of colors. Each company of horses has been selected of one color entire. There is a company of bays, a company of blacks, one of whites, one of sorrels, one of greys, one of cream color, &c. &c. &c. which render the companies distinct, and the effect exceedingly pleasing. This regiment goes out under the command of Col. Dodge, and from his well attested qualifications, and from the beautiful equipment of the command, there can be little doubt but they will do credit to themselves and honor to their country, so far as honor can be gained and laurels can be plucked from their wild stems in a savage country.

The object of this summer's campaign seems to be to cultivate an acquaintance with the Pawnees and Camanches. These are two extensive tribes of roaming Indians, who, from their extreme ignorance of us, have not yet recognized the United States in treaty, and have struck frequent blows on our frontiers, and plundered our traders who are traversing their country. For this I cannot so much blame them, for the Spaniards are gradually advancing upon them on one side, and the Americans on the other, and fast destroying the furs and game of their country, which God gave them as their only wealth and means of subsistence. This movement of the dragoons seems to be one of the most humane in its views, and I heartily hope that it may prove so in the event, as well as for our own sakes as for that of the Indians.

I can see no reason why we should march upon them with an invading army, carrying with it the spirit of chastisement. The object of government undoubtedly is to effect a friendly meeting with them, that they may see and respect us, and to establish something like a system of mutual rights with them. To penetrate their country with the other view, that of chastising them, even with five times the number that are now going, would be entirely futile, and perhaps disastrous in the extreme. It is a pretty thing, and perhaps an easy one, in the estimation of the world, for any army of mounted men to be gayly prancing over the boundless green fields of the west; and it is so for a little distance; but it would be well that the world should be apprized of some of the actual difficulties that oppose themselves to the success of such a campaign, that they may not censure too severely in case this command should fail to accomplish the objects for which they were organized.

In the first place, from the great difficulty of organizing and equipping, these troops are starting too late in the season for their summer's campaign, by two months. The journey which they have to perform is a very long one, and although the first part of it will be picturesque and pleasing, the after part of it will be tiresome and fatiguing in the extreme. As they advance to the west, the grass, and consequently the game, will be gradually diminishing, and water in many parts of the country not to be found.

As the troops will be obliged to subsist themselves a great part of the way, it will be extremely difficult to do it under such circumstances, and at the same time to hold themselves in readiness, with half famished horses, and men nearly exhausted, to contend with a numerous enemy, who are at home, on the ground on which they were born, with horses fresh and ready for action. It is not probable, however, that the Indians will venture to take advantage of such circumstances, but I am inclined to think that the expedition will be more likely to fail from another source; it is my opinion that the appearance of so large a military force in their country will alarm them to that degree, that they will fly with their families to their hiding places amongst those barren deserts, which they themselves can reach only by great fatigue and extreme privation, and to which our half exhausted troops cannot possibly follow them.

From these haunts their warriors would advance and annoy the regiment as much as they could, by striking at their hunting parties and cutting off their supplies. To attempt to pursue them, if they cannot be called to a council, would be as useless as to follow the wind; for our troops, in such a case, are in a country where they are obliged to subsist themselves; and the Indians, being on fresh horses, with a supply of provisions, would easily drive all the buffalo ahead of them, and endeavor, as far as possible, to decoy our troops into the barren parts of the country, where they could not find the means of subsistence.

The plan designed to be pursued, and the only one that can succeed, is to send runners to the different bands, explaining the friendly intentions of our government, and to invite them to a meeting. For this purpose several Camanche and Pawnee prisoners have been purchased from the Osages, who may be of great service in bringing about a friendly interview.

I ardently hope that this plan may succeed, for I am anticipating great fatigue and privation in the endeavor to see these wild tribes together, that I may be enabled to lay before the world a just estimate of their manners and customs.

I hope that my suggestions may not be truly prophetic, but I am constrained to say that I doubt very much whether we shall see any thing more of them than their trails, and the sites of their deserted villages.

Several companies have already started from this place, and the remaining ones will be on their march in a day or two. General Leavenworth will accompany them two hundred miles, to the mouth of False Washita, and I shall be attached to his staff. Incidents which may occur I shall record for you. Until then, adieu.   Your friend and servant,

GEO. CATLIN.

LETTER XV.

Two stories and a half.

My Dear Sir,

I thought, at the date of my last, that I should not again write you before our return from the prairies, but an occurrence which took place last evening furnishes me with a little amusing material.

It was about half an hour after tattoo, when I was about returning to my bunk, somewhat fatigued with the toils and heat of the day, when two of my companions, Corporal Ned Stephens and Harry Benson, came into the barrack-room and gave me the wink to follow them.

Accordingly, throwing my guard-cloak around me, I left the quarters, and in a few moments our party was joined by our friend Long Ned, who had been waiting without the sentry-walk for our arrival.

"Boys," said he, "this is perhaps the last evening that we shall spend here. Now, as you know we have a long journey in prospect, and have had some months of temperance in arrears, I've no notion of letting this last chance slip by of partaking of a little *rational enjoyment.* What do you agree to?"

"Let's go to Rodger's," said Corporal Stephens, "and talk about old times, over a venison steak and a drop of whiskey."

"Not so," said Benson. "The M—— lost some cool hundreds last night at poker,* in camp, and is to meet some brother officers at Rodger's to night. So that won't do."

* A favorite game of cards at the south and west.

"Well," said Long Ned, "the moon shines bright, and as the weather bids fair, let's take an out-door sitting for want of better quarters. So toss up who goes for the whiskey, and then hurra for the hollow behind the *bayou*."

This was agreed to, and it fell to my lot to act the part of caterer. So off they started for the *bayou*, while I trudged across the prairie to our mutual friend old Rodger's cabin.

It was strictly forbidden that any man should leave the barrack-ground after dark without a written pass, upon any pretence whatever; and moreover, whiskey was a contraband article among the soldiers, probably because the officers deemed the supply not more than sufficient for *home consumption;* therefore the business that I had in hand was one of double risk and severe penalty, in case of detection.

However, I walked boldly up to the house and commenced reconnoitering. First I creeped under the window, and saw that the room was lighted, but could not distinguish any one distinctly; presently I heard the Major and Captain, talking loudly, and soon discovered what was going on.

"I'll stake you another ten," cried the M——.

"Done," said Captain ———.

"Twenty more," said the M——.

"Done," said the Captain.

"Fifty more" said the M——.

"Done," said the Captain.

The M—— hesitated; the coolness of the Captain threw him off his guard; at last he struck his fist upon the table and roared at the top of his voice,

"I'll stake you another hundred."

"Done," said the Captain.

The M—— dared not risk more, and throwing down his cards exclaimed,

"There's four kings! What have you got?"

"Only four aces!" said the Captain coolly, as he began to scrape the money together.

"D—m——n!" roared the M——, at the same time splitting the pine table with a blow of his fist.

That's enough, thought I, the M—— has lost again, and we shall probably have an hour's extra drill in the morning to make up for it.

Some one now came into the hall, and I skulked down into the grass until I should see who it might be; the fellow, however, came into the moon-light, and I discovered him to be one of old Rodgers' slaves.

"Ben—Ben—Ben," I whispered as loud as I dared—"Ben—Ben, I say." He heard the last call, and came to where I was sitting in the grass.

"Ben," said I, "here's a dollar—hurra for a quart of whiskey in a twinkling.'

The fellow was used to such calls and obeyed *instanter;* and in a few minutes more I was "making tracks" toward the trysting place.

A more lovely and retired spot could not have been selected for the carousal of a party of skulking soldiers, than the hollow behind the *bayou.* There I found Long Ned, as usual, master of ceremonies, upon the stump of an old oak tree, and the rest of the company reclining upon the grass, after the fashion of a Gipsey group. After the bottle had gone around, it was proposed that every man should tell his story; this was carried, and Corporal Stephens being second in rank, was appointed to speak first; and after prefacing his story with sundry clearings of the throat, and divers flourishes, commenced.

"Gentlemen, and fellow-soldiers, like Irving's Jack Buckthorne, I was born to great expectations, which, to anticipate my story a little, is all that I ever realized. I had the misfortune to have a rich uncle, who, after I had paid all the attention to, that I was able whilst living, left me the price of a Bible in his will."

"Ha! ha! ha!" roared Long Ned, loud enough to be heard at the barracks.

"No laughing matter, gentlemen, I assure you," exclaimed the corporal; "why, he cut me off without a shilling."

"The old man," said Benson, "had too much love for you to put temptation in your way—here's his health," he continued, putting the bottle to his mouth.

"Stop! stop!" cried the corporal, "he's been dead these six years."

"Well, then, we'll drink peace to his ashes, provided there's any thing left of him."

"Well, as I was saying, the old gentleman left me the price of a Bible, and the rest of his property all went to a fellow that he had only seen once in his life."

"There's disinterested benevolence for you!" interrupted Long Ned.

"Benevolence with a vengeance!" roared the corporal. "Squandered—clean wasted!—why it didn't last the cub two years after the old gentleman's death."

"So much the better for you—who knows what you might have come to if you had got the money," said Benson.

"Gentlemen," cried the corporal, "let's drop that subject—I hate to dwell upon such things too long— so let's proceed. Well, I had picked up a little Latin at school, and so, thinks I, here it is with me, neck or nothing, so off I started for New-York; and opened a grammar school for young gentlemen."

"You a grammar school! ha! ha!—but go on," said Benson.

"Yes, gentlemen, I might have done very well too, hadn't things turned up rather badly the first quarter."

"No doubt," said Long Ned, in his sleeve.

"Then I set about writing pieces for newspapers."

"Worse and worse," again interrupted Long Ned.

"Better and better, if you please," continued the corporal; "this brought me two dollars a week, besides the old paper, which made up a half dollar more."

"So you turned editor, eh?" asked Benson.

"Why not exactly editor either. I manufactured accidents, and fires, and providential escapes, and the like. In this way I went on pretty comfortably for about two years, when one day, as I was coming through the Park, I saw a great crowd of people, and thinks I to myself, here is something in my line, and so I elbowed through the crowd, and who do you think I saw there in the clutches of a police officer, and so drunk that he could hardly stand, and as ragged and shabby as a beggar? Why no other than the heir to all my uncle's property."

"That was an item for you," said Long Ned; "your hand must have trembled as you wrote the fellow's name."

"Why," said the corporal, "Gentlemen, to tell you the plain truth, that very circumstance immortalized me. I went to my office (I occupied one corner of the editor's) and then I sat down and wrote a long article upon the 'dreadful effect of young men being left large fortunes.'"

"How did it go down?" asked Benson.

"Go down! why, sir, it was copied into every paper in the country in less than a month, and on account of the number of subscribers that it brought the paper, I was allowed a dollar a week more pay—why, I was a made man; I left the victualing-shop where I had lived upon sixpenny cuts of roast beef and turkey for the two years past, and took lodgings in a regular boarding-house—took an office upon my own account, and issued prospectuses for a new weekly paper. I determined that I would no longer waste my brains for other people, so the next week saw my name in full at the head of the ——— Magazine. The first difficulty that I met with was to procure paper; I had spent all my spare funds in the purchase of divers incidental little affairs that are alone to be appreciated by one who has had to buy the same—so, to get the paper I had to pawn an old family watch that had descended down to me, as Mrs. Somebody would say, through a long line of distinguished ancestors. On this I got ten dollars, and that was enough to buy paper for the first week's issue, hoping to realize enough from the proceeds of them to pay for the second."

"Well," said Long Ned, who had listened attentively to this detail, "how did you make out?"

"Aye, there's the rub! Make out? Why, sir, the very elements were opposed to me, a rainy day spoiled it all; the boys that I had engaged to sell the papers refused to go out in the rain, and so things went on till afternoon, when a colored man came into the office to buy a paper for his master, who had read a flaming puff that I had written for the T———, then the paper most in vogue; this inspired my drooping spirits, and off I started with a bundle of papers under my arm, determined to try my own luck; but, alas alas! my courage soon failed me; three or four people to whom I offered my papers for sale, looked them over attentively with a very polite '*I believe not.*' This was too much; back I posted to the office, when, lo! it was as clear of furniture as a poet's purse of money. 'What is to pay here?' I cried, in a rage, to the little rascal that I had left in charge.

" 'Mr. Smith, sir, came and took the chair and table away on a cart, sir,' he answered, as he trembled all over, for he saw that I was in a rage.

" 'And what had Mr. Smith to do with my furniture?' I raved.

" 'Why, sir, he said 'twas all he was likely to get for printing the magazine, sir.'

" 'The villain!' cried I, 'I will prosecute him for damages;' and I cast my eyes sorrowfully at the pile of magazines on the floor. This Mr. Smith was the only man that had offered to trust me in the first place, and now to turn his back upon me in my misfortune, it was too much; I started out, determined to commence a suit against him for damages. On my way from my empty office to the lawyer's, who should I meet but an old school-mate of mine, dressed with a blue round jacket trimmed all over with gold lace."

" 'My good fellow,' said he, 'how are you? Very glad to see you! How well you look! Things turned out well with you since you left the country?'

" He would have gone on talking for an hour if I hadn't stopped him; so I told him every thing that had happened, and just how I was situated.

" 'Now,' said he, 'let me advise you as a friend—enlist with me.'

"'Enlist!' I answered in astonishment, 'no, no. I am determined to work my way in the world, and be somebody. Enlist indeed!'

"'Good morning, sir,' said my military friend drily, when he found that I wasn't to be caught so easy.

"But, gentlemen, to cut a long story short, things went on worse and worse with me, and at last I began to think of the proposal in good earnest; eight dollars a month, thinks I, besides rations, this was too much; so I went to look after my friend, but he had gone, his company had been filled up, so I determined to enter the service; off I started to find another recruiting officer, and in a word, here I am."

"Bravo! bravo!" shouted the whole party, and my friend Harry Benson was next called on to tell his life and adventures.

Now, my dear M——, if you have never been away from home, and among strangers, or on ship board, you cannot appreciate the zest with which a yarn is swallowed by such an audience, and the more especially if you have ever been familiar with the scenes and *dramatis personæ* of the tale. But, not to interrupt my friend Harry any longer, let us listen to his story. Thus he commenced:

"I was born in the city of Dublin, in the *swate* little island of Erin, and my father followed the respectable calling of a shop-keeper. But I was born to be a great man, and so I mean to be yet. Look there," said Harry vehemently, (as he pointed to a mole upon his right arm,) "do you see that? Well, if you do, that's enough. If there is a word of truth in the dream-book, Harry, says I to myself, you'll live to see the day when you'll be a great man."

"Ha—ha—ha!" roared all the party except Harry,

who went on as soberly as if he had been saying his prayers.

"Did you ever read Bonaparte's memoirs? because, if you did, you couldn't help knowing that he was a great man," continued he. "Well, now I read them when I was a boy, and immediately, says I, Harry, you was born to be a great man, and so you shall be. Now, just as I was thinking all this over in my own mind, who should come into the room but the old gentleman.

"'Now,' says he to me, 'Harry,' says he, 'how do you like Mr. Ferris?'

"'Is it how do I like him, do you say? Why, he's a decent man enough for a shop-keeper,' says I, 'but he's not at all like Bonaparte neither.'

"'And what do you know about Bonaparte, you limmer of Satan?' said he.

"'Is it what do I know about Bonaparte?' says I. 'Why, didn't I just finish reading his memoirs, and havn't I got a mole on my right arm to boot,' says I; 'and didn't the fortune-teller in Bow-street say to me,' 'Harry,' says he, ' you was cut out for a great man; now see that your father don't spoil the pattern?'

"'Now hark'e,' said the old gentleman, in a peculiar accent that I shall never forget, 'I am going to bind you to Mr. Ferris to-morrow.'

"'Bind me to Mr. Ferris! What! make a haberdasher out of a man with a mole on his right arm!' and all the horrors of a seven years' apprenticeship arose before me.

"'Make yourself in readiness,' said the old gentleman, and left the room.

"Harry, says I, you're in a bad fix this time, notwithstanding. Seven years, thinks I—what's to be done? However, to cut it short, gentlemen, the next morning when the old man came where I was, I wasn't there, that's all."

"Well," cried Long Ned impatiently, "where did you go?"

"Leave me alone for that," said Harry, "where should a gentleman go that had the mark of being a great man all over him; why I went to London and made my first inquiry for the horse guards, and in a crack Harry Benson was on the high road to promotion, having enlisted as a private in his majesty's —— regiment of foot, and in less than a month I got to be third corporal! Thinks I all this time, Harry, what might the old gentleman say if he knew where you was; but better so, thinks I, than measuring tape behind Mr. Ferris's counter."

"Well, Harry," said the corporal, "how did you get to America—between two days, eh?"

"*The divil a man*," said Harry, in reply to this insinuation, "can say that Harry Benson is a deserter. No, no, honor among thieves; I procured an honorable discharge from his majesty's service and sailed next day for America. Having been a soldier at home, I was soon induced to become a soldier here. You know as well now as I can tell you, how they talked to a fellow when they wanted to enlist him, and so I shall save myself the trouble of telling it."*

---

* The history of Harry Benson's exploits while in his majesty's service have been wound into a most interesting narrative by my excellent friend Mr. John M. Moore, and published in his highly entertaining paper. The incidents as related above, although in some respects differing from those related of him in the European, may be relied on as authentic, as I got them from Harry's own mouth.

"Harry," says the corporal, "don't your conscience sometimes trouble you?"

"Now and then," answered Harry, "but I keep it for the most part smothered in whiskey."

Harry's story gave universal satisfaction, and after another round from the bottle, Long Ned hem'd and began.

"My father was a major in the British lancers," he commenced, and seemed to stretch himself three inches above his usual height. "When I was twelve years old he was stationed at Castle Cornet, in the island of Guernsey, from whence I was sent to college at London; here I stayed till I was seventeen, when I got the appointment of cornet in the —— dragoon guards, and shortly after was appointed riding-master to the regiment, in which station I remained for nearly five years; but becoming tired of the inactive service of a heavy dragoon, I obtained a transfer into an East India regiment, and went to Maidstone for the purpose of joining them; but there altering my mind, I obtained a commission in a regiment then fitting out to join the Liberals in Portugal, in the service of Don Pedro. About the middle of July we set sail from London, over a hundred strong, and arrived some two or three days after at Plymouth; from here we took ship, and were nine days upon our passage to Oporto. Thus far we had not lost a single man. Coming in view of the city, I was struck with the grandeur of the scene, built upon its seven hills, and at this time surrounded by more than fifty thousand of the enemy's troops, who were continually pouring in tremendous volleys of shot and shell. Perceiving our ship, they did us the honor to send us a shell in our direction, which carried away the jib-boom. We lay till night off the city, and then disembarked amid the fire of the enemy's musketry, but fortunately we only lost two men. We marched into the town, and when we went through the streets were cheered by the ladies from the windows and balconies, who waved their white handkerchiefs and cried, *Viva la Constitution! Viva la Anglais! Viva la Don Pedro!* We quartered that night in an old convent situated a little without the town, called the *Convent de Seminario*. The second day after our arrival I was appointed adjutant of the regiment, and met the enemy five days afterwards in a skirmish, near a little fort on the opposite side of the river Duro, called the *Sara Convent*, garrisoned by about eight hundred men. Then as——

"Halt!—stand!—take them all prisoners!" cried the sergeant of the patroll, who had overheard us laughing, and now commanded that we should be taken to the guard-house.

"Sergeant, a word in your ear!" said Harry. "It's somewhat cold I think to-night."

"Cold!" re-echoed the sergeant, "why it's hot enough to roast eggs!"

"That's just what I mean," said Harry; "so take a drop of the *creatur* and say no more about it."

During this conversation Long Ned and the corporal had slipped slyly away, and skulked into camp, whilst Harry Benson and myself were the only ones of the party left in the custody of the patroll.

"It can't hurt you, sergeant," continued Harry, "so put your lips to the bottle and take a wee taste."

The sergeant yielded, and, of course, after him all the rest of the guard, therefore the next morning found us, as usual, at roll-call, nevertheless sorry that Long Ned's story had been interrupted.

LETTER XVI.

Various incidents on the march from Fort Gibson to the Pawnee Village.

Camp Washita, July, 1834.

My Dear Sir,

Our command has just halted, and I seize the opportunity to write you a line to accompany a few leaves of my journal, and never upon a spot more romantic was a letter ever penned. A grove of forest trees, the first that we have met for several days, afford us a delightful and refreshing shade; our men and horses are lying upon the grass in every direction, and a more lovely scene you may not well imagine.

A baggage-wagon is to be sent back to Fort Gibson to-day, and the driver has consented to be the bearer of this. I have but a moment, however, to devote to you, and must content myself with transmitting the enclosed extract from my notes, which I have been somewhat particular to take.

Encampment, west bank of the Arkansas,
June 15, 1834.

The three last recruited troops arrived at Camp Jackson on the afternoon of the 12th, and pitched a temporary encampment on the left of our barracks. Three days having been allowed them to prepare for the summer campaign, we set forward this morning, and crossing the Neosho at Fort Gibson, travelled between three and four miles and pitched our tents along the west bank of the Arkansas. The eight troops which form the command (company "K" having been left at Camp Jackson) are nearly full, and, together with the other personages who accompany the regiment, form quite a formidable and imposing cavalcade; of these personages I will take occasion here to remark at length hereafter, all the representatives of friendly Indian tribes who intend to accompany us on the campaign not yet having arrived. The country on the west side of the Arkansas is occupied by the Creeks and Osages; the land is somewhat higher than on the opposite bank, and is remarkably rich, but the Indians take but little pains to improve it, only raising sufficient corn for their own scanty consumption The Cherokees, on the opposite side, are by far a more industrious and enterprising race, and many of them live much in the manner of their civilized neighbors.

A portion of the prairie over which we travelled today presented a truly beautiful appearance; it was covered with the prickle-pear, the broad yellow blossoms of which species, when reflected on by the sun, exhibited the appearance of a burning sea of gold, and presented a lively and grateful contrast to the dense billow of green beyond it.

We remained at our encampment on the bank of the Arkansas until the morning of the twenty-first, when we were joined by the Indian chiefs and others who are to accompany our regiment upon the campaign; and all arrangements being completed, we took up the line of march toward the Washita river, over the new road which, agreeable to the order of General Leavenworth, had been laid out, and at eight o'clock on the morning of the twenty-first we were again defiling over the prairie. Toward evening we crossed the north fork of the Canadian, and having, during the day, accomplished twenty miles travel, encamped, about sundown, about one mile west of its banks. This river, which is at times a considerable stream, was at this period, however, quite low, owing to the peculiar dryness of this season, and we had but little difficulty in fording it, the water scarcely reaching above our horses knees. This portion of the country abounds in buffalo, which, from various appearances, seem to have been quite numerous here this season; the soil is peculiarly rich, but for the most part lies in a state of unprofitable idleness, and so, in all probability, it will continue while in the hands of the indolent and half-civilized Indians who hold it. But such, probably, is not long destined to be the case, for the country is by far too inviting to escape the notice of the throng of settlers who almost daily keep moving toward the west. A few short years will probably so far change the aspect and character of this region, that many an humble and adventurous squatter will rear his log-cabin at the very base of the Rocky Mountains.

Colonel Dodge, with a small detachment of forty men, left us at this camp and hurried forward to the Washita, where he expected to be reinforced by a division of two companies of infantry, under command of General Leavenworth.

Among the Indians who form part of our command, are representatives from the tribes of the Osages, Cherokees, Delawares, Senecas, and Mohawks.

The Cherokee party being under the command of a chief called *Dutch*, a man remarkable among them for his prowess and courage, as well as for the many successful enterprises which he has carried on against the neighboring tribes, and also a fellow of fine personal appearance.

George Bullett, whose Indian name is Pon-da-gne-se, is the principal leader of the Delawares.

A Frenchman, named *Beatie*, who has lived many years among the Osages, has command of this party; he is also a celebrated hunter, and possesses great skill in his profession.

De-nath-de-ago is in command of the detachment of Senecas.

We have also with us the two Pawnee girls that we took from the Osages last May, and hope that we shall hold out some inducement to that savage tribe, by their restoration, to give up the white prisoner which they captured last summer; and perhaps serve to give a pacific tone to our whole intercourse with them.

Scarce any thing worthy of remark took place during the next two days travel, except the appearance of a prairie mound, at the foot of which we encamped on the evening of the twenty-third. It was about four hundred feet in height, rising somewhat in form of a pyramid. From the summit of this mound the eye could range over a wide and lovely extent of country in either direction. On one side a magnificent valley extended for several miles, while in the distance a range of blue hills formed the outline of the landscape.

From Camp Cass, on the twenty-fourth, we marched westwardly about eighteen miles, over a richly diversified country; alternate patches of prairie and timber-land afforded a grateful relief to each other, and after dark, on the evening of the next day, we forded the stream of the Canadian.

We passed through an Osage village on our route between the Canadian and the False Washita—a nation that have perhaps profited as little by civilization as those who have never been visited by the whites. They still retain most of their wild habits, living mostly upon game. They possess a vast extent of country, almost entirely uncultivated. During the winter they clothe themselves in the skins of the buffalo and other wild animals, but, in the warm season of the year go almost entirely naked, painting their bodies and faces in the most grotesque and unmeaning manner. The village contained about three hundred beings, male and female, including children. They offered us many trifles of their own manufacture in exchange for tobacco and butcher-knives. Many of the men left their village and accompanied our regiment, and many trifling articles which they could not obtain from us by traffic, they found means of pilfering.

This people reminds me of the wandering Gypsies, hunting and theft being their only means of subsistence. During the summer they wander about from place to place, providing for to-day without a thought of to-morrow. Frequently, during their wanderings, they fall in with other tribes, who infest the prairies either for plunder or other mischievous purposes, and engage in the most cruel and sanguinary wars. It was during one of these intestine broils that this tribe took from the Pawnees the two girls, prisoners, who accompany our regiment.

On the twenty-seventh we crossed the Blue River, which region about there is richly impregnated with iron ore, and here we had the honor to kill the first buffalo that had been attacked by any of our men since the commencement of the march.

On the thirtieth we were joined by General Leavenworth, who declared his intention of accompanying the command, in person, to the Pawnee village. We learned that some companies of infantry were to accompany us. Lieutenants Northrop and Steen joined us from the west side of the Washita, which river we forded with much difficulty, and the loss of ten or twelve of our horses, which were drowned.

This river is not very wide, and the water, which is of a muddy red color, runs between high and prominent banks of a miry nature, which made it very inconvenient for our horses to land.

We remained in camp all day on the second of July, and were engaged pretty much all the time on the third, in making preparations for our crossing this stream. The water being quite deep, we were obliged to swim our horses. Our baggage-wagons (which are the greatest drawback to a military expedition that can be experienced) we were obliged to transport by means of a raft, constructed of canoes lashed together and covered with plank; we also used a canvass boat, covered with gum elastic, belonging to Lieut. Col. Kearney, which we found to answer an excellent purpose. Having, at length, ferried over all our movables, we encamped for a few days upon the bank.

Our regiment is now re-organized. We leave one hundred and forty-nine men at this camp, on duty, and eighty-six sick. General Leavenworth also remains here. Six companies of forty-two, rank and file, set forward this morning. Having abandoned our baggage-wagons, we shall make more rapid headway.

On the seventh of July, the weather being extremely oppressive, we commenced our march from the Washita. It having become far advanced in the day before we set out, we traveled but about eight miles, when, after encamping and strengthening our guard, the greater portion of the command worn down by fatigue and the extreme heat of the weather, lay stretched asleep upon the grass. Many suspicious signs were noticed, such as pony tracks, recent fires, &c. and, in fact, an Indian spy, probably a Pawnee or Camanche, was discovered lurking near the encampment, and pursuit was made after him, but to no effect. The night being extremely dark, and in an enemys country, anxiety naturally pervaded every rank; all was still and silent; the smouldering embers of our fires, occasionally stirred by the evening breeze, shot forth a momentary flickering, which only served to render the night still more dark and gloomy. Naught could be heard save the steady step of the sentinel, or the occasional tramping of the horses, which were picketed at our heads, in the centre of the encampment. It had probably reached the hour of mid-night, when we were startled from our sleep by the report of a gun; our horses broke their fastenings and ran in every direction; all was confusion and dismay; each man seized his carbine, and prepared himself for an immediate attack; the bugle sounded the assembly-call; the several companies arranged themselves opposite to their respective divisions; every one expecting that the Indians were upon us. In this state things remained for some time, when the alarm began, in a manner, to abate, and the tumult was ascertained to have been caused by a sentinel's having fired upon a horse that had slipped his fastening and wandered without the guard. The horse immediately, when shot, run violently among the other horses, causing them to become frightened and dispersed in every direction.

Our horses being, at this juncture, our chief dependence, required us to use active and immediate exertion to regain them; fearing, too, that they might fall into the hands of the enemy, we divided ourselves in small parties, and taking different routes, set out in search of them; after being on the watch all night, we found all of them again, with the exception of ten.

We remained in camp all day, and next morning set out at early dawn. We had proceeded but a few miles, when we discovered a party of mounted Indians on our left, (probably Pawnees,) and were immediately ordered to halt. A party of about forty dragoons, under the command of Captain Hunter, was ordered to advance toward them with a flag of truce. When they had proceeded about two miles, they despatched a messenger back to the regiment, with the report that they could distinguish three white flags among the Indians; but this was probably a mistake, for we lost sight of them shortly after, and saw no more of them for several days; but from this time forward did we carry, in advance, and on either side of us, a flag of truce.

I have but a moment to spare as the wagon is about to start. I will not probably be able to forward you another letter until after our return to Fort Gibson. I will, however, mark down in my journal all incidents that may occur, of an interesting nature, on the route. The weather is excessively warm, and we are about entering the Grand Prairie. Our little band is daily diminishing in numbers on account of sickness. We are obliged to construct temporary sheds of poles covered with boughs and leaves, under which the sick men are sheltered from the scorching sun. As I before mentioned, General Leavenworth remained at the sick camp, on the Washita.

LETTER XVII.

Continuation of march from the Grand Prairie to the Pawnee Village, and return march to Fort Gibson.

Fort Gibson, A. T. 1834.

My dear Sir,

Since the date of my last we have had many a toilsome and weary day. We have, indeed, fulfilled, to the letter, one count in the specified object of our enlistment, that is, "to scour the prairies and forests of the west." You can be as little aware of the diversity of scenes through which we have passed, as of the varied reflections which they give rise to.

Sometimes the mind will seem unloaded with a single burden, wholly absorbed in the excitement and novelty of the scenes around it; then again will a cloud pass over this sunny, but too transient dream, and relapse into the dull monotony of sad reflections. When the day had sunk to rest, and the gray mists of evening gathered around; when the weary horses and their no less jaded riders might be seen reclining upon the grass around the encampment, then came the hour of reflection. Such is the time when our inmost souls open themselves upon us, and all that years had garnered up in our bosoms flit before us in an instant Often, at such a moment, have I again in fancy mingled with those whom memory has treasured in her fondest embrace; but, even then, when the mind had become dead to the scenes around, would oftentimes our happiest reflections be dissipated in an instant by the echo of some envious bugle note.

My last, if I remember aright, left us at the bank of the Washita, from which camp we again continued on our march toward the west. The next day we saw, in the distance, a number of buffalo, and several hunting parties were detached from our regiment to pursue them. Captain Boone took charge of the small party of six, to which I was attached, and directed his course through a dense thicket of briers, almost impassable, for the purpose of finding two which had been killed by the Indians of our party the previous night, which having found, we returned with as much of the meat as we could carry on our horses, towards the regiment, which had already taken up the line of march, and depositing it, again set out in quest of more; we rode through several thickets so matted together with an undergrowth of nettles and briers, as almost entirely to forbid a passage; our horses were so torn by them that the blood literally run in streams down their legs and breasts; we ourselves not entirely escaping, our hands and faces being more or less scratched and torn by them. We fell in with but one drove of buffalo during the morning, which having been previously fired at and pursued by the Indians, we were unable to approach near enough to fire among with any effect. We traveled in different directions about twenty miles, when toward evening, entering the Grand Prairie, we unexpectedly found ourselves in the midst of no less than two thousand of these prodigious animals.

Within an hundred paces of us stood a fierce bull, of enormous size, weighing not less than twenty-five hundred pounds; this was the first favorable opportunity that we had yet had of viewing closely one of these mammoth creatures. They did not at all appear frightened at our approach, and continued quietly feeding upon the prairie-grass, which was here ate off quite short, owing to the great number of the herd.

These animals appear well accomplished for the country in which they live; their heads and necks, even down as far as their shoulders, are covered with a long shaggy hair, as is also their fore-legs, down as far as the fet-lock joint, which serves to protect their flesh from the thorns and briars, through which they make their way without the least inconvenience or harm.

As we came in sight of this immense drove, we alighted from our horses, and one of the party advanced slowly and cautiously through the tall grass along the skirt of the wood, and fired three successive balls into the bull, which stood nearest, before he ran, which, however, weakened him considerably; at this we all gave chase upon our horses, and fired eleven balls into his body before he fell; we now approached as near as our horses would allow, and with one well-directed aim laid him prostrate and lifeless. Leaving some of the party to hold the horses, the remainder commenced the job of butchering him. In removing the hide from the left shoulder, we discovered the steel point of an Indian arrow embedded in the flesh, and from the callous appearance of the flesh around it, imagined that it must have long remained there.

We loaded our horses with as much of the meat as they could carry, and night approaching, we directed our course toward the encampment, and having arrived there, found that several of the other hunting parties, that had in the morning started in different directions, had returned no less successful than ourselves.

One of our men this morning picked up upon the prairie, under a little brush thicket, several pieces of a pair of saddle bags, which, no doubt, had belonged to a citizen named Murtin, who had been murdered by the Pawnees but a few weeks before, on the Washita river.

The barbarous acts of these savages are not alone confined to their own dominions, but extend as far east even as the waters of the Arkansas, their principal aim is to intercept the Santa Fe traders, when their object is plunder. As I have remarked in a previous letter, company "A" of our regiment accompanied one of these parties this summer; but of late years the strength of these expeditions has been fully able to effectually repulse any attack on the part of the Indians.

About an hour after sunset we pitched our encampment, and after having used more than ordinary exertions to secure our horses, and doubling the guard, the greater portion of the command sought repose, which, after a day of great excitement and extreme fatigue, was peculiarly grateful.

The next morning we merged from the little skirt

of wood and entered upon the grand prairie, a level and unbroken sea of green as far as the eye could extend. In every direction might be seen herds of deer and buffalo, and occasionally a drove of wild horses; these animals are very numerous here, and several have been taken by the Indians of our party; they are remarkably fleet and beautiful, and not stunted and thick-legged as those usually rode by the Indians, which deformity is caused by their breaking them much too young, and before their limbs have attained their proper growth.

The next day we started early upon our march, and when about six or eight miles upon our route, we discovered on an eminence about three miles in advance of us, a party of mounted Indians, apparently about forty in number. We moved cautiously toward them, and halting our main-body about a mile distant from them, sent forward our van-guard in their direction. They had advanced but a little distance, when the Indians sent forward a party of about the same number to meet them; but becoming suspicious, they several times retreated, after having come within a few hundred yards of our guard. After repeated fruitless attempts to treat with them in this manner, the guard was recalled, and a single officer detached to meet them. The leader of the Indian party set forward from his followers, and in the centre between the two parties they met.

This was a moment of intense and breathless anxiety, and upon the event of their meeting evidently depended the whole issue of our expedition; every voice was hushed, and even our horses seemed instinctively to maintain order and silence.

The hand of friendship was cordially proffered on

our part, and fearlessly accepted by the chief, and in a few moments more, with a confidence but little to be expected from these savages, they were riding in the very centre of our columns. From our interpreters we learned that they belonged to the Camanche tribe, and had left their settlement on a hunting expedition for buffalo.

We made known to these Indians that the object of our visit to their country was to hold treaties with the several different tribes, and endeavor if possible to make an established peace, not only between the various nations themselves, but with the whites upon the border-settlements. They seemed much pleased with our design, and offered to conduct us to their own wigwams, and to point out the road to the Pawnee villages, and we immediately set forward under their guidance.

The Camanches are a very numerous tribe, and extend themselves over that vast extent of country extending between the Red River and the north fork of the Washita, which you may easily point out upon the map. They have no established villages, but wander about from place to place, living chiefly upon game and wild fruit. They are armed with bows and arrows, and spears, and clothe themselves in the skins of the buffalo, elk, and deer. They are of a bright copper color, their faces broad and large; they are generally muscular men, and differ only in appearance from their squaws in the manner of wearing the hair, the latter having their heads cropt very short, whilst the former wear their hair in long tufts. They are the allies of the Pawnees, Kioways, and Arripahoes, and together, when prepared for battle, form a host not easily conquered. Among the Camanche women we discovered several Spanish females who had probably spent the greater portion of their lives among the Indians, and had assimilated their manners to their wild habits.

The Camanche, when mounted, presents a fine classic appearance; with his covering of variegated hide, his broad shining face, his spear and target, he is apt to remind one of the more chivalrous days of ancient Britain, when the tilt and tourney claimed no less the prowess of the bold than the plaudits of the fair; when the knight templars laid lance in rest, and sovereigns marshalled their followers on the plains of Palestine.

The events of this day have been of a very interesting character, and we begin to have greater hopes of success in attaining the grand object of our expedition, that is, to obtain an interview with the Pawnee tribes, and if possible effect an amicable treaty.

It rained violently throughout the next night, and rendered the route much more toilsome to traverse. We remained in camp until 7 o'clock the next morning, and then again, under the guidance of our Camanche friends, set forward on our march. Colonel Dodge found to-day, upon inquiry, the Kiowas, Camanches, and Pawnees to be allies, and with the single exception of their speaking different languages, they may in a manner be called one nation. The Camanches, however, are much the finest looking, and a more noble and generous tribe than either of the others; and withal, the largest, therefore the colonel resolved to delay his visit to the Pawnee villages until he had first visited the wigwams of the Camanches.

As we were this day riding over the prairie, my attention was attracted by a folded piece of paper blowing about in advance of the regiment, and dismounting to procure it, I was surprised to find a half sheet of foolscap with eight or ten stanzas of what probably was intended for poetry scrawled upon it. In any other place I would have thrown it aside as a foolish piece of ignorant composition, but reflecting upon the strange situation in which I had discovered this rare specimen of poetic genius, I determined to preserve it* as a memento of the wild west, if I should ever again be permitted to return to the abodes of civilized life.

Reading it over several times to myself before I could distinctly decipher the connection and spelling, I at length made known to my troop the prize which I had found, and reading it several times more aloud at the instigation of Corporal Tim, we had many a hearty laugh over the mock pathetic strains of this most harmonious piece of composition. You shall have one stanza, I will not trouble you with more, as it is so foolish an affair; but, considering the novelty of its discovery, I assure you I never read it without indulging a hearty strain of laughter. It began thus:

> "As i walked out one mornin arely
> all down by the side of a river clere
> Thare i espyed a lovely damzle
> and she was like a lilly fare
> i stept up to her and says i fare lady
> Will you be a seaman's bride
> Says she i wont because i tell you
> ive got an other bow beside."

* I gave this strange production to the editor of a popular weekly paper, upon my return to New-York, who promised it a place in his columns, but unfortunately it was swept out of the office among the rubbish, being, as I have before observed, quite soiled and discolored.

From the above you may form some idea of the style of the remainder, but the drift of the story is this: The accepted lover of the lady has been a long time absent at sea, and his faithful and patient fair one is anxiously awaiting his return. As I have shown you by the above stanzas, the story opens by the rejection of another suitor, who seeks in vain to make the lady believe that her betrothed perished at sea. She, however, faithful to her plighted troth, refuses to listen to the addresses of her new admirer, who strives, as the tale proceeds, to impress the truth of his story upon the mind of the lady, until at length she declares that she will never marry any other than her own *Riley*, who could not have been so cruel as to have died at sea and left her disconsolate. At this the new suitor throws off his disguise and proclaims, to use his own words,

> "i am the man what you call Riley
> i am your own sea-faring mar."

The lady immediately recognizes her lover, and much happiness ensues.

I would not willingly so long have detained you with this love-sick tale, but for the peculiar circumstances connected with it. The paper upon which it is written has become altogether discolored by time and exposure, but how it ever came to be in this wild western prairie I can but little imagine. I have, however, attributed it to some of the wagoners who attended the Santa Fe traders across the prairie upon their trading expeditions, or else to one of the troop of rangers who last summer pranced over these regions.

The story, however, independent of its orthography,

contains an excellent moral; it teaches the endurance of patience under trials, and an unwavering attachment to the object of our affections. This production has served to illumine many a dark moment, and never fails to produce a cheerful effect upon the risible faculties of the audience in hearing.

Camp Camanche, July 13, 1834.

Our camp is pitched upon the border of a deep creek, the banks of which are quite high and precipitous, and we are nearly surrounded on the other three sides by a deep ravine, thus being encased within a strong natural entrenchment; we are, however, but little afraid of any thing like an attack from the Indians, the kindness shown us by the Camanches is too evident to be dissembled, and we feel but little alarm on that score. We are suffering considerably for want of water, as well as provisions; we have been several days out of bread-stuff, and subsist entirely upon fresh meat.

We fell in with twelve more Camanches to-day, who were upon a hunting expedition; they were very friendly, and shook hands with the soldiers, and joined our party. The Pawnee girl (one of the two that we took from the Osages last spring) recognized an old acquaintance among this party, and was enabled, through an Osage who speaks English, to interpret their "talk." A few miles travel now brought us to the Camanche lodge, where we were received in the most friendly manner by almost an hundred mounted men, who, evidently with strong signs of fear, came out to meet us from their camp, which is pleasantly situated in a valley. This day, as Lieutenant Wheelock observed, was a very interesting one, absolutely so, and peculiarly so, when six nations, some of whom had but recently been at war with each other, shake hands cordially together; a form, it is true, but a type, it is believed, of permanent peace, which must promote the interest of the whole country.

The Camanche camp, which is composed of about from two to three hundred wigwams of poles covered with tanned hides, is but a short distance from the spot upon which we pitched our encampment, and special orders have been issued that no soldier, or even officer, without special permission, shall visit it after dark; our own camp is surrounded by a chain of sentinels, and every precaution taken to guard against any thing which might occur; herds of horses, not less than three or four thousand, are grazing around the encampment. From all appearance, this tribe have been but a few days at this camp; their great chief is now absent upon a hunting expedition. The American flag is waving over the lodge; how they procured it I am unable to say, unless from the Santa Fe traders, whom they make it a business to plunder. The morning that we arrived here was thick and hazy, yet still the landscape could be discerned as being bold, rugged, and beautiful. On our right and rear lay a vast prairie of unvaried green; its tall grass, when swept by the breeze, waving like the surges of the ocean to the verge of the distant horizon, and sparkling with its fragrant and delicate flowers as far as the eye could reach. On the left, in the distance, could dimly be discovered an arm of the Rocky Mountains, the loftiest of whose summit seem to rend the clouds; and, on our front, separated by a small stream of water, lay the wigwams of the savages.

Several of our men have purchased from the Indians the horses which they catch wild, and are willing to dispose of for even a blanket or butcher-knife. At this time our provisions were almost entirely exhausted, and we were obliged to trade with them for dried meat, which they offered in exchange for tobacco, &c. We purchased it as buffalo, but, in all probability, the greater portion of it was horse meat; however, our appetites were too voracious to distinguish the difference.

Having a great number of sick men in the regiment we constructed a small shed of a frame covered with brush, and left them under a strong guard at this camp, whilst, the third day after, the remainder of the command set forward, under the guidance of an Indian pilot, towards the villages of the Pawnees. Our course lay directly across this chain of stupendous and rocky mountains. We had been now nearly a month without a morsel of bread, and sometimes meat was so scarce as to allow not more than a pint of broth a day for a man. Sickness and desertion had much reduced our little band, and our horses were almost worn out with fatigue. Our situation was now extremely precarious; starvation seemed to stare us in the face on the one hand, and should the Indians prove unfriendly, we had but little chance of escape on the other; however, with only one hundred and fifty men, we determined to penetrate into the country of that nation which particularly formed the subject of our treaty.

Arrived at the foot of the mountains, we were obliged to dismount and lead our horses, with the utmost difficulty, over immense ledges of over-hanging rocks, of stupendous size, by which we were encircled on every side; at one moment we would be sunk in a valley from which it seemed impossible to extricate ourselves, and perhaps the next, upon a pinnacle overlooking a little world; the scenery around us surpassed in grandeur and magnificence any thing that can be imagined, much less described; and a few days after, traveling over this toilsome and intricate route, we arrived at the very spot that contained the whole object of our expedition — *the village of the Pawnee Picts.*

These Indians, which may more properly be called Toyash, are not so fine-looking as the Camanches, but they are their allies and friends, as well as of the Kiowas. The passage which leads to their village is through a narrow defile over a sweep of perpendicular rocks, almost inaccessible to human feet. The village is situated most delightfully in a rich bottom, embedded in the midst of these immense ledges of rocks and mountains. Here, according to previous appointment, Col. Dodge met in council the chiefs and warriors of the Toyash nation, to which place now many of the Camanches began to arrive. At this council Col. Dodge, Major Armstrong, (the Indian agent,) and General Stokes, (the Indian commissioner,) presided. The scene was one glowing with interest, and cannot at all be imagined by one that is ignorant of the vehemence of Indian eloquence and the wild scenes of Indian landscape.

After the council, composed of these three distinct races of human beings, "civilized, half civilized, and wild," was in readiness, Col. Dodge spoke as follows.*

* I must here acknowlege my indebtedness to Lieut. Wheelock, from whose journal of the expedition I have procured the replies of the Indians to the inquiries of Col. Dodge.

"We are the first American officers who have ever come to see the Pawnees: we meet you as friends, not as enemies; to make peace with you, to shake hands with you. The great American captain is at peace with all white men in the world; he wishes to be at peace with all the red men in the world. We have been sent here to view this country, and to invite you to go to Washington, where the great American chief lives, to make a treaty with him, that you may learn how he wishes to send among you traders, who will bring you guns and blankets, and every thing that you want. The great American chief wishes also to make peace between you and the Osages; you have been at war with the Osages; and to secure peace between you and the Cherokees, Senecas, Delawares, and Choctaws, and all other red men, that you may meet together as friends, and not shed each other's blood, as you have done. On our way to your village we met a party of Camanches. We showed to them a white flag, which said to them, 'we wish to be friends.' Their principal men were gone to hunt; we treated their old men, women and children, with kindness; we gave them presents; they had many horses, we could have taken all their horses from them, but did not; we showed to them that we wanted to be at peace with them; they told us that you were their friends; we were glad to hear it; we have come to your town, and found you as defenceless as the Camanches; we have treated you as we treated them. The American people show their kindness by actions, and not by words alone. We have been told that a white man was made prisoner by you last summer; that a boy was made prisoner by you last spring; we have come now to require the boy at your hands, for we are told that he is in your town. Give us the white boy, and we will give you the Pawnee girl that we have brought with us; we wish to shake hands with you, and be friends; you must now give me a positive and direct answer in regard to the white man who was taken last summer, and the boy who was taken last spring."

The chief We-ter-ra-shah-ro replied. " I know nothing of the man who you say was taken last summer; the white boy is here."

Colonel Dodge resumed. " I wish the boy brought to me; I will then give to you the Pawnee girl. This act, together with all the information you can give concerning the man who was taken last summer, will be the best proof that you can give of the sincerity of your disposition to shake hands and be at peace with us. I cannot leave the country until we obtain possession of the boy, and gain information respecting the man who was taken last summer; his name was Abby; he was taken between the Blue river and the Washita, about this time last year."

Chief. I know nothing of it. I believe they were Camanches who took the man. (On receiving some intelligence from one of his friends, the chief continued:) I remember now, the Oways, who live south, did it.

Colonel Dodge. Do the Oways hunt on the grounds between the Blue and Washita rivers?

Chief. They hunt there, and I have heard that they took the man Abby, and when they got near their camp, they killed him.

Colonel Dodge. How far do the Oways live from here?

Chief. They follow the buffalo as the Camanches

do; they have a town. [Here a pistol was accidentally fired in the council-lodge, which caused much confusion. It was soon explained, however, and business proceeded. The white boy who had been sent for, was brought in and presented to Col. Dodge; the boy was entirely naked, about seven years of age; his name is Matthew Wright Martin.]

Chief. I am glad to shake hands with you, with the red men that you have brought with you, the Osages, Delawares, and Cherokees; the principal chief is not here; but you are as gladly received as he would have welcomed you; the chief has gone to the country of the Pawnee O'Mahaws; he believed that you had gone that way; the father of the Toyash girl went with the chief to seek his daughter.

Col. Dodge. How did the Camanches obtain the American flag I saw flying in their camp?

Chief. The Pawnees from La Platte sent two flags, one for the Wacoahs, and the other to the Camanches.

Col. Dodge. Do the Spaniards come here to trade with you?

Chief. They do; they left us not long since, and went west.

Col. Dodge. The Americans will give you better and cheaper goods than the Spaniards do. Tell me if you know where the ranger (Abby) was taken, and how he was killed.

Chief. I have inquired, and have learned this day, that the Indians who live near St. Antoine, in Mexico, captured Abby, and that they killed him on Red River.

Col. Dodge. What Indians kill our Santa Fe traders?

Chief. There is a roving tribe of very bad Indians

called Wakinas; they range north of the country of the Arkansas." Col. Dodge here presented the girl to her friends, whereupon they conducted her from the council.

Col. Dodge. I am very much pleased at the exchange of prisoners. I hope the friends of the girl will be happy with her; she is a good girl; I wish her well. I will restore the little boy to his mother; her heart will be glad, and she will think better of the Pawnees; a bright sun has shined upon us this day; I hope the Great Spirit will let it shine continually upon us. You have some Osage prisoners; the Osages have some Pawnee prisoners; we will exchange and give you your Pawnee friends, and you shall restore the Osages to their friends. How many Osages have you?

Chief. There are Osages here; they are men who were raised here and do not wish to leave us. The Delaware woman and boy that we took, died of the small pox.

Col. Dodge. The American president will have a treaty of peace made between you all; then you will meet and exchange prisoners; this will be done when the next grass grows. The Osages who are with the Pawnees, who then wish to return to the Osages, can come back to their people.

Chief. We wish to have it done soon.

Col. Dodge. The American president wishes to see some of each nation shake hands before him; he will give presents to those who visit him, and fix a permanent peace between their nations. Peace cannot be made with all the tribes, till a large white paper be written, and signed by the president and the hands of the chief. Will your chiefs go with me now to see the American president? I wish also to take with me some Camanche chiefs. The president will be happy to see you, and will make you, as I told you before, presents of handsome guns, coats, &c.

This is the proper time to make peace with the red men and the white men; if you do not seize this opportunity you may never have another. The bright chain of friendship can now be made bright between all the Indians and the white men."

Chief. We do not like to pass through the timber; it will be hard for our horses to pass through the thick timber country between us and the white men.

Col. Dodge. There are roads—a big road is now being made.

Chief. We have met here as friends, we hope to remain so. The Great Spirit has seen us, as we now see the white men, Cherokees, Osages, Delawares, and Senecas as friends, we hope to remain so.

Col. Dodge. I hope so. How came you by the negro who is here with you?

Chief. This Camanche brought him; he found him on the Red River; you can take him and do as you please with him.

The council here closed.

July 23d.—We-ter-ra-shah-ro and two other principal men met Col. Dodge at his tent this morning, and held farther talk with him. The four leaders of the bands of Indians who were with us were present at the talk, and participated therein. Col. Dodge spoke as follows: " Toyash chiefs, I told you yesterday that I wished to show the road that leads to the great American captain, and make you acquainted with the Indians that live on the way thither—have you thought of going with me? Our great father wished you to see the red men who live on the way, that you may be better able to settle all difficulties with them. You shall be well treated; presents shall be made to you, and you shall be sent back in safety. Peace cannot be made unless some of you go; I am not the great captain, he only can make peace with you and other red men; I wish only a few of you to go with me; I wish you to go willingly and as friends; had I chosen to force you to go, it would have been easy for me to do so; you see I do not wish to force you."

After a good deal of consultation, one of the chiefs (a Wacoah) consented to go. Here the following interesting ceremony took place. The boy whom we recovered yesterday is the son of the late Judge Martin, of Arkansas, who was killed by a party of Indians some weeks since; the son was with his father on a hunting excursion, and being parted from him, [his death however he did not witness, and is now in ignorance of it,] says, that after being parted from his father, the Indians who had taken him were disposed, save one, to kill him; this one shielded him, and took care of him in sickness; Colonel Dodge, as a reward for his noble kindness, gave him a rifle, and at the same time caused the little boy to present him, with his own hand, a pistol. Colonel Dodge now assured the chiefs that they should receive further presents if they would go with him to his country; that he regretted he had nothing of value with him, but begged them to accept of some rifles and pistols, which they did with much evident satisfaction. We-ter-ra-shah-ro and the other chief men with him, here consulted some time together on the subject of visiting the president. We-ter-ra-shah-ro spoke, "We have been at war with the nations which we see around us to-day: we wish now to make peace with them."

Colonel Dodge answered him. " It is the wish of the president that you make peace with them; that you present to each other clean hands: it is to effect this that I wish you to go with me."

The chief resumed. " We wish much to make peace with the Osages, we have been long at war with them; we wish to see the lands of the Creeks and Cherokees also, to shake hands with all. We want now to hear those Indians who came with you to speak to us." The chief men of the four parties spoke as follows:

Dutch, the Cherokee, thus spoke: "I am now going to tell you what the chief of the Cherokees bade me to say to you if we met as friends. He says to you, he wishes his people to come to you without fear, and that you should visit them without fear. My heart is glad that we are all willing to be friends; a long time ago it was so, there was no war between us. I am rejoiced, and my people will be rejoiced when they hear that it may be so again. Look at me, you see I speak the truth. I have nothing more to say."

Beatte, leader of the Osage band, said, " We came for peace. I have brought a few Osages, who were not afraid to come among you, with hearts inclined for peace. We look on our friend, Colonel Dodge, as our father; he is a true father to us all. I hope you will believe all that he has to say to you, and trust that he will prove a father to you. We wish you to visit our people, to see how we live since the white men have been our friends; they have made us happy, they will make you happy; you shall go with our father as he wishes; you must then come and see the Osages. I have said all that I can say."

Monpisha, an Osage youth, spoke to the Toyash men. "We shake hands with pleasure; I am nothing but a boy, my father was an Osage chief; we wish to be peaceable men, and friends. Our good father has made, in coming to you, a great road: we hope it will never be stained with blood. My father told me he was once a wild Indian; that white men taught him to be happy, instructed him how to build houses, raise cattle, and live like white men. I was sent to the white man's school, (missionary school,) was taught to read and write: this will be extended to you, if you make peace with white men; your buffalo will be gone in a few years; your great father, the president, will give you cattle, and teach you how to live without buffalo."

George Bullet (Pon-da-gne-se) spoke. "When I tell the Delawares that we are friends, and can now hunt without warring together, they will be happy; our children will hereafter be happy, and not fear each other; we will no more fear the prairie Indian, and you will not be afraid of us."

Colonel Dodge resumed. "I am lad to hear what our friends say to you. I must say to you now, that I am very sorry that a few of our horses got into your cornfield last night. I shall pay you for the damage done—it was not my wish to disturb your property in any manner. White men will always be just to you. I must also repeat that I regretted that the pistol was accidentally fired in the council-lodge yesterday; I did not wish to alarm your people: I was pleased with the coolness of your chief; he was not alarmed. I wish you now to consider if some of you will go with me."

The chiefs signified that they would go home and

decide who should accompany the command on its march back, and accordingly left our camp.

Many Camanches arrived to day; amongst them the principal chief Ta-we-que-nah, and two other chiefs. Colonel Dodge held the following talk with them in his tent.

" The great American Captain has sent me to view this country, and to offer the hand of friendship to all the red men who are here ; he wishes to see you all at peace with each other ; he desires you to come and see him, that he may fix a permanent peace with your tribes; he will make you presents, and he will send traders among you, who will serve you with a great many things that you want to make you happy. The President, who is a good father to you, wishes to see you at peace with the Osages, Cherokees, Delawares, and all red men. We have endeavored to give you evidence of our friendship—we did so when we passed your camp; you were not at home, your women and children were defenceless, we treated them kindly; we confided in you too, our sick men we left behind near your camp."

Ta-we-que-nah replied. " I passed a night in your camp with your sick men ; they treated us with kindness."

Col. Dodge. You say that the Indians over Red River are your enemies, they kill you when you meet; these are Mexican Indians, and do not make treaties with our great father the President ; but he will protect you when you make peace with the Osages and other tribes that have been at war against you. The flag that you have, came to you from the great father at Washington. The Pawnee O'Mohaws have such a flag, and all other red men who are our friends whenever you show it, you will be known as friends. I was glad to see the flag over your camp.

The chief spoke: "I wish to be at peace with you. There are many bands of Camanches, I shall visit them all this year, and will say to them what you have said to me; they will all be glad to make peace with you. I am an old man now, but never, since I was a boy, did I kill one of your people. You ask me who killed the ranger, Abby; I can tell you, for I remember when this white man was taken; the Texas Camanches took this white man and carried him over the Red River, and there killed him."

Col. Dodge. I wish some of you to go with me, that you may see our country, and that peace may be made strongly between you and the red men, as well as between ourselves; the Pawnee O'Mohaws met the Osages, and Delawares, and Cherokees on our lands, and there made peace; they were enemies before, they are now friends, and do not hate each other. We wish you to come to us, and make, in the same way, peace with us.

Te-we-que-nah. You have a girl who was taken from our friends the Kiowas. I have a Spanish girl; I will give you the Spanish girl in exchange for the Kiowa girl that you have brought with you.

Col. Dodge. I wish to secure your friendship and the friendship of the Kiowas. I wish you to accompany me. I wish some of the Kiowas to go also; but I do not mean to sell the girl to them; I mean to give her to her relations and friends without price; I will give the girl to her tribe; they shall see how much their friends we are.

Ta-we-que-nah. If I go with you I shall be afraid

to come back through the timber. I cannot go myself; my brother will go with you.

Col. Dodge. I pledge myself that you shall be safely conducted back.

Here the talk was interrupted by a band of some twenty or thirty Kiowas rushing on horseback into camp, and almost into the door of Colonel Dodge's tent; the squaws and children fled in great alarm. The indignation of these Indians against the Osages had kindled to a great pitch, and could scarcely be kept in respectful bounds in their relation to us. The Osages, not many months previously, had murdered a large number of the women and children of the Kiowas whilst the men were absent hunting. We held in possession, of which they were informed, a Kiowa girl, who was taken on the occasion of the massacre alluded to: the Kiowas having just arrived, were not aware of the intention on our part to restore the girl, and consequently presented themselves in a warlike shape, that caused many a man in the camp to stand by his arms. Col. Dodge, however, immediately addressed them with assurances of our friendly disposition, and gradually led them into gentleness. They are a bold, warlike-looking Indian. Some of their horses are very fine; they ride well, and were admirably equipped to-day for fight or flight; their bows strung and quivers filled with arrows. They kept their saddles chiefly. A relation of the Kiowa girl embraced her, and shed tears of joy at the intimation that she should be restored to her father and friends. She proves to be a relation of one of the chiefs. An arrangement was now made for a general council to be held the next day, between the Camanche, Toyash, and Kiowa nations.

July 24*th.*—At ten o'clock the chiefs of the council began to assemble at the place appointed for the meeting, which was in a wood about two hundred yards from our camp. The father of the Kiowa girl, having learned that she was to be restored, in a speech addressed to the Kiowas, whose numbers every moment increased, gave vent to his joy, and praise of his white friends. All came mounted and armed. Many of our officers were present. There were not less than two thousand mounted and armed Indians around the council. Great excitement prevailed among the Indians, but especially with the Kiowas, who embraced Colonel Dodge, and shed tears of gratitude for the restoration of their relative. An uncle of Wa-ha-sep-ah, a man of about forty years of age, was touchingly eager in his demonstrations, frequently throwing his arms around Colonel Dodge, and weeping over his shoulders, invoking blessings upon him in a manner the most graceful and ardent; the women came in succession, and embraced the girl, who was seated among the chiefs. The council being now in order, and the pipes having made their rounds, Colonel Dodge addressed the Camanche chief, who sat on his right, and who interpreted his words to the Kiowas, whilst a Toyash Indian, who speaks the Caddo tongue, communicated with the Toyash men from Chiom, through one of our Cherokee friends, who speaks English and Caddo: " I am glad to see together the great chief of the Camanche nation, the chiefs of the Kiowa and Toyash people, and the American officers who are with me; we have been strangers until now. I am glad to meet the captain of the Camanches, (Ta-we-que-nah.) You must be a great man, and have much power with all the tribes around you. I ask you to urge to these Indians what I have said to you, that we are your friends, and that, to secure our mutual and lasting friendship, it is better for some of each of you to go with me, as I have before mentioned to you."

Here another band of Kiowas, about sixty in number, rode up, led by a principal man, handsomely dressed. He wore a Spanish red cloth mantle, prodigious feathers, and leggings that followed his heels like an ancient train. Another of the chiefs of the new band was very showily arrayed; he wore a perfectly white dressed deer skin hunting shirt, trimmed profusely with fringe of the same material, and beautifully bound with blue beads, over which was thrown a cloth mantle of blue and crimson, with leggings and moccasons entirely of beads. Our new friends shook hands all round, and seated themselves with a dignity and grace that would well become senators of a more civilized conclave.

Colonel Dodge resumed. " Kiowa chiefs! I herewith present to you your relation; receive her as the best evidence of the sincere friendship of Americans. Our great captain, the President, purchased this girl of the Osages, who took her from your people, and has sent me to restore her to the arms of her friends, who love her. The Camanche chief, Ta-we-que-nah, offered me yesterday, in exchange for her, a Spanish girl; I would not accept of his offer, for the delivery of the girl is an act of justice, and is but one of the many acts of kindness that the great American Captain will be glad to show to you. You, and the Indians who came with us, have long been at war with each other; it is time you were at peace together; it is the wish of the President to secure a permanent good understanding among you all. He will send traders among you. You want guns, blankets, &c. the buffalo are becoming scarce; there are less and less every year. You shall have cattle which you can keep with you; you can plant your corn and cultivate the soil, as the Cherokees and other Indians do. Here is a young man (Mr. Chadwick) who has come out with me to see you, and who will return next summer, and bring goods and trade with you. I now wish you to consider the invitation given you to go with me, and assure you you shall receive presents, and be safely conducted through the timber country." One of the chiefs inquired, " Will you go to-morrow?"

Colonel Dodge. I wish to go as soon as practicable, as we have far to go; I wish you to visit General Leavenworth, another of your friends, and a captain under the great Captain; he wishes to see you; he has never seen you; I should be glad to introduce to him two chiefs from each nation, or one chief and some of the warriors of each people.

Titche-totche-cha, chief of the Kiowas, signified his willingness to go. We-ter-rah-shah-ro, an old chief, (70 years of age,) urged his red brethren to rely on the truth of Colonel Dodge's words: " he is a good man," said he; " believe his words."

The father of the Kiowa girl begged Colonel Dodge to accept of a present, which the Colonel declined, repeating what he had before said, that he did not wish for ransom or reward; that the child was given to the father as an evidence of the good feeling of his people for them.

Tiche-totche-cha spoke: " The American captain has spoken well to-day; the white men have shown themselves our friends. If a white man ever comes to my country, he shall be kindly treated; if he wants a horse, or any thing that I have, he shall not pay for it; I will give him what he wants. The council here closed, we returned to our camp, and left the Indians to decide in regard to accompanying us. It is on all accounts desirable to move from here: our provisions prove unhealthy for our men, consisting entirely of green corn and dried horse and buffalo meat; the weather has been excessively hot and dry; our men, many of them sick, are without a physician or medicines; two or three officers are, and have been for several days, ill of fevers. The Camanche squaws are very troublesome, they steal every thing that they can secrete. The Toyash women are infinitely more respectable; the difference in these three tribes seems to be somewhat thus: the Camanche is an arrogant, jealous, savage Don; the Toyash, a savage farmer; whilst the Kiowa, more chivalric, impulsive, and daring than either, reminds one of the bold clannish Highlander, whose very crimes are made, by the poet, captivating; this tribe has roamed more towards the Rocky Mountains until within a few years past."

Our treaty being concluded, amicable relations being effected between ourselves and the Indians, we began to feel that the main object of our expedition was settled, and congratulated ourselves upon our success in having so happily treated with the hitherto deadly enemies of the whites. The difference in our number was very striking, with only one hundred and fifty men capable of bearing arms, we had marched into the midst of not less than fifteen hundred of the savages. We remained at their village four days, during which time we were scantily supplied with buffalo or horse meat, corn, pumpkins, watermelons, &c. which they cultivate in small patches. In exchange for which, we bartered almost every thing that we possessed, even to the very buttons from our clothes. Colonel Dodge having obtained the consent of several of their chiefs, we made preparations for our homeward march.

Buffalo, elk, antelope, deer, and wild horses are very plenty in this part of the country, many of which were taken by the Indians belonging to our party, as well as by some of the dragoons themselves. The next morning, at an early hour, the chiefs of three different tribes visited our camp, and received presents of guns and pistols, and other articles, from Colonel Dodge. " Fifteen Kiowas, including their chiefs, were the first mounted and ready to accompany us. The Camanche chief, very cautious, and apparently suspicious, deferred his coming till late, when four Camanches and a squaw joined us; there was much delay on the part of the Toyash; at length the old chief, We-ten-ra-shah-ro, a Wacoah chief, (of a small band who speaks the same language as the Toyash people, and live near their town,) and two Toyash warriors, rode into our camp prepared to move with us. The command, with the Indians, the white boy and the negro in company, marched at three o'clock, and halted at five, encamping on the borders of a creek about six miles distant.

Here I must break off; in a few days I will resume my description of our homeward march, till then
I remain as ever,
Your friend.

LETTER XVIII.

Continuation of march.—Arrival at Fort Gibson.

Fort Gibson, August, 1834.
My Dear Sir,

After the conclusion of the treaty, a detailed account of which I gave you in my last, we made preparations for our homeward march, and, in company with several of the chiefs of the Pawnees, Camanches, Wicos, and other wild tribes, in addition to our red friends of the Delawares, Osages, &c. who had accompanied us from the fort, we began to retrace our steps, and to look forward with no small degree of anxiety and satisfaction to the time of our arrival at Camp Jackson.

On the 28th of July we again set forward from the encampment of the previous night, situated about six miles distant from the Pawnee village, and directed our course towards the north-east. Nine o'clock found us upon the march, and at about four in the afternoon we again pitched our tents about twelve miles distant upon the prairie: the weather was extremely warm, and its effects equally discernible upon the horses, as their worn out riders. We suffered very much for want of water, and were grateful for the scanty draughts which we here and there could procure from the stagnant pools along the trail.

Deer and buffalo were quite abundant upon this portion of the prairie, and we took the precaution to lay up a full supply of meat for our march. One of our men this day killed a large panther, which animals are not uncommon hereabouts.

It would be doubtless tedious to you were I to recapitulate all the minor events of our homeward route;

I will therefore condense as much as possible the account of our different days travel towards Fort Gibson. The Pawnee Indian who had served us for a guide, left us after the third day, and his place was supplied by a Toyash, who appeared to have a much more intimate knowledge of the country than his predecessor, leading the command over a fine level country instead of the ravines and rocky precipices over which the Pawnee had before led us. During the next afternoon a delightful shower of rain fell, which was an event for which we had been long and anxiously waiting. The next day we forded the "Roaring River," a name given to it by the Indians, probably on account of the swiftness of its current, which, in times of a freshet, becomes quite rapid—this is one of the tributary streams of the Red river, between which and the north fork of the Washita the dominions of the Camanches extend. By the by, this tribe are very much disliked by the Toyash; being a more powerful tribe, they take advantage of them, and plunder and cheat them with impunity. The Kiowas are a nation of a very different character, being much more honest and tractable. The Pawnees are smaller, and of a darker color, and not at all as fine looking as the Camanches.

The weather still continuing excessively hot, we remained encamped during the two succeeding days, and the greater part of the command were employed in killing buffalo and curing the meat.

During our homeward route, we kept farther toward the north than we had in going out; and upon crossing the Canadian river, we were distant an hundred miles from the point which we had forded during our westward march. Although the heat was so extremely oppressive during the day, yet at night the covering of a blanket was quite comfortable. It was remarked that this portion of the country was remarkably free from flies, musquitoes, or any of the more common plagues of summer in our climate.

During our respite of a couple of days, as we were one evening enjoying the welcome rest, and preparing for the toils and fatigue of the succeeding day, we were suddenly alarmed by the cry of one of the sentinels, of " Secure your horses,"—every man sprung to his feet and seized his bridle. An immense herd of buffalo were rushing across the prairie in the direction of our camp, and knowing the course which these animals pursue, we were at first alarmed for the safety of our encampment. Our horses were picketed upon the prairie around, and would probably be again dispersed, had it not been for the exertions of the mounted sentinels, who with great difficulty changed the direction of the herd, and thereby saved us from the effects of another *stampedo*. This is an evil to be guarded against with the greatest care upon the prairies ; instances not being unfrequent when caravans have been run down and trampled upon by the immense herds which roam wild upon these extensive plains.

The assembly-call next morning summoned us again to commence the journey of another day; the short respite that we had enjoyed, had served to give our horses as well as ourselves much additional strength, and at about ten o'clock we again continued our route across the prairies. We this day passed several large herds of buffalo, among which the Indians of our party dashed and killed a large number. One Kiowa Indian with three arrows brought to the ground three of these prodigious animals, making each shot tell effectually.

The next day (August 5th) we remained in camp, and again were the greater part of us engaged in preparing buffalo meat. It was during our stay at this place that the mournful intelligence of the death of General Leavenworth was announced to our regiment; he was attacked with a bilious fever, and expired at Camp Smith, where he had remained with a small detachment, not far from the Cross timbers. This piece of intelligence cast a gloom over the regiment. I believe that I have before remarked to you, that he was a man universally beloved by those under his command, as well for his unassuming manners, as for the natural mildness and clemency of his disposition. Captain Deane, of the third infantry, who brought the news, also gave intimation of the death of Lieutenant McClure, of company " B," who died on the 20th July, (the day previous to the death of General Leavenworth,) at a sick camp on the bank of the Washita, where upwards of an hundred and fifty of our men had been left sick. Lieutenant McClure was a much esteemed officer, of a mild and amiable disposition and gentlemanly deportment, but of too weak and slender a frame to bear up against the toils, fatigues, and privations of a campaign over the scorching and boundless prairies, and through the deep forests of this western world.

On the 7th of August we passed through the last of the Cross timbers, and next day struck upon the road directing to Fort Gibson. If the eye of the soldier had before been sunken and dilated with fatigue and anxiety, it now brightened at the prospect of an approaching season of rest, and dwelt familiarly upon scenes around, that told of the drawing to a close of his trials and privations; hardship had wrought many a wrinkle, and hunger and fatigue had reduced almost to a skeleton many a frame : but now, like the first glad glimpse of land to the sea-tossed mariner, the destined goal seemed at hand. From the 7th to the 14th nothing of interest transpired, and on the afternoon of that day we pitched our encampment upon the same spot from which the command had set out two months before, and brought to a welcome termination this toilsome and dangerous march.

Our route, which had oftentimes been over briars and through bushes and thorns, had proved terribly fatal to clothing, and the greater part of the command were, at this time, literally half naked.

Fourteen miles travel next day brought us to the bank of the Neosho, opposite to Fort Gibson, and here we pitched our encampment. The weary dragoons shook hands with the soldiers at the fort, and the savage Indian from the Pawnee Peeks grasped the hand of his half civilized brother from the Arkansas.

Immediately upon our arrival runners were sent to all the different tribes of this region of country to attend a grand council at the fort, and in a few days a large number of delegates from the Choctaws, Cherokees, Creeks, Osages, Delawares, and other tribes, were assembled.

But there was one meeting far more sweet than the soldier with his friend, or the red man with his brother —'twas the meeting of a mother and her son. O who can paint the rapture of the hour, when to the arms of a fond mother flew the long-lost child of her affections; that child which had been snatched from the arms of a father by the rude grasp of the savages; the father murdered, and the almost infant boy borne to their wild abodes.

If, in the hour of her first wild transport of despair, that mother had sunk under the burden of her grief, when the double loss of husband and of child burst upon her at once, how amply was the pang of her anguish allayed by the restoration of her boy, at a moment when she was perchance wiping the tear-drop from her eye, as the thought of his early fate intruded upon her hour of reflection. None but a mother can appreciate the agony of her sorrow or guess at the transport of her joy; her darling boy, whom she had mourned over as murdered by the savage Indians, thus suddenly restored to her arms unharmed, as at the day of his departure. But, alas! why dwell upon the thought; the tear-drop even now falls from mine own eye, as I pen these reflections.

The facts in the case are simply these. Judge Martin, a wealthy planter of Louisiana, had accompanied some friends early this spring upon a hunting expedition up the False Washita, and whilst, together with his little son, he had become separated from the party, he was surprised by the Indians, and cruelly murdered; his little boy taken prisoner, and carried with them to their savage haunts. The circumstances of his re-capture you have already learned in a previous letter.

I must here close, and subscribe myself, as ever,
Your friend, &c.

LETTER XIX.

[The following interesting letter from Mr. Catlin, written to a friend in New-York after his return to Fort Gibson, may not be out of place in this connection,—therefore I have taken the liberty to insert it.]

Fort Gibson, Sept. 8, 1834.

MY DEAR SIR,

Trusting that a few lines from the western frontier will at all times be acceptable to you; and supposing, too, that at this time they would be particularly so, I have ventured to drop you a few words more on the subject of the Pawnees, &c.

Since I wrote my last letter, wherein I gave a very brief account of our campaign, and successful acquaintance with the Camanches, Pawnees, Kiowas, &c. we have had a bustling time with the Indians at this place, Colonel Dodge sent runners to the chiefs of all the contiguous tribes of Indians, with an invitation to meet the Pawnees, &c. in council at this place. Seven or eight tribes flocked to us in great numbers on the first day of the month, when the council commenced; it continued for several days, and gave these semi-civilized sons of the forest a fair opportunity of shaking the hands of their wild and untamed brethren of the west—of embracing them in their arms with expressions of friendship, and of smoking the calumet together, as the solemn pledge of lasting peace.

Colonel Dodge, Major Armstrong, (the Indian agent,) and General Stokes, (the Indian Commissioner,) presided at the council, and I cannot name a scene more interesting and entertaining than it was; where, for several days in succession, free vent was given to the feelings of men *civilized, half-civil,* and *wild*—where the three stages of man were fearlessly asserting their rights, their happiness, and friendship for each other. The vain orations of the half polished (and half breed) Cherokees and Choctaws, with all their finery and art, found their match in the brief and jarring gutturals of the wild and naked man.

After the council had adjourned, and the fumes of the peace-making calumet had vanished away, and Colonel Dodge had made them additional presents, they soon made preparation for their departure, and on the next day started, with an escort of dragoons, for their own country. This movement is much to be regretted; for it would have been exceedingly gratifying to the people of the east to have seen so wild a group, and it would have been of great service to them to have visited Washington,—a journey though, which they could not be prevailed upon to make.

We brought with us to this place, three of the principal chiefs of the Pawnees, fifteen Kiowas, one Camanche, and one Wico chief. The group was undoubtedly one of the most interesting that ever visited our frontier; and I have taken the utmost pains in painting the portraits of all of them, as well as seven of the Camanche chiefs, who came part of the way with us and turned back. These portraits, together with other paintings which I have made, descriptive of their manners and customs—views of their villages —landscapes of the country, &c. will soon be laid before the amateurs of the east, and, I trust, will be found to be interesting.

Although the achievement has been a handsome one, of bringing those unknown people to an acquaintance and a general peace, and at first sight would appear to be of great benefit to them, yet I have my strong doubts whether it will better their condition, unless, with the exercised aid of the strong arm of government, they can be protected in the rights which by nature they are entitled to.

There is already in this place a company of eighty men fitted out, who are to start to-morrow, to overtake these Indians a few miles from this place, and accompany them home, with a large stock of goods, with traps for catching beaver, &c. calculating to build a trading house amongst them, where they will amass, at once, an immense fortune, being the first traders and trappers that have ever been in that part of the country.

I have traveled too much among Indian tribes, and seen too much, not to know the evil consequences of such a system. Goods are sold at such exorbitant prices, that the Indian gets a mere shadow for his peltries, &c. The trappers, and other men in the employment of these traders, are generally the lowest and most debased class of society, who corrupt the morals of the savage without setting them one good example. The Indians see no white people but these, and of course judge us all by them: they consequently hold us, and always will, in contempt, as inferior to themselves, as they have reason to do, and they neither fear nor respect us. When, on the contrary, if the government would promptly prohibit such establishments, and invite these Indians to our frontier posts, they would bring in their furs, their robes, horses, mules, &c. to this place, where there is a good market for them all—where they would get the full value of their property—where there are several stores of goods—where there is an honorable competition, and where they would get four or five times as much for their articles of trade as they would get from a trader in the village, out of the reach of competition, and out of sight of the civilized world.

At the same time, as they would be continually coming where they would see good and polished society, they would be gradually adopting our modes of living—introducing to their country our vegetables, our domestic animals, poultry, &c. and at length our arts and manufactures; they would see and estimate our military strength and advantages, and would be led to fear and respect us. In short, it would undoubtedly be the quickest and surest way to a general acquaintance—to friendship and peace, and at last to civilization. If there is a law in existence for such protection of the Indian tribes, which may have been waived in the case of those nations with which we have long traded, it is a great pity that it should not be rigidly enforced in this new and important acquaintance which we have just made with fifteen or twenty thousand strangers to the civilized world; yet (as we have learned from their unaffected hospitality when in their villages) with hearts of human mould, *susceptible* of all the noble feelings peculiar to civilized man.

This acquaintance has cost the United States a vast sum of money, as well as the lives of several valuable and esteemed officers, and at least some fifty or sixty of the dragoons; and for the honor of the American name, I think we ought, in forming an acquaintance with these numerous tribes, to adopt and *enforce* some different system from that which has been generally practiced on and beyond our frontiers heretofore.

What the regiment of dragoons has suffered from sickness since they started on their summer's campaign, is unexampled in this country, and almost incredible. When we started from this place, ten or fifteen were sent back the first day, too sick to proceed; and so afterwards our numbers were daily diminished; and at the distance of two hundred miles from this place we could muster, out of the whole regiment, but two hundred and fifty men who were able to proceed, with which little band, and that again reduced some sixty or seventy by sickness, we pushed on and accomplished all that was done. Since our return, the sick have been brought in by dozens and scores from the points where they had been left, and although the dragoons who were well enough to leave have all marched off from this post, (some to Leavenworth, three companies twenty miles distant from this, and three companies to the Des Moines on the Mississippi, to their wintering quarters,) they have left at this place one hundred and forty or fifty sick, who are burying two to three and four per day of their numbers. A great many have died, and many more poor fellows must inevitably sink into their graves. The disease seems to be entirely of a bilious nature, and contracted by exposure to the sun, and the impurity of the water which, in many parts of our route, we were obliged to use. The beautiful and pictured scenes which we passed over had an alluring charm on their surface, but (as it would seem) a lurking poison within, that spread a gloom about our encampment whenever we pitched it.

We sometimes rode from day to day, without a tree to shade us from the burning rays of a tropical sun, or a breath of wind to regale us, or cheer our hearts—and with mouths continually parched with thirst, we dipped our drink from stagnant pools that were heated by the sun and kept in fermentation by the wallowing herds of buffalo that resort to them. In this way we dragged on, sometimes passing picturesque and broken country, with fine springs and streams, affording us the luxury of a refreshing shade and a cool draught of water.

The sickness and distress continually about us, spread a gloom over the camp, and marred every pleasure which we might otherwise have enjoyed; for the country abounds, most of the way, with buffalo, deer, turkies, bear, &c. Bands, too, of the snorting wild horses were almost hourly prancing before us, and I found them to be the wildest and fleetest inhabitant of the prairie of the west. The Pawnees and Camanches take vast numbers of them, but the finest and fleetest of them they cannot catch. I approached several times very near to these herds without being discovered, and with a good spy-glass examined them with great pleasure; some of them were very handsome, their manes falling almost to the ground; but when we visited the Camanche village, I looked through their almost incredible herds of horses that were grazing about them (perhaps three thousand, or near it) for the " *splendid,*" " *Arabian,*" &c. horse, of which I have heard so much at the east, as belonging to that country, but I could see or hear nothing of it; and I am strongly inclined to think that it is, in a measure, a *horse* of *imagination.*

The horses of the Camanches are principally the wild horse, and a great many from the Spanish country. They are all small, and most of them miserable and mean. Several of the best of them were purchased by our officers, and having brought them in, can sell them for sixty or seventy-five dollars only.

In haste,—for the present, adieu.
Your friend and servant,
GEORGE CATLIN.

LETTER XX.

Remarks upon Prairies—and settlement of the West.

In my notes thus far, upon our journey over these wild regions of the west, you may have perceived that my attention has been directed more to the movements of the regiment than to the description of country over which we have passed. The eye of the botanist might have dwelt delightedly on the rich variety of plants and flowers, and shrubs and trees, which stud this fertile region; and his pen would perchance have classified and delineated their *genera* and properties; and so might the geologist have marked the soil and *strata* of the earth, and told us of its peculiar formation and ingredient. But I know nothing of these things; I can only tell you, that here a stream meanders, or that there a deep dark forest gathers its apparently interminable shade; that on one side, the lovely prairie rears upon its bosom its myriads of fragrant flowers, or upon the other, that the towering mountain seems to pierce the blue ethereal.

Thus you perceive, that, in answer to your scientific inquiries, I can only speak in general terms, that is farther than I have already intimated in previous letters. In relation to soil, I can only say, that for the most part, throughout that whole extent of country between the Mississippi river and the Rocky Mountains, it is extremely rich and productive, especially upon the prairies and bottom lands: there are, however, many places which are so barren and unprofitable, that for miles in extent nothing but dwarf-oaks can be discerned; but, generally speaking, this is a luxuriant and fruitful region, and destined, at a day not far distant, to repay the labor of the husbandman with a golden harvest.

Upon the prairies, the productions that cover different portions are peculiarly distinct; sometimes the tall grass, unmingled with a varied blade, will cover them for miles and miles, like a rich green carpet over a level floor; then again, where the immense herds of cattle are found, the pasturage is cropped close to the earth. On others, the hazle bushes and briars are intertwined, whilst again the broad yellow blossoms of the prickle-pear reflects from the sun's rays the appearance of a molten sea of gold, and affords a lovely and brilliant contrast to the dense mass of green around. But the loveliest of all the prairies are those which are varied by gentle undulations, and covered with the blended hues of tender and fragrant flowers, out-vieing in magnificence the richest and rarest exotics, and sending forth upon the breeze an odor that well might shame the perfumed harem of an eastern despot. Here the gentle hare-bell and the simple violet mingle their varied hues with the deep carnation of the gaudy piony. Here the daizy and the butter-cup appear in sweet simplicity, under the over-hanging tendrils of the fragrant sweet-brier. The virgin-lilly here stands the unsullied emblem of virtue and purity, whilst the gently blushing rose, as if conscious of its royalty, proudly rears its fragrant bud as in guardianship over its fragile court.

Sometimes the nettle will usurp the prairie for many a mile, under the thorny leaves of which the strawberry grows luxuriantly, a living commentary upon the botanical acquirements of the bard of Avon, who says:

"The strawberry grows underneath the nettle,
And wholesome berries thrive and ripen best
Neighbored by fruit of baser quality."

A grateful contrast is sometimes afforded to the level monotony of the prairie, by the intervention of the canebrake along the margin of the transparent rivers which glide through this region of our land, which wears its garb of green throughout the whole year, and remains verdant and beautiful when all else seems dead, save the aspiring missletoe which shoots in luxuriant bunches from the top branches of the tallest oaks, and seeming to delight most to flourish when all around it is wrapt in the mantle of winter.

But feeble indeed would be my effort to pourtray the lovely appearance of these boundless fields of verdure, and well might I shrink from the task, when our own Irving and Cooper have culled their fragrant flowers to adorn their magic pages; when our own Bryant has woven their glories into the delightful harmony of poetic verse; and other pens have told of the days when the prancing steeds of the mail-clad warriors of De Soto gaily pranced over the prairies.

To one who has never wandered farther toward the west than that portion of our country forming the middle district, provided that he possesses a disposition savoring of romance, and a desire to view the ever-varying scenes of nature; nothing could perhaps contribute so greatly to his gratification, and at the same time furnish him with so much useful instruction, as a journey through the vast valley of the Mississippi, and thence westward over the prairies. Considering the rapidity not only with which towns and cities have sprung into existence within a few years past, but the formation of new states and territories, adding new links to our already vast chain of dominion; we have but to stretch forward the eye through the vista of a dawning day, when the whole of the hunting ground of the red man shall give way to the furrow of the plough.

Where but a few years ago vast and impenetrable forests extended over that immense region only known by the broad appellation of "*the west*," now is centered the very heart and glory of our country; and taking as our data the result of past experience, may we not be allowed to look forward with an equal degree of certainty through the next twenty years, and view that whole territory extending between the Mississippi river and the Rocky Mountains, dotted with cabins and cornfields; not accessible only through the medium of a trail or foot-path, but divided into districts, and intersected with roads, and affording conveyances for the transportation of our mails, with safety and rapidity, from the whole line of our Atlantic shore to the no longer "unexplored regions of the west."

I cannot help here recurring to a passage in the

"Heart of Mid-Lothian," in which Sir Walter, in remarking upon the improvements of the age, thus speaks:"

"The times have changed in nothing more (we follow, as we were wont, the manuscript of Peter Pattison) than in the rapid conveyance of intelligence and communication betwixt one part of Scotland and another. It is not above twenty or thirty years, according to the evidence of many credible witnesses now alive, since a little miserable horse-cart, performing with difficulty a journey of thirty miles *per diem*, carried our mails from the capital of Scotland to its extremity. Nor was Scotland much more deficient in their accommodations than our richer sister had been about eighty years before." But, need we go across the water to learn that locomotion, during the last thirty years, hath overleaped every other improvement, and that the rate that of yore was traveled *per diem*, now may be accomplished within the *hour?* Shades of the Knickerbockers, what a change hath taken place! Had Rip Van Winkle but taken a deeper potation, and continued his nap till now, the old gentleman would surely have died of grief and disappointment. To have opened his eyes upon this age of rail-roads, and twelve-mile trotters; of steam engines, and percussion locks; of lucifers, and loco focos; of aerial voyages, and safety-valve diving bells; and in short, in this age of improvement and rapidity, would of a truth, been too much for the nerves of even the mild, easy-going, indifferent, honest Rip.

But, notwithstanding the mighty change that hath come o'er this land, the Rocky Mountains are not much nearer to their cousins along the Hudson than they were in the days of honest Rip Van Winkle. There hath been a boundary to these doings, and as yet no rail-road intersects the western prairie beyond the Arkansas and the Mississippi. No post-coaches rattle along the Macadamized turnpike over the Pawnee Peaks. There the elk and the bison still range, and the Indian hunter still dwells amid the wild region that encompasses them. But every year hath made encroachments upon this vaunted region; emigration hath "poured like a torrent down upon a vale," from every quarter of the globe, upon the skirts of this wild dominion; and should prosperity and peace follow up the unabated progress of our country's advancement, but a few years more will not only find the well guarded trading party, or the troop of mounted and armed soldiers traversing these regions, but the sound of the hammer of the artizan shall ring across the prairie, and the woodman's axe shall resound through the forest.

Indulge me, if not with me, for a moment, whilst I look through the horoscope, and tell what is now hidden behind the curtain of futurity. See that wild and lovely prairie, waving as the air breathes upon its deep green mantle, spangled with its ten thousand times ten thousand flowers, of the brightest hue, and yielding a delicious fragrance; like a boundless ocean, no pathway divides it. Look again, see those towering piles of castellated rocks, beetling above the cloud-capped summit of the mountain; that roaring torrent dashing from crag to crag, from precipice to precipice. Look through that opening vista, and see, like Ossa upon Pelion, mountain rearing its crest above mountain. Stretch forward your eye, and look along that deep green vale, studded with groves, and watered with crystal streams. Climb to yonder pinnacle, and gaze upon the world beneath it—no human habitation, no vestige of improvement greets your view; nature still reigns triumphant over the broad expanse. Let me draw aside the curtain—fifty years hath flown away, many a head hath been laid low in the dust, and many a new actor hath made his debut upon the stage of life—what seest thou? " On yonder pinnacle of the mountain, from whence I gazed upon the trackless prairie, stands a proud dwelling, with its towers and porticoes—its halls are filled with groups of visitors; I see a stairway leading up the mountain, carved in the solid rock, and as it winds amid the clusters of trees, I can see many groups resting, as they ascend the summit. See yonder steam-car darting across the prairie, having in its train an hundred passengers. Yonder canal connects the Columbia with the Mississippi, and those boats are carrying bales, and boxes of merchandise to the various towns along its line. There, amid the crumbled fragments at the mountain's base, are a group of students gathering specimens for their cabinet—and see that happy and merry group of boarding-school girls frolicking over the prairie. What a change! The splendid steamer now disturbs the waters of the Mackenzie and the Columbia; civilization hath strode across the land: yonder shriveled Indian is the last of his race; his people are no more—his hunting ground hath yielded to the plough—his wigwam is destroyed—and he stands solitary and alone, the last relic of a mighty race.

Is all this visionary? No, he who watches the signs of the times, and reflects for a moment over the events of years gone by; then bends forward his eye to look through the intervening space of a few years more, must readily imagine that such must, and inevitably will be the result.

But to take a more minute and scientific view of these mountains, I will direct your attention to a few remarks which are not so much the result of actual observation on my part, as what I have been enabled to derive from statistics which I have collected from the compilations of others. "The Rocky Mountains form the most interesting and prominent feature in the physical geography of North America. Though much nearer the western than the eastern shore of that great continent, they appear to form, in relation to the distribution both of plants and animals, a strongly-marked line of demarkation, which presents a barrier to the progress of migration of many species.

"No doubt, the direction of this vast chain being from south to north, it lies in the line of, rather than at right angles to, the usual course of navigation, and therefore offers a less formidable barricade than if it were stretched across the continent. As it is, however, the natural productions which occur on the plains, on the different sides of this lengthened range, exhibit a considerable dissimilarity. Nature has, under the regulation of the laws of Providence, no doubt made many exceptions in favor of this rule, in favor of species which occur on both sides of the chain; but the distribution both of plants and animals, if not regulated, is at least modified by the intervention of these mountains."

The careful geographical observer can doubtless trace this chain of mountains throughout the entire length of our continent, beginning with the most eastern ridge, and journeying from the Green Mountains to the towering pyramids which skirt the borders of the Hudson, thence over the toilsome Alleghanies, and so on in a continuous range to the farthest western acclivity on the boundary of the Arctic Sea, forming a mighty ligature which binds in social compact the extended borders of our republic. This peculiar ridge, however, which stretches from Mexico to the Mackenzie River, in a line parallel with the Pacific Ocean, is as yet but imperfectly explored. Although the soldier and the trader have ventured to traverse the broad regions which lie between them and the Mississippi, and although the emigrant and the squatter have climbed their summit, or reared an humble cabin at their base, yet still the summer's verdure and the winter's snow have both alternately to clothe the prairie a few years more before they shall be despoiled of their far western locality. Their highest summit is something more than 15,000 feet above the level of the sea. The following extract which I shall take from the work published by Mr. Tytler, contains observations which neither my own situation or acquirements would have enabled me to make; you must therefore excuse me for the length to which I may extend it. This being a leisure day with me, I can devote a portion of it to your service; I am not, however, as you may perceive, egotist enough to exclude the remarks of others upon this subject to give place to my own; and therefore, as it may throw some light upon the history of this region of country, I the more cheerfully send you the statistical observations of the above named gentleman. Speaking of the Rocky Mountains, he says: "Though much inferior in height to the Andes of the southern continent, of which, however, in a general sense, they may be regarded as the northern continuation, they greatly exceed in elevation the other mountain-chains of North America. This, indeed, becomes apparent from a consideration of the courses of the great rivers of the country, all of which, with the exception of the lake-born St. Lawrence, derive their sources and primary streams from the Rocky Mountains, however different may be the direction in which their waters flow. The Columbia, for example, which falls into the Northern Pacific Ocean in the 46th parallel, derives its primary streams from the western slopes of the same rocky chain, the eastern sides of which give rise to the waters of the Missouri, which, following a south-easterly and southern direction, terminate their long-continued course of 4500 miles in the Gulf of Mexico. The Saskatchawan, in both its great branches, likewise flows from the eastern slopes of the Rocky Mountains, and, uniting its streams a short way below Carlton House, it flows through Lake Winipeg, and then, assuming the name of Nelson River, it empties itself, in the vicinity of Cape Tatnam, into Hudson's Bay. In like manner, the Mackenzie, which, in respect of size, may be regarded as the third river in North America (being inferior to the Missouri and St. Lawrence alone,) derives its two main branches, the Elk and Peace Rivers, from these mountains; and ere long, flowing northwards and in a north-westerly direction, it opens its numerous mouths into the Polar Sea, after a course of nearly 2000 miles. It may be mentioned as a singular fact, that the Peace River actually rises on the western side of the Rocky Mountain ridge, within 300 yards of the source of the Tacootchesse, or Fraser's River, which flows into the Strait of Georgia, on the western shore.

"At a considerable distance below its issue from

Great Slave Lake, and where the Mackenzie makes its first near approach to the Rocky Mountains, it is joined by a large stream which runs a little to the northward of the Peace River, and flows along the eastern base of the mountains. It was called the River of the Mountains by Sir Alexander Mackenzie; but it has since, on account of its great magnitude, become more generally recognised by the traders under the name of the South Branch of the Mackenzie. The Mackenzie also receives several other large streams in the course of its seaward journey, and among others Great Bear Lake River, whose head-waters draw their source from the banks of the Coppermine River, and Peel's River, which issues from the Rocky Mountains in latitude 67°. 'Immediately after the junction of Peel's River,' Dr. Richardson observes, 'the Mackenzie separates into numerous branches, which flow to the sea through a great delta composed of alluvial mud. Here, from the richness of the soil, and from the river bursting its icy chains comparatively very early in the season, and irrigating the low delta with the warmer waters brought from countries ten or twelve degrees farther to the southward, trees flourish, and a more luxuriant vegetation exists than in any place in the same parallel on the North American continent.' In latitude 68°, there are many groves of handsome white spruce-firs, and in lititude 69°, on the desolate shores of the Polar Sea, dense and well-grown willow-thickets cover the flat islands; while currants and gooseberries grow on the drier hummocks, accompanied by showy epilobiums and perennial lupins. The moose-deer, the beaver, and the American hare follow this extension of a life-sustaining vegetation, and the existence of these herbivorous animals induces a corresponding increase in the localities of wolves, foxes, and other predaceous kinds.

"The above mentioned are the principal rivers which traverse the fur-countries of America. There are, however, a few others of smaller size, the banks of which yielded their share of the natural history collections, and may therefore be briefly noticed. Hayes River takes its origin from the neighborhood of Lake Winipeg, and, after running a course almost parallel to that of Nelson's River, it falls into the same quarter of Hudson's Bay. York Factory, so frequently mentioned in the narratives of our northern expeditions, stands on the low alluvial point that separates the mouths of these two rivers. The Missinnippi, or as it is sometimes called, the English River, falls into Hudson's Bay at Churchill. Its upper stream is denominated the Beaver River, and takes its rise from a small ridge of hills, intermediate between a bend of the Elk River and the northern branch of the Saskatchawan. Lastly, the Coppermine River derives its origin not far from the east end of Great Slave Lake, and pursuing a northerly course, already made familiar to our readers, it flows through the Barren Grounds into the Arctic Sea. It is inferior in size to several branches of the Mackenzie; and as there are few alluvial deposites along its banks, it is deficient in that comparative luxuriance of vegetation which, along the banks of the Mackenzie, induces several species of herbivorous quadrupeds to seek a higher latitude than they elsewhere attain. Did our limits permit, we could dwell with pleasure on this example of the interconnection or mutual dependence of the links of a lengthened chain of facts in natural history.

"There are various practicable passages across the

Rocky Mountains. Sir Alexander Mackenzie crossed them in the year 1793, at the head of the Peace River, between latitude 55° and 56°. The same route was followed in 1806 by a party of the North-west Company who went to form a settlement at New-Caledonia. It is still occasionally used by the servants of the Hudson's Bay Company. In the year 1805 Lewis and Clarke effected a passage at the head of the Missouri, in latitude 47°, on their way to the mouth of the Columbia. Dr. Richardson informs us, that for several years subsequent to that period, the North-West Company were in the habit of crossing in latitude $52\frac{1}{2}°$, at the head of the north branch of the Saskatchawan, between which and one of the feeding streams of the Columbia there is a short portage; but of late years, owing to the hostility of the Indians, that route has been deserted, and the Hudson's Bay Company, who now engross the whole of the fur trade of that country, make use of a more lengthened portage between the northern branch of the Columbia and the Red Deer River, one of the branches of the Elk or Mackenzie. We are likewise informed that attempts have been recently made to effect a passage in the 62d parallel of latitude; but although several ridges of the mountains were crossed, it does not appear that any stream flowing towards the Pacific was attained.

"The latest journeys across the Rocky Mountains with which we happen to be acquainted, are those of Messrs. Drummond and Douglas, two skillful and enterprising botanists, both belonging professionally to that high class of practical horticulturists for which Scotland has been long famous, and of which she is so justly proud.

"Mr. Drummond acted in the capacity of assistant-naturalist to Sir John Franklin's *second* overland expedition, and it was to his unrivalled skill in collecting, and indefatigable zeal, that Dr. Richardson was indebted for a large proportion both of the botanical and zoological productions. He continued at Cumberland House in 1825, and occupied himself collecting plants during the month of July, after the main-body of the expedition had departed northwards. He then ascended the Saskatchawan for 660 miles, to Edmonton House, performing much of the journey on foot, and amassing objects of natural history by the way. He left Edmonton House on the 22d of September, and crossing a thickly-wooded swampy country to Red Deer River, a branch of the Elk or Athabasca, he traveled along its banks until he reached the Rocky Mountains, the ground being by this time covered with snow. Having explored the portage-road for fifty miles across the mountains towards the Columbia River, he hired an Indian hunter, with whom he returned to the head of the Elk River, on which he passed the winter, making collections, under privations which, Dr. Richardson observes, 'would have effectually quenched the zeal of a less hardy naturalist.' He revisited the Columbia portage-road during the month of April, 1826, and continued in that vicinity until the 10th of August, after which he made a journey to the head-waters of the Peace River, during which he *suffered severely from famine*. But, nothing daunted, our enduring countryman, as soon as he had obtained a supply of provisions, hastened back to the Columbia portage, with the view of crossing to that river, and botanizing for a season on its banks. However, when he had reached the west end of the portage, he was overtaken by letters from Sir John Franklin, informing him that it was necessary to be at York Factory in 1827. He was therefore obliged to commence his return, greatly to his own regret; for a transient view of the Columbia had stimulated his desire to investigate its natural treasures. 'The snow,' he observes, 'covered the ground too deeply to permit me to add much to my collections in this hasty trip over the mountains; but it was impossible to avoid noticing the great superiority of the climate on the western side of that lofty range. From the instant the descent towards the Pacific commences, there is a visible improvement in the growth of timber, and the variety of forest-trees greatly increases. The few mosses that I gleaned in the excursion were so fine that I could not but deeply regret that I was unable to pass a season or two in that interesting region.' He now reluctantly turned his back upon the mountains, and, returning by Edmonton House, where he spent some time, he joined Dr. Richardson at Carlton House, on his homeward journey. Mr. Drummond's collections on the mountains and plains of the Saskatchawan amounted to about 1500 species of plants, 150 birds, fifty quadrupeds, and a considerable number of insects. He remained at Carlton House for six weeks after Dr. Richardson had left that place, and, descending to Cumberland House, he there met Captain Back, whom he accompanied to York Factory. He had previously, however, had the pleasure of being joined by a countryman and kindred spirit, Mr. David Douglas, the other indefatigable collector to whom we have already alluded. Mr. Douglas had been engaged in gathering plants for three years for the Horticultural Society, in North California and on the banks of the Columbia River. He had crossed the Rocky Mountains from the westward, at the head of the Elk River, by the same portage-road previously traversed by Mr. Drummond, and having spent a short time in visiting the Red River of Lake Winipeg, he returned to England along with Mr. Drummond, by the way of Hudson's Bay. 'Thus, a zone of at least two degrees of latitude in width, and reaching entirely across the continent, from the mouth of the Columbia to that of the Nelson River of Hudson's Bay, has been explored by two of the ablest and most zealous collectors that England has ever sent forth; while a zone of similar width, extending at right angles with the other from Canada to the Polar Sea, has been more cursorily examined by the expeditions.'

"That widely-extended tract of territory which lies to the eastward of the Rocky Mountains, and to the north of the Missouri and the Great Lakes, is now well known to the Hudson's Bay traders, with exception of the shores of the Polar Sea, and a corner, bounded to the westward by the Coppermine River, Great Slave, Athabasca, Wollaston, and Deer Lakes, to the southward by the Churchill or Missinnippi, and to the northward and eastward by the sea. When viewed under a zoological aspect, we find that this north-eastern corner, more particularly known under the name of the 'Barren Grounds,' carries its purely arctic character farther to the south than any of the other meridians. This very bare and desolate portion of America is almost entirely destitute of wood, except along the banks of its larger rivers. The rocks of this district are primitive, and rarely rise to such an elevation as to deserve the name of mountain-ridges, being rather an assemblage of low hills with rounded summits, and more or less precipitous sides. The soil of the narrow valleys which separate these hills is either an imperfect peat-earth, affording nourishment to dwarf birches, stunted willows, larches, and black spruce-trees,—or, more generally, it is composed of a rocky debris, consisting of dry, coarse, quartzose sand, unadapted to other vegetation than that of lichens. The centres of the larger valleys are filled with lakes of limpid water, which are stored with fish, even though frequently completely land-locked. More generally, however, one of these lakes discharges its waters into another, through a narrow gorge, by a turbulent and rapid stream; and, indeed, most of the rivers which irrigate these barren grounds may almost be viewed as a chain of narrow and connected lakes. The rein-deer or caribou, and the musk-ox, are the prevailing quadrupeds of these unproductive wastes, where the absence of fur-bearing species has prevented any settlement by the traders. The only human inhabitants are the caribou-eaters,—a people composed of a few forlorn families of the Chipewyans.

"From the district above described, a belt of low primitive rocks extends to the northern shores of Lake Superior. Dr. Richardson calculates its width at about 200 miles; and he states that, as it becomes more southerly, it recedes from the Rocky Mountains, and differs from the Barren Grounds in being well wooded. It is bounded to the eastward by a narrow strip of limestone, beyond which there is a flat, swampy, and partly alluvial district, forming the western shores of Hudson's Bay. This tract, from the western border of the low primitive tract just mentioned to the coast of Hudson's Bay, has been named the *Eastern District*, and presents us with several animals unknown to the higher latitudes.

" The Eastern District is bounded to the westward by

a flat limestone deposite; and a remarkable chain of lakes and rivers, such as the Lake of the Woods, Lake Winipeg, Beaver Lake, and the central portion of Churchill or Missinnippi, all of which lie to the southward of the Methye Portage, marks the line of junction of the two formations. This district, which Dr. Richardson has named the *Limestone Tract,* is well wooded, and produces the fur-bearing animals in great abundance. The white or polar bear, the arctic fox, the Hudson's Bay lemming, and several other species disappear, while their places are filled up by bisons, bats, and squirrels, unknown to the other regions.

"Intermediate between the limestone tract and the foot of the Rocky Mountains there occurs a wide expanse of prairie land. So slight are the inequalities of its surface, that the traveler, while crossing it, is obliged to regulate his course either by the compass or the observation of the heavenly bodies. The soil is tolerably fertile, though, for the greater proportion, dry and rather sandy. It supports, however, a thick grassy sward, which yields an abundant pasture to innumerable herds of bison and many species of deer; and the grizzly bear, the fiercest and most powerful of all the North American land-animals, properly so called, inhabits various portions of this wide-spread plain. Prairies of a similar aspect, and still greater extent, are known to border the Arkansa and Missouri rivers. They are said to become gradually narrower to the northward, and in the southern portion of the fur-countries they extend for about fifteen degrees of longitude, from Maneetobaw, or Maneetowoopoo, and Winipegoos Lakes, to the base of the Rocky Mountains. These magnificent plains are partially intersected by ridges of low hills, and also by several streams, of which the banks are wooded; and towards the skirts of the plains many detached masses of finely-formed timber, and pieces of still water, are disposed in so pleasing and picturesque a manner as to convey the idea rather of a cultivated English park than of an American wilderness. There is, however, so great a deficiency of wood in the central parts of these plains, that 'the hunters,' says Dr. Richardson, 'are under the necessity of taking fuel with them on their journeys, or in dry weather of making their fires of the manure of the bison. To the northward of the Saskatchawan, the country is more broken, and intersected by woody hills; and on the banks of the Peace River the plains are of comparatively small extent, and are detached from each other by woody tracts: they terminate altogether in the angle between the River of the Mountains and Great Slave Lake. The abundance of pasture renders these plains the favorite resort of various ruminating animals.'"

Having thus indulged myself, and perhaps wearied you, by entering into this detailed statement, I cannot allow myself to dismiss the subject without adverting to a thought which has often crossed my mind, in relation to the inducements held out to emigrants, as well as the poorer classes of our own population, to settle here upon these fertile regions. Instead of toiling for a scanty pittance, as the greater portion of our laboring people have to do, who are located in large towns or cities, and continuing their toilsome labors from dawn till evening, throughout year after year, without perhaps ever having it in their power to lay by a dollar for a future day, they might here become the happy, and even affluent settlers of a soil which scarce needs the labor of cultivation to yield an abun-

dant harvest: however, this portion of our country is daily becoming better known, and more justly appreciated; every year extends the limits of our settled frontier, and succeeding years are destined to increase with a rapid ratio the tide of western emigration: the buffalo and the Indian, alike the enemies of civilization and settlement, are fast receding before the tide of enterprise, and the industrious honey-bees, the forerunners of white emigration, are humming over the flowers of the prairie, and depositing their delicious burden in the hollow caverns of the old oak trees. But I will dwell no longer upon the glories of this vaunted region, and, as usual, close this epistle, by subscribing to it the name of
Your friend.

LETTER XXI.

Remarks upon the Worship, Exercises, Oratory, Poetry, and condition of the Indians.

Fort Gibson, 1834.

MY DEAR SIR,

I will now attempt to fulfill my promise in regard to furnishing you with something connected with the Indians. I have become myself much attached to them, and I assure you, have taken great pains to become acquainted with their habits, manners, superstitions, legends, and, in a small degree, with their language. People at the east know but little about what is doing in this remote region, and consequently can feel but little interest for the poor Indians.

An old number of a Scotch paper that I have with me, thus defines the Indian race: "America, which is perhaps the finest country of the world, when first discovered, was found to be only thinly inhabited by a few scattered tribes who dwelt upon the sides of their majestic rivers or magnificent lakes, or, like other uncivilized people, led a solitary and savage life, amidst the intricate paths of its extensive forests. We are all aware how its different regions became populated by emigration from other countries, but with these settlers we shall not interfere, as it is the original natives of America alone who here claim our attention and interest. It is presumed, as we already explained, that this continent was peopled by migrations from the north-east part of Asia; a fact borne out by the circumstance, that when America was discovered, the natives were found to be acquainted by tradition with the most remarkable events related in Mosaic history: in addition to which, the American language appears to have been founded on the Asiatic. The natives of America possess a large and robust frame, and a well-proportioned figure; their complexion is of a bronze, or reddish copper hue, as if it were rusty colored, not unlike cinnamon or tannin; their hair is black, long, coarse, and shining, but not thickset on the head; their beard is thin, and grows in tufts; their forehead low, and their eyes lengthened out, and their outer angles turned upward to the temples; their eyebrows are high, their cheek-bones prominent; their nose is a little flattened, but well marked; their lips extended, and their teeth closely set and pointed: in their mouth there is an expression of sweetness, which forms a striking contrast to the gloomy, harsh, and even stern character of their countenance: their head is of a square shape, and their face is broad without being flat, and tapers towards the chin. They have a high chest, massy thighs, and arched legs; their foot is large, and their whole body squat and thick set. The stature and complexion of the native American differs materially in different parts of the continent; but on the whole, they bear in their physical and moral character so strong a resemblance to each other, that there can be but little doubt that they derived their origin from the same stock."

As civilization advances, the Indians recede; and from the simple fact that the experiment has never been fairly tested, we are apt to imagine that they are incapable of being civilized. Every succeeding year diminishes the extent of their dominions, and in a few more they will be forced to cross the Rocky Mountains, and move their wigwams to the very shores of the Pacific. Now, whatever of profit such a change shall yield to the man whose whole soul is wrapt up in his avarice and gold; whatever it may add to the power and splendor of our country to extend her territory over this now wild and romantic region; still I hold, that, to the mind of the philanthropist and the christian, the extermination of the Indian race under such circumstances must ever be a sorrowful subject of reflection.

Uncontaminated by the vices and vicious habits introduced amongst them by the whites, the Indian character has much in it to be admired, and but little to be condemned. They indeed lead a wandering unsettled life, but in many respects live more naturally than their civilized neighbors. They enjoy life upon an extended scale, neither pampering their appetites with dainties, nor trammeling their minds and actions with foolish and useless notions of fashion and etiquette. There is a something of nobleness about them in almost every thing they do. Educated to the chase, they depend upon their skill and exertions for sustenance; and even their wild sports relish of the more classic games of the Greeks as formerly practiced at their Olympic festivals. Although the superstitious ceremonies and observances practiced amongst them may appear vain and foolish to those unacquainted with their import, still there is a wild and glowing vein of romance connected with them from which one hardly wishes to draw the veil. We all have our beliefs and disbeliefs, our likes and dislikes, our ceremonies and superstitions, to a greater or less degree; and, in comparison with the rest of mankind, the superstitions and ceremonies of the Indians are neither the most groundless or unnatural. The untaught savage looks abroad upon creation, and feasts his eyes upon her beauties, her grandeur and magnificence on the one hand, and upon her no less to be admired variety and harmony on the other. An innate principle teaches him that there is a being who created all these objects. He discovers the unseen hand of an over-ruling agency operating upon the whole creation. He watches the seasons as they roll around in regular and rapid succession. He knows not of an immaterial God, therefore he seeks to find in the material world an object worthy of his adoration and his love. He gazes upon the sun as the most powerful and prominent object in creation, and he worships it as his god. The light of science has never dawned upon his intellect, and as amid the grassy ocean of the prairie he beholds the glorious and resplendent luminary of day coming forth in solitary brightness, shedding his lustre and influence upon every object in creation, and after having performed his diurnal course, descend on the other side of the heavens—as he gazes, he believes, and in his belief is happy and contented ; would that I might, in regard to them, add with the poet,

" Where ignorance is bliss, 'tis folly to be wise."

In his native ignorance, the Indian is moved only by the impulse of his animal nature, and it must be allowed by every candid and observing commentator upon their character and habits, that they have not, as a people, been the gainers by their intercourse with the whites. I do not deny that civilization has in many instances done much to soften down and meliorate the condition of the Indian ; but these good effects are more than counterbalanced by the misery and wretchedness that have been entailed upon them by the introduction of all the worst habits and vices of the whites, who, wherever they have settled among them, have taught them, in most instances, scarcely a single counteracting virtue. " Who can believe," (asked a writer on the Indian character some time ago,) " that the introduction of ardent spirits amongst them has added no new item to the catalogue of their crimes, nor subtracted one from the list of their cardinal virtues ?"

Few, comparatively, have the opportunity, fewer the inclination, to visit and observe the Indians in their remote haunts, or even, perhaps, upon our immediate frontiers. All who have done so must be convinced that wherever, and for whatever purpose, the Indian and the white man come in contact, the former, in all that relates to his moral condition, is sure to become irretrievably and severely a sufferer. Every unbiassed inquirer, who will avail himself of the abundant evidence before the public, will be convinced that for more than two hundred years, in despite of all the benevolent exertions of individuals, of humane associations, and of governments, the direct tendency of intercourse between the two races has been the uniform and rapid deterioration of the Indians.

However far these remarks may tend to show what has been the effect of such an intercourse, still I am far, very far from being of opinion that the Indians are not susceptible of being so far benefited by civilization as to adopt not only the habits of life of the whites, but even to be made to understand and become partakers of the great truths and promises of revelation. But the truth is, that the character and business of that class of men who, for the most part, have dwelt and traded amongst the Indians, was not calculated to leave a proper influence upon their minds. Generally, the men who have carried on the trading intercourse with them were those who, impelled only by the hope of gain, ventured to penetrate the deep recesses of unexplored forests, to traverse the parched and boundless prairie, to ford the mighty rivers of the west, indifferent to every privation and hardship; and who cared nothing for the ignorant beings with whom they traded, farther than to obtain their peltries upon the terms most advantageous to themselves, leaving behind them a few trinkets and more than enough liquor to poison their habits, thus enriching themselves but morally destroying the Indians. Instead of carrying with them those things that might serve to add comfort in some degree to their condition, the traders usually go laden with only such gaudy and glittering toys as are calculated to catch the attention of the ignorant people with whom they trade; and to avoid the prohibition of government in regard to the vending of liquor, they artfully deal it out to the Indians gratuitously, for the purpose of trafficking with them the more advantageously while under its pernicious influence.

Nothing can exceed the extent of torture that the Indian will inflict upon himself to satisfy either his vanity or some superstitious belief. Many instances of this may be found in the records of their history, one of which I will mention: " A devotee caused two stout arrows to be passed through the muscles of his breast, one on each side near the mammæ. To these arrows, cords were attached, the opposite ends of which were affixed to the upper part of a post, which had been firmly implanted in the earth for that purpose. He then threw himself backward into an oblique position within about two feet of the soil, so as to depend with the greater portion of his weight by the cords. In this situation, the most excruciating that can be imagined, he continued to chant and to keep time with the music of the gong, until, from long abstinence and suffering, he fainted. The by-standers then cried out, 'Courage, courage!' with much shouting and noise; after a short interval of insensibility he revived, and proceeded with his self-inflicted tortures as before, until nature becoming too exhausted, he again relapsed into insensibility, upon which he was loosened from the cords and carried off amid the acclamations of the whole assembly."

There are also many instances of the most unfeeling cruelty practiced by the white settlers toward the Indians, one of which I listened to with deep attention, as related by an old Indian, who appeared to be almost sunk under the weight of years. The story impressed my mind so deeply that I determined to transcribe it for your consideration, but subsequently, in looking over the library at the fort, I chanced to open upon the very same anecdote,* for which I would refer you to the second volume of Major Long's expedition.

* "In 1814 a trader married a beautiful squaw of one of the most distinguished families of the Omawhaw nation. This match, on the part of the husband, was induced by the following circumstances. Being an active, intelligent, and enterprising man, he had introduced the American trade to the Missouri Indians, and had gained great influence amongst them by his bravery and ingenuous deportment; but he at length perceived that his influence was gradually declining, in consequence of the presence and wiles of many other traders to whom his enterprise had opened the way, and that his customers were gradually forsaking him.

Thus circumstanced, in order to regain the ground that he had lost, he determined to seek a matrimonial alliance with one of the most powerful families of the Omawhaws. In pursuance of this resolution he selected a squaw whose family and friends were such as he desired. He addressed himself to her friends according to the Indian custom, and informed them that he loved their daughter, and that he was sorry to see her in the state of poverty common to their nation, and although he possessed a wife among the white people, yet he wished also to have one of the Omawhaw nation. If they would transfer their daughter to him in marriage, he would obligate himself to treat her kindly; and as he had commenced a permanent trading establishment in their country, he would dwell during a portion of the year with her, and the remainder with the white people, as the nature of his occupation required. His establishment should be her home and that of her people during his life, as he never intended to abandon the trade. In return he expressed his expectation that the nation would give him the refusal of their peltries, in order that he might be enabled to comply with his engagements with them. He further promised that his children should be made known to the white people, and probably be qualified to continue the trade after his death.

The Indian seems to act throughout upon the text, that "sufficient for the day is the evil thereof." If he has been successful in the chase, he returns to his wig-

The parents replied with thanks for his liberal offer, and for his disposition to have pity on them, they would not object to the connection, and hoped that their daughter would accept of him as a husband. The parents then retired and opened the subject to their daughter; they assured her that the proposed husband was a great man, greater than any of the Omawhaws, that he would do much for her and for them, and concluded by requesting her acquiescence in the wishes of the white man. She replied that all they said was without doubt true, and she was willing to become his wife.

The agreement being thus concluded, the trader made presents agreeable to the custom of the nation, and conducted his interesting prize to his house.

The spring succeeded, the trader departed for the settlements, leaving her at his trading house.

The ensuing autumn she had the pleasure to see him return, having conceived for him the most tender attachment. Upon his visit the following season, she presented him with a fine daughter, born during his absence, which she had nursed with the tenderest care.

With her infant in her arms, she daily seated herself upon the bank of the river, and followed the downward course of the stream with her eye, to gain the earliest notice of his approach. Thus time passed; on the second year, the father, upon his return, was presented with a son, and obtained his squaw's reluctant consent to take their daughter with him on his return voyage to the country of the white people. But no sooner did he commence his journey than her maternal fondness overpowered her, and although she had another charge upon which to lavish her kindness, yet she ran crying and screaming along the bank of the river after the boat, tearing out her long flowing hair, and appearing to be almost bereft of reason. On her return home she gave away every thing she possessed, cut off her hair, went into deep mourning, and remained inconsolable. She would often say that she well knew that her daughter

wam in cheerfulness, but if unsuccessful he never murmurs. The games of the Indian are manly and beautiful, and as I have before remarked, they resemble

would be better treated than she could be at home, but she could not help regarding her own situation as if the Waconda had taken away her child for ever.

One day she was engaged with six other squaws in agricultural labors, her infant boy being secured to his cradle-like-board, which she had carefully reclined against a tree at a little distance; they were discovered by a war party of Sioux, who rushed towards them, expecting to gratify their vengeance by securing their scalps. An exclamation from her companions directed her attention to the common enemy, and in her fright she precipitately fled; but suddenly recollecting her child, she swiftly returned full in the face of the Sioux, snatched her child from the tree, and turned to save its life, more precious than her own. She was closely pursued by one of the enemy, when she arrived at a fence which separated her from the field of the trading house. A moment's hesitation here would have been fatal, and exerting all her strength, she threw the child with its board as far as she could on the opposite side. Four of the squaws were tomahawked, and the others escaped, among which was the mother, having succeeded in bearing off her child uninjured.

The trader, on his arrival at the settlements, learned that his white or civilized wife had died during his absence, and after the usual formalities, and devoting a short time to sorrow, he again united himself with another highly respectable and amiable lady. The second season after, his wife accompanied him on his annual voyage up the Missouri, to his trading house, the abode of his squaw.

Previously to his arrival, however, he despatched a message to his dependants at the trading house, to prevent his squaw from appearing in the presence of his wife. She was accordingly sent off to the village of her nation some sixty or seventy miles off. She could not remain long there, but soon returned with her little boy on her back, and accompanied by some of her friends, she encamped near the husband's residence. She sent her son to the trader, who treated him affectionately. On the second day the trader sent for his squaw, and requested that she would accompany her friends back to their village.

in many respects those practiced at the Olympic circles, and so celebrated in the annals of Grecian history. They are bold, athletic, and daring, and in many

She departed without a murmur, as it is a custom among the Omawhaws to send away one of their wives, whilst they remain for a time with a more favorite one.

About two months afterwards the trader recalled her. Overjoyed at what she supposed to be her good fortune, she lost no time in presenting herself before the husband whom she tenderly loved; but great was her disappointment, when the husband demanded the surrender of the child, and renounced for the future any association with her, directing her to return to her people, and provide for her future well-being as best she might.

Overpowered by her feelings on this demand and repudiation, she ran from the house, and finding a canoe on the river shore, she paddled over to the opposite side with her child in her arms and made her escape to the forest.

The night was cold, and attended with a fall of snow and hail; reflecting upon her disconsolate condition, she resolved to return again in the morning, and with the feelings of a wife and a mother to plead her cause before the arbiter of her fate, and endeavor to mitigate the cruel sentence.

Agreeable to this determination, she once more approached him upon whom she believed she had claims paramount to any other individual. "Here is our child," said she; "I do not question your fondness for him, but is he not still more dear to me? You say that you will keep him for yourself, and drive me far away from you. But no, I will remain with him, I can find some hole or corner in which I can creep and be near to him, and sometimes see him. If you will not give me food, I will, nevertheless, remain and starve before your eyes.

The trader then offered her a considerable present, desiring her at the same time to go and leave the child. But she said, "Is my child a dog, that I should sell him for merchandise? You cannot drive me away; you may beat me, it is true, and otherwise abuse me, but I will still remain with you. When you married me, you promised to use me kindly as long as I should be faithful to you; that I have been so no one can deny.

respects display much of agility and strength, as well as cunning. The young Indian may be often seen darting like lightning across the prairie bestride a wild horse, with no other equipment than a halter, and displaying wonderful skill in his management and manœuvres. I might notice here also the hurling of the tomahawk, and the unerring aim with which they shoot their arrows, even whilst at full speed upon their horses. In the use of fire-arms, the Indians that

Ours was not a marriage contracted for a season; no, it was to terminate only with our lives. I was then a young girl, and might have been united to an Omawhaw chief; but I am now an old woman, having had two children, and what Omawhaw will regard me? Is not my right paramount to that of your other wife? she had not heard of me before you possessed her. It is true, her skin is whiter than mine, but her heart cannot be more pure towards you, nor her fidelity more rigid.

"Do not take the child away from my heart; I cannot bear to hear it cry, and not be present to relieve it—permit me to keep it until spring, when it will be able to eat, and then, if it must be so, take it from my sight, that I may part with it but once."

The trader seeing her thus inflexible, told her that she might remain there if she pleased, but the child must be sent immediately down to the settlements.

The affectionate mother had thus far sustained herself during the interview with the firmness of conscious virtue, and successfully resisted the impulse of her feelings; but nature now yielded, the tears coursed rapidly down her cheeks, and clasping her hands together, and bowing her head, she burst out into an agony of grief, exclaiming, "Why did the Waconda hate me so much as to induce me again to put my child into your power."

The feelings of the unhappy mother were, however, soon relieved. Mr. Dougherty communicated the circumstances to Major O'Fallon, who immediately and peremptorily ordered the restoration of the child to its mother, and informed the trader that any further attempt on his part to wrest it from her should be at his peril.

are in the habit of using them, have often attained great perfection.

I might here say a word upon the subject of literature, but in this department the Indians have but little to boast, their legends and traditions being generally preserved in rude characters, upon the surface of rocks and trees. Their oratory is pompous, and upon any occasion of more than ordinary importance, it sometimes appears vehement and ardent; but at the best it consists of but little more than the frequent repetition of disconnected sentences, from which, either to extract information or instruction, one must analyze with the most critical exactness.

If aught that come from the lips of the Indians may be dignified with the name of poetry, it may most frequently be heard in their moments of excitement, when the phrases that they utter are highly imaginative and musical. Those who have been intimately acquainted with the character and habits of this people, have generally remarked that the circumstances that give rise to the most poetical exclamations among them are "not always of the most grave and serious occurrences of life, but that love in its disappointments and success, sorrow, hope, and even intoxication, choose the same method of utterance."

However, to speak of the Indians as a people, it would be as far from truth to ascribe to them any peculiar characteristics, as it would be to speak of the likes, and tastes, and motives, and feelings of all the white race of civilized beings under heaven in general terms. To ascribe to them, as a mass, magnanimity, would be perhaps as untrue as it would be, on the other hand, to say that they were all savage and blood-thirsty, and incapable of any noble feelings. Therefore the

Indians of almost every tribe differ in stature, color, habits and temperament, to even a greater degree than the whites; so it may at once be seen how unjustly any epithet or specification of character must be applied to them as a race.

The Indians, through superstitious notions, take no note of their age, and consequently no accurate account can be given of their longevity, although they are in general longer lived than the whites, a fact which may be attributed to their temperate habits, wholesome food, and constant exercise. The squaw is commonly as rugged as the man, and performs most of the duties and labors that among us belong to the occupation of the other sex; and, even during the most trying and interesting stages of her maternal state, she relaxes nothing from her accustomed toil, neither carrying a lighter burden or making a shorter journey. There are many anecdotes that go to show great generalship on the part of the Indians, as they have been frequently engaged in intestine broils; but, from what I can discover, the mode of warfare most usual amongst them displays but little tact or skill, as they never attack in solid column, or in line, but in the moment of attack they disperse with a tremendous yell, and each Indian picks his enemy.

Several years ago, a very ferocious and terrible savage reigned as chief of the Omawhaws. One day his squaw displeasing him, in a violent rage he drew his knife and plunged it into her heart; not apparently caring for what he had done, he sat doggedly, and gazed upon the lifeless body before him; for three successive days did this blood-thirsty chief, the terror of his tribe, remain in profound silence with his head buried in his hands and during the whole time, refused to have the dead body of his squaw removed from before him. In vain did his people petition him to unveil his face, but he either heard them not, or cared not for their entreaties: at length, after every remonstrance on the part of his people had failed, and every other means had proved ineffectual, they brought an infant child, and the mother gently raising the leg of the chief, placed the neck of the infant beneath it; this appeared to awake his sensibilities. He roused himself from his lethargy, and after haranguing his people, again resumed his ordinary avocations.

I will close these remarks upon the customs and economy of the Indians by again reflecting, for a moment, upon what not only may, but upon what ought to be done to better their condition—upon what the whites owe to them, and not only to them, but to themselves and to their God to do for them. That they are capable of being instructed in the great truths of the Christian religion is beyond a doubt; that its influence upon their minds and lives would be productive of the happiest results is also true; it therefore only remains for them to be instructed, and for us to provide a way for its accomplishment. Do we not owe it to them to bestow upon the scattered remnants of their people the same blessings that we enjoy? We settled upon their shores, and they received us kindly: we were hungry, and they gave us meat; thirsty, and they gave us drink. We gradually increased in numbers, and they yielded territory. As we have extended in power and strength, the Indians have receded. The white man now claims the soil. The Indian has crossed the waters of the Mississippi and the Arkansaw; still the white man's course is onward, and as he advances the aboriginal recedes. A few years more will drive the scattered remnant of their tribes into the Pacific. For full two hundred years have the Indians been driven before the influence of civilization, and how little has been done to meliorate their condition! All the objections used against striving to educate and civilize them are, in my opinion, groundless.

I have here only touched upon some of the more obvious and striking features of Indian character and manners. I hope upon my return to be able to give you many anecdotes relating to this interesting class of our fellow beings.

I remain yours, &c.

LETTER XXII.

Montgomery's Point, Mississippi River, 1834.

My dear Sir,

You may wonder at the postmark of this letter, but exercise a little patience and I will unravel the mystery. I am here in waiting for conveyance to New-Orleans; but the question with you is how I came here. I will tell you.

A few evenings since I was somewhat indisposed, and retired to the log hut that had been constructed for the accommodation of invalids, for the purpose of being somewhat more retired and undergoing a little medical regimen. This building, which had received the rather pompous title of "the hospital," was situated somewhere about midway between the camp and the sutler's store, consequently all who passed to and fro had to pass by the door. As I was next evening seated upon the prairie a little distance from the road, two or three of my comrades passed by, and with a significant look, wished me much joy at my good fortune and passed on. Imagining that they alluded to the privilege of my being free from duty whilst under the doctor's hands, I thought nothing of the salutation, and resumed the train of thought that their interruption had broken off; presently along came another party on their diurnal visit to the sutler's, and repeating in substance, although not in phraseology, the same salutation, continued on their walk. I thanked them for their good wishes, and once more turned to my own reflections, well knowing that a sick soldier who has the good fortune to quarter in the hospital, is rather looked upon as occupying an enviable situation; I again imagined that their remarks alluded to the respite from company duty that my indisposition had gained for me. A few moments after, along came one of my own troop, my friend Corporal Tim, who I have already introduced to you in a previous letter. "Hollo," said the corporal, as he came within hail, " shall you go through Rochester ?"

" Go where?" I inquired, surprised at the question, but imagining that I had misunderstood it.

" Through Rochester," repeated the corporal; "but I'll talk to you as I come back," he continued, as he hurried on to the sutler's.

That's somewhat strange, thought I. I then recollected that the corporal had relatives living in Rochester, but his term of service would expire before mine, and I again wondered what could be the meaning of the question; but, thought I, I shall find out when he returns. I was again left alone, but in another minute along came a whole bevy of "*hoosiers,*" as the Indiana boys are classically termed, each in turn, as he passed throwing out some dark hint which seemed to have a hidden interpretation beyond my ken. The frequency of their salutations at length annoyed me. I imagined that they were spoken ironically, and began to wonder what offence I had committed that would warrant my deposition from the snug quarters in the hospital to the somewhat less enviable precincts of the guard tent. I ransacked my memory, but although I jolted over several minor derelictions from the "rules and articles," still I remained in the most profound ignorance of the commission of any flagrant act of disobedience that would warrant my apprehension.

In this state of nervous impatience I remained for some ten or fifteen minutes, when along came another member of my own troop, holding a letter in his hand and scarce able to speak for want of breath.

"Shall you go by the way of New-Orleans or down the Ohio?" was his first inquiry.

"What do you mean?" I asked somewhat impatiently.

"Hav'n't you heard?" said he, with much evident astonishment.

"Heard what?"

"No matter," said he, apparently enjoying my excitement.

"If you have any thing to tell me, out with it," cried I, "and not make a fool of me any longer."

"Ask Washburn," said he, throwing me the letter, and starting off at a run toward the sutler's.

What can all this mean, thought I, half guessing at the truth but not daring to cherish the idea, lest it should prove only a delusion. Can it be, that in a moment when expectation least had life, that her warmest desires were to be gratified, and "hope" again sprung into existence in a heart to which "for a season" it had "bade farewell." Memory began to wander back through the fond remembrance of years gone by, whilst fancy reanimated the forms of other days, and cast her silken chains over a heart too apt to chase the phantoms of a visionary brain.

How strange the sensation created by the alternate conflict of hope and fear! one moment vivid as the lightning's flash, the next darker than the night of Egypt's desolation; now in the transport of imagination, one minute lighter than the thistle's down, the next, like an incubus, the heart falls back upon itself and sinks into the vortex of despondency; now memory revels in the glowing imagery of the past, hope gaily points through the vista of a sunlit future; but, as from a dream too bright to last, we wake to sober reality, the gloom of which is oftentimes enhanced by the attendance of the unreal images that had for a moment usurped its dominion.

Thus was it with me; I stood, scarce willing to believe, and still more unwilling to doubt. In this mood I remained for some time pondering the riddle in my mind, the solution within my grasp, but still fearing to unravel it, lest in the end I should fall from the pinnacle of the airy tower that I had raised. Thus I remained till the return of Corporal Tim from the sutler's, and running half way to meet him, I demanded the meaning of his previous interrogatory.

"What," said Tim, somewhat in astonishment— "are you really in ignorance?"

"Ignorant," I replied, "of any thing that could warrant such an inquiry; therefore I beg of you to tell me at once the meaning of these strange insinuations which have kept my mind in a state of continual excitement."

"Well," said the corporal, "to relieve your mind, I'll tell you—you are at liberty; I've seen your discharge."

"Corporal," said I, "I little thought that I should be the first to return; but if it is so, I shall often think over the days that we have spent together.

I must own, my dear M. that I could not refrain from shedding tears; not tears of joy at the prospect of returning to the land where all the recollections and enjoyments of youth are centered, but tears of sorrow at the thought of bidding farewell to many a companion whom I had learned to love, and, strange to say, sorrow at the idea of quitting a mode of life replete with trials and privations. I felt now the full force of the closing lines of the "Prisoner of Chilon,"

> "With spiders I had friendship made,
> "And watched them in their sullen trade;
> "Had seen the mice at moonlight play,
> "And why should I feel less than they?
> "We were all inmates of one place,
> "And I the monarch of each race;
> "Had power to kill, yet, strange to tell,
> "In quiet we had learned to dwell.
> "My very chains and I grew friends,
> "So much a long communion tends
> "To make us what we are—even I,
> "Regained my freedom with a sigh."

I now ventured, despite of the doctor's injunctions, to walk into camp, and accordingly taking the corporal's arm, sallied into the quarters.

No sooner had I crossed the threshold than a volley

of congratulations and inquiries saluted me ; each soldier in turn prefacing his *pax vobiscum* with request that I would be the bearer of some communication or other to brothers, sisters, mothers, sweet-hearts, cousins in abundance, literally overwhelming me with questions, to all of which I had a ready answer : at length the commotion subsided, and having become assured that my discharge had in reality received the signature of the colonel, I commenced making immediate preparations for my departure. I have before remarked to you, that I carried in my knapsack a few volumes, which were almost the only books in the regiment ; these, and several other articles, I distributed around as keepsakes among my companions, and taking off my military garb, put on a suit of citizen's clothing, which I had reserved for the purpose of a homeward tour, whenever such an event might take place. A few moments afterward, I was summoned to the captain's tent. I had always been a favorite with the captain, and had enjoyed many privileges, for which I shall ever remember him with feelings of kindness. I believe that I have never given you any description of this officer.

Perhaps no other man in the army could assume the stern dignity of a commander, with a better grace than Captain Sumner : his appearance seemed at once to command respect, and throughout all grades I believe that he enjoyed it. I shall never forget the first time that I ever saw him ; it was on board the Helen Mar, upon our journey down the Ohio River ; he surveyed me from head to foot, with one of the most searching glances that I ever encountered ; inquired my name, and what I had formerly been engaged in ; then turning to the orderly sergeant who stood beside me, he said, "Issue his clothing, and let him mess in Corporal Smith's squad." This now vividly recurred to my mind, as I entered his tent for the purpose of receiving his parting instructions: he extended his hand to me, and told me that I was now free to return home, if I wished to do so. I had, during my whole term, enjoyed much of the captain's society, having been his confidential clerk; and had, ere this, learned that he was no stranger to the manners of a polished and refined society; and his deportment toward me at this time was the more gratifying, especially in contrast to the rigid system of non-intercourse which must necessarily exist for the preservation of discipline and good order between the officer and those under his command: but now this was gone; the sternness of the commander had fled, and his conduct was such as at once bade me remember that I was in the presence of an equal.

It would be tedious to recapitulate all the substance of our interview, suffice it that I left the tent with a government draft for the amount of my pay and traveling fees, payable wherever Uncle Sam had funds.

The last night that I spent in camp was rendered more pleasant by the many expressions of kindness which I received from my late fellow-soldiers. I went around from tent to tent with different feelings from any with which I had ever before strolled through the encampment, feeling that it was for the last time. There is a feeling embodied in that sorrowing word farewell, that is the same in all situations, only perhaps varied by the intensity of anguish occasioned by the pang of separation; and I can truly say that there were many in the camp with whom I had contracted the tie of friendship too strongly to break it off thus suddenly without the intrusion of a tear.

Luckily a steamer arrived late in the evening at Fort Gibson, upon her course down the Arkansas; accordingly the next morning I tied up the few articles of clothing which I had reserved from my knapsack, and once more bidding adieu to my companions, took a last look at the encampment, and wended my way to the fort, having previously taken leave of my excellent friend, Lieutenant Burgwin, who, I assure you, I parted with more unwillingly than any other officer of the regiment.

About noon the Galliopolis left the fort dock, and sailing about two miles down the Neosho, between the deep green canebrake on the one side, and the corn fields of the Creeks and Osages on the other, entered upon the broad waters of the Arkansas. I kept my eye fixed upon the star-spangled flag as it floated above the turrets of the fort, until the intervening foliage hid it from my view, and just as we were merging from the crystal stream of the Neosho into the muddy water of the Arkansas, the last notes of the dinner-call at the fort died upon the ear.

As we left in the distance the encampment, with its bustle, its excitement, and its revelry—as the onward progress of our boat was hurrying us farther and farther from the scenes and forms with which I had so long been familiar, I began to look forward to the day when I should again mingle in the scenes endeared by early recollections, and hallowed by the fond remembrance of those who had been the companions of my childhood and the friends of early youth. There is something in the anticipation of again returning to one's home after a long separation which is calculated to arouse in the mind the most pleasurable sensations, and not the least, I assure you, among the anticipated joys of my return, do I value the privilege of again meeting with those of my friends with whom those years of my life were spent, which may indeed be termed the spring time of existence. But there is one thought which is painful in this prospect; how many, whom we left behind when we set out upon our journey, do we part with for ever! how many who were last to grasp the hand of friendship at our departure, who, alas! we find not among those who welcome our arrival! As Irving has most feelingly and beautifully expressed it, we ask, Where are they? and we are pointed to the grave. But this melancholy strain but ill suits me at this time; I would fain look upon the sunny side, and anticipate only enjoyment.

The monotonous banks of the Arkansas present but little to divert the mind of the traveler; here and there a bluff, now and then a cabin varies the scene, but for the most part the deep forests of cotton wood extend along its borders, interspersed with patches of cane. We sailed quietly along during the day, passing, in the afternoon, Fort Smith, a station about fifty miles below Fort Gibson, and on the evening of the next day stopped for a few hours at the city of Little Rock.

This little group of dwellings, which has been somewhat prematurely denominated by the title of a city, is situated upon a prominent bluff on the west side of the river, imbedded, as it were, in the deep foliage of the cotton wood, a species of tree much resembling our poplar, though much more diffuse in the distribution of its limbs. This place, which has been selected as the capital city of the Arkansas Territory, is destined, from its location and peculiar advantages, in common with almost all our western towns, to increase with great rapidity; enjoying, as it does, the benefit of direct water communication with New Orleans in one direction, and many hundred miles up the Arkansas on the other, and surrounded by a rich and beautiful tract of country on either side of the river, it must become ere long the mart of extensive traffic, when the rapidly increasing tide of emigration shall have extended its renovating influence over this now but thinly populated region.

Continuing our sail down the river, we discovered but little to attract the eye during the remainder of the day, until, just as the sun was setting, we came within view of the most lovely and romantic spot upon which my eye ever rested. It was a little bay setting in from the river, under the overhanging archway of a natural cavern or grotto, from the ceiling of which the pendant tendrils of the creepers and vines formed a fringe to the foliage above. The variegated tints of the leaves and shrubbery blended the hues of green, and purple, and crimson, and gold. The chirping notes of the sweet warblers of summer echoed and re-echoed through the dell. The still unrippled waters lay like a marble pavement to this fairy grot, and reflected back the proudly arched necks of the pelicans as they floated upon its surface.

Had the genius of romance sought a dwelling-place amid the solitudes of this western world, this spot would surely have been suited to her taste. This rural glen would indeed have been no unfit haven for the immortal Nine: true, here was no towering brow of high Olympus, but a vale as rich as that of Tempe smiled on one side, and the waters as gentle as Penæus glided on the other. Here the clustering arbors of woodbine and honeysuckle formed grottoes as romantic as the bowers of Arcadia, and the deeper foliage of the cypress and the elm might vie with the far-famed groves of Thrace.

Perchance one might often pass along this stream without observing this fairy glen, but the watchful eye of a romantic observer would hardly escape the view when gliding along the western shore toward the gathering hour of twilight. We were soon, however, borne out of sight, and the shades of evening gathered deeper and deeper over the scene.

There was no moon, and the evening was too dark to allow of any observations along the banks of that portion of the Arkansas through which we were now gliding; and there being no feature of interest on board our boat, we sought repose at an early hour.

After a sail of two days more, we emerged from the stream of the Arkansas into the more turbid waters of the Mississippi, and beating for several miles against its powerful tide, arrived in a few hours at this place, which derives its name from the owner of the soil, and is somewhat of a noted place in this part of the country. I have been here now two days waiting for a steamer bound down the river, the Galliopolis being destined for the Ohio, and I having determined to return by the way of New Orleans.

You must excuse the protracted, and perhaps uninteresting details of this letter, as I have endeavored to extend its limits for the purpose of keeping my mind occupied, the more effectually to get rid of time. I feel like a fish out of water, and the hours drag along as if in mockery of my impatience. I hope soon to meet you. If I should write again, it will probably be from New Orleans: till then, adieu.

Your friend, &c.

LETTER XXIII.

New-Orleans, 1834.

My Dear Sir,

As I get nearer and nearer towards home, I find my anxiety increasing : I think that, of all unpleasant sensations, impatience is the worst, the more especially if we have not the immediate means of gratifying it.

I would not have troubled you with another letter, had I not the same excuse that I plead at the termination of my last, that is, to make the hours pass, if possible, more quickly, by striving to keep the powers of the mind in active operation. Of all places which it has as yet been my fortune to visit, I have met with none to compare with this. Here the white, the black, and the mulatto ; the Frenchman, the yankee, and the creole, are mingled together. The sun is pouring out its rays to the temperature of somewhat less than boiling heat, and the musquetoes and gallinippers are so thick that the aerial animalculæ must enjoy a tight squeeze ; but I find that I am anticipating my story.

After a sojourn of five days at Montgomery Point, I took passage on board the steamer bound down the Mississippi, and to my surprise fell in with an old acquaintance ; but, from the alteration in his appearance since last we met, I had to ponder some minutes before I could recognize in the form before me the features of our quondam friend " *Billy Sheridan,*" as he is familiarly styled by the boatmen—a character, you may remember, with whom I fell in upon the Ohio River, on my journey at the commencement of my tour. He then composed one of the crew of the "*Slow and Easy,*" and, together with " Captain Jo. Chunk," and "Ben," formed the entire propellers of that aptly-christened broad-horn: he had, however, soon after changed his quarters, and had since been boating upon the Mississippi.

Of all the species of mankind existing under heaven, the western boatmen deserve a distinct and separate cognomen. They are a sort of amphibious animal—kind-hearted as a Connecticut grand-mother, but as rough as a Rocky Mountain bear. In highwater they make the boat carry them, and in low water they are content to carry the boat—or in other words, they are ever ready to jump in and ease her over the sand-bar, then jump on board and wait patiently for the next. Spending the greater portion of their time on the water, they scarce know how to behave on shore, and feel only at home upon the deck of their own craft, where they exercise entire sovereignty.

This race of beings are chiefly to be met with on board the lumber craft and broad-horns, and differ materially from the steamboat hands, whom they look upon as sworn enemies, for having monopolized the waters of the Mississippi for the most part, and thereby wrested the business from the hands of the legitimate boatmen. They are a hardy and enterprising set of men, afraid of nothing, and, when upon their own deck, as proud as Lucifer himself—not much degenerated since the days of *Mike Fink*, who was looked upon as the most fool-hardy and daring of his race. By-the-by, a little history of this man may not be amiss, it may be new to you, though well known by every school-boy throughout the west.

I can give you but a faint idea of the character of Mike myself, but it would have done your heart good to have heard Captain Jo. Chunk tell the story of some of his daring exploits.

"There ar'nt a man," said Captain Jo. " from Pittsburgh to New Orleans, but what's heard of Mike Fink; and there ar'nt a boatman on the river, to this day, but what strives to imitate him. Before them 'ere steamers come on the river, Mike was looked up to as a kind of king among the boatmen, and he sailed a little the prettiest craft that there was to be found about these ere parts. Along through the warm summer afternoons, when there war'nt nothing much to do, it used to be the fashion among the boatman to let one hold up a tin cup in the stern of the boat, while another would knock out the bottom with a rifle ball from the bow; and the one that missed had to pay a quart for the good of the crew. How-some-ever," continued Captain Jo. "this war'nt sport enough for Mike, and he used to bet that he could knock the tin cup off a man's head; and there was one fellow fool enough to let him do it: this was a brother of Mike's, who was just such another great strapping fellow as himself, but hadn't as much wit in his head as Mike had in his little finger. He was always willing to let Mike shoot the cup off his head, provided that he'd share the quart with him; and Mike would rather give him the whole of it than miss the chance of displaying his skill.

" Down there, at Smithland, behind the Cumberland bar," continued Captain Jo, "used to be Mike's headquarters; and one day when he had made a bet that he'd shoot the tin cup off from a fellow's head, he happened to fire a little too quick, and lodged the ball in his brains. A man who stood a little way off and had an old grudge against Mike, leveled his rifle and shot him dead on the spot; and this was the end of Mike

Fink, the first boatman who dared to navigate a broadhorn down the falls of the Ohio."

I was led to reflect that the daring and fool-hardy spirit of Mike Fink had not become extinct among the boatmen, when our steamer came to, for a few hours, at Natchez, on her way down the Mississippi. This city, which on the heights displays a beautiful appearance, is nevertheless more noted on the river here for the character of the lower town, or "Natchez under the hill," which the boatmen make a kind of rendezvous, and is the frequent theatre of a royal row. At the time of our stop there, over fifty boats of different descriptions were lying off in the river opposite this place. Close to the wharf, upon the deck of a broadhorn, stood a fellow of powerful muscular appearance, and every now and then he would swing around his arms and throw out a challenge to any one "*who dared to come and take the rust off of him*," styling himself the "*roarer*," and declaring that he hadn't had a fight in a month, and was getting lazy.

The men standing around seemed neither disposed to take much notice of this fellow nor to accept his challenge; and from this I imagined that he was a regular bruiser, and no one cared to oppose him. For some time he continued throwing out his challenge, and interlarding his speeches with the usual boast of a western bruiser, that is, that he was "half horse, half alligator, half steamboat, and half snapping-turtle, with a little dash of lightning, &c. &c."

Presently a little stubbed fellow came along, and hearing the challenger dare any one to rub the rust off of him, stepped up, and in a dry kind of style looked up in his face and inquired, "Who might you be, my big chicken? eh!"

"I'm a high-pressure steamer," roared the big bully.

"And I'm a snag," replied the little one, as he pitched into him, and before he had time to reflect he was sprawling upon the deck.

A general shout of applause burst from the spectators, and many now, who before had stood aloof from the braggadocio, jumped on board the boat and enjoyed the manner in which the little fellow pummeled him.

This scrape appeared to be the signal for several other fights, and in the evening a general row ensued, which ended in the demolition of several edifices and the unhousing of several scores of their inmates; however, during the night our boat left the town, and I learned nothing farther connected with this scrape.

It is strange, however, that a man whose early habits and education must have destined him for a nobler sphere, as was evident in the case of "Billy Sheridan," should have chosen to associate himself with a set of men like these; but probably this independent sort of life was best suited to his deranged state of mind, and he was undoubtedly happier than he could have been in the midst of the sycophantic throng in which he had spent his early years, and whom he heartily despised. I was told that he had given himself up a slave to rum, and that, through feelings of charity, he was allowed to remain on board the boat.

I could not help thinking, in looking upon this man, how many votaries were bowing before the shrine of intemperance, and prostituting upon her altars the talents and energies that nature gave them for nobler purposes, and perhaps a more striking instance of the blighting effects of drunkenness may not often be met with than in the character of this paradox of genius and degradation.

That this man was indeed the son of the celebrated

Sheridan I know not, but so he himself affirmed, and his appearance and attainments were striking commentaries upon the truth of his assertion. He recognized me the moment that I came on board the boat, and saluted me by the title of Lieutenant, (which you may remember is not the first time that I have been thus styled.) His usual custom upon clear nights is to retire, when relieved from work, to the upper deck of the boat, and stretching himself upon his back, spend the greater portion of the night in gazing at the stars and communing with his own imagination. One of his incoherent rhodomontades I one evening overheard, but to attempt to narrate it would be as hopeless an undertaking as that of turning the tide of the Mississippi athwart its channel; his mind would wander from starry realms of space down to the confines of dull earth with a velocity equalled only by its own wild flight over the records of past years, reanimating the court of St. James with many a brilliant but departed form, whose spirit-stirring eloquence had left an indelible impress upon his memory. Then he would seem to wander through the solemn aisles of the abbey, and hold converse with the spirits of the departed dead; but, quicker than the ray of light darting through the unmeasured fields of space, would his rapid imagination ascend to the starry zone and pour forth, in broken and disconnected strains, some wild apostrophe, till his exhausted frame would sink into repose.

Journeying down the Mississippi, especially during the warm season of the year, the monotony of its banks afford scarce enough novelty to keep the active mind of an impatient traveller from a tedious looking forward toward the end of the route. We now were sailing down that portion of the river which glides between that alluvial tract extending on one shore from the neighborhood of Baton Rouge, and on the other from the confluence of the Chafalia, which is supposed to be the ancient bed of the Red River, and may be discerned upon the map in somewhere about the thirty-first degree. This country is denominated the Delta, and is composed of two strips of land which extend on either side of the river to the Balize, gradually becoming narrower and narrower until they disappear beneath the surface, many miles out into the Gulf of Mexico.

Major Stoddard, who many years ago wrote a very able treatise upon the state of Louisiana, in speaking of this region of country, says that "nothing is more certain than that the delta has gradually arisen out of the sea, or rather that it has been formed by alluvious substances precipitated by the waters from the upper regions. It is calculated that from 1720, a period of eighty years, the land has advanced fifteen miles into the sea, and there are those who assert that it has advanced three miles within the memory of middle-aged men. The eastern part of New Spain, along the gulf, exhibits abundant proofs of similar advances, owing perhaps to the constant accumulation of sand by the trade winds, which is driven to the shore by the perpetual motion of the waves in that direction.

It is remarkable that the banks of the river are much more elevated than the circumjacent country; this is occasioned by a more copious deposition along the margins than at a distance from them; they are thickly covered with grass, and a vast variety of ligneous plants, which serve to filtrate the waters in their progress to the low grounds and swamps, and to contain the greatest proportion of the alluvious substances. Hence the land along the banks to a certain depth, generally from four hundred to seven hundred yards are excellent for tillage, while the whole country to the rear of them is alternately covered by lakes and impassable swamps.

"The waters precipitated over the banks never return into the same channel. Those from the west bank of the Mississippi find innumerable passages to the gulf; while those from the opposite bank fall into the lakes, which may be considered as arms of the sea, and bid fair to be reclaimed in time from the ocean. That the Delta has been thus reclaimed, may be inferred from a variety of circumstances, particularly from the existence of a vast number of logs and trees at unequal depths under the ground, multitudes of which are found beneath the level of the ocean. These are buried in a sub-stratum of black earth, and already begin to be decomposed and converted into fuel."

Such is the history of the Delta as related about twenty-five years ago; probably since that time the alluvial has extended much farther, and more dense accumulations have been formed. The theory of Major Stoddard is undoubtedly correct concerning it. The muddy waters of the Mississippi, below the confluence of the Missouri, hurrying down its tide the turbid waters of that immense river, laden with a sedimental substance which gradually settles upon its banks, forming continuous strata of rich earth, and extending its limits every year farther and farther out into the ocean, literally bearing the soil of the Rocky Mountains upon its bosom, and depositing it at the farther extremity, to lengthen out the course of its mighty channel.

This portion of the Mississippi, if not the most interesting, is at least the most cheering to the eye of the northern traveler: here commences a beautiful range of plantations, which continue until we arrive at New-Orleans, and the waving crops of sugar-cane and snowy blossoms of the cotton fields, the lovely villas of the planters, and the prettily arranged out-houses, present a combined aspect of opulence and verdure.

We arrived at this place about sunset, the weather extremely warm and oppressive. My first inquiry was for the paymaster, but, to my extreme disappointment, he was absent at Baton Rouge, and would not return for several days; this made my situation extremely awkward, as I had no money with me, and had depended upon my draft to pay my passage down the river. I was obliged to remain on board the boat until the return of Major Randal, who cashed my draft and enabled me to feel free from all responsibility.

This city, which is now, as the world knows, the great mart of southern traffic, is built upon a portion of the Delta, or loose soil, somewhat more elevated than the land upon the opposite shore, about one hundred and ten or twelve miles from the sea, that is, allowing for the windings of the river. In 1720 it was commenced by the French, and two years afterward became the seat of government. According to the account given by Major Stoddard, it contained about a thousand houses and eight thousand inhabitants, including the colored population, when it fell into our hands.

The account given by him, however, in 1812, will but little accord with the present condition of the city. If you will excuse it, I will trouble you with an extract from his work, which will furnish you with some little idea of the history of this city up to that date. He says:

"Six complete squares are embraced by the city. The fronts of these are three hundred and nineteen English feet in length, and extend north, thirty-two degrees east, and south, thirty-two degrees west, and are intersected by twelve streets at right angles. Each square is divided into twelve lots. Five of them measure sixty by one hundred and twenty feet. On the opposite side are two key lots, which measure sixty by one hundred and fifty feet. The streets are thirty-seven feet and a half in width. On the back part of the city are two narrow rows of buildings, converging to a point.

"The ground plot of the city may be considered as a plain, inclining north-west two points west. It has a descent of about six feet from the bank of the river to the palisades in the rear of the buildings, and about three feet more to St. John's creek at its medium height. The lands in all the low country gradually descend from the river, and soon terminate in lakes or swamps.

"Nearly the whole of the old houses are of wood, one story high, and make an ordinary appearance. The suburbs on the upper or north end of the city have been built since the fire in 1794, and contain about two hundred and fifteen houses, mostly composed of cypress wood, and generally covered with shingles or clapboards. Among them is one elegant brick house covered with tile. Several of them are two stories high, and two in the same quarter three stories high. One of them cost eighty thousand dollars, and the rest from fifteen to twenty thousand dollars. They are plastered on the outside with white or colored mortar; this, as frosts are seldom severe in the climate, lasts many years; it beautifies the buildings, and preserves the bricks, which, from the negligence or parsimony of the manufacturers, are usually too soft to resist the weather.

"In New-Orleans, as in all other parts of the low country, the houses have no cellars under ground; water is generally found within two or three feet of the surface, especially in wet seasons. The wells rarely exceed fifteen feet in depth. The water in them is clear, free from salt, but unpleasant to the taste.

"The following are the public buildings; the cathedral, the town-house, the prison, the barracks, the hospital, the convent and church, the charity hospital and church, the government house and stores, and some others of inferior note, which will be cursorily mentioned.

"The cathedral stands at the head of a spacious open square, about four hundred feet from the river. This building is of brick, extending about ninety feet on the street, and one hundred and twenty back of it. The roof is covered with flat and hollow tile, supported by ten large brick columns, which are plastered, and afford an agreeable appearance. Each front corner has a tower considerably elevated, and the southerly one contains two small bells. This church has likewise a small organ, but on the whole is much less decorated than other catholic places of worship. It was governed by a bishop, two canons, one grand vicar, one parish priest, and four subordinate priests. Considerable funds in houses appertain to it. The bishop received an annual salary of four thousand dollars, charged on the revenues of some southern bishopric; the canons about seven hundred and twenty dollars, and the other priests about three hundred and sixty dollars each, exclusive of casual benefits arising from marriages, burials, and the like. There were likewise a few capuchins, and friars of the order of carmelites, who were paid by the crown.

"The town-house is rather an elegant building, two stories high, and about ninety feet long, with an arched portico, both above and below, along its whole front. The upper arches are glazed, which adds much to the beauty of the structure. The Spaniards occupied one part of the ground story as a guard-house, and permitted a notary to occupy the other as an office. The upper story was appropriated to the use of the cabildo.

"In the rear of the town-house, and adjoining to it, is the prison. Under the Spanish government it was a wretched receptacle of vice and misery; like the grave, it received many tenants who were soon forgotten by the world: some of them perished with age and disease, and others by the hands of assassins. Criminals, under sentence of death, were often kept immured within its walls for years, owing either to the tardiness or lenity of the tribunal at the Havanna, without whose approval no sentence of death could be carried into execution.

"The public barracks are situated at the lower end of the front street. They are accommodated with a spacious area, surrounded by a brick wall, as also an extensive parade-ground between them and the river. The buildings are of brick, and one story high, covered with shingles, and calculated to receive about fifteen hundred men. They were built by the French, and have a spacious arcade in front and rear.

"The building denominated the king's hospital, is on the same line, but higher up. It was originally intended as a receptacle for the sick and diseased belonging to the army and navy. It will accommodate about one hundred and fifty patients, and affords to the miserable a tolerable asylum.

"The convent of the Ursuline nuns is situated on the upper side of the barracks, and beyond the hospital, which stands nearer the line of the street. This was likewise built by the French: it is of brick, and spacious, covered with shingles, and two stories high. An extensive garden is attached to it, extremely productive of fruit and vegetables. It will accommodate about fifty nuns, and from seventy to eighty young females, who resort to it for their education. Attached to the convent is a small house containing three rooms, divided longitudinally from each other by double gratings about six inches asunder, with apertures about two inches square, where strangers may see and converse with the nuns and boarders on particular business. Near to the main building, and on the street, stands an old school-house, where the female children of the citizens appear at certain fixed hours to be gratuitously instructed in writing, reading, and arithmetic. This religious institution is possessed of considerable funds. Each nun, on taking the final vow, or black veil, deposits fifteen hundred dollars, if she be able, which becomes part of the common stock, and cannot be alienated. The church belonging to the convent is small, and was the gift of a gentleman who died a few years ago at New-Orleans. He was in early life a notary, and by various speculations amassed an immense property, and failed at last to leave an unspotted name behind him. He likewise built the cathedral church and charity hospital, and endeavored by acts of beneficence, near the end of his days, to atone for the errors of his youth.

"The charity hospital stands on the westerly or

back part of the city. Poor Spanish subjects, and sometimes strangers, (provided they paid half a dollar per day,) were admitted into this asylum. Those entirely destitute were admitted gratis. They had medicine, sustenance, and other aid afforded them.

"The government house stands on the front street, and on the fifth square, reckoning from the upper side, and one hundred feet from the river. It is an ancient building, erected by the French, and two stories high, with galleries or arcades round the whole of it. The lower front was formerly occupied by the governmental secretary and the clerks of offices. This structure is indifferent, both as to architecture and convenience.

"On the south-westerly part of the same square were the lodges and stables of the regular dragoons, which, with the garden belonging to the government house, occupy about four-fifths of the square.

"On the corners of the second and third squares, lower down, are the public stores, built of brick, extending about thirty-five feet on front street, and about two hundred feet on a cross street. They are one story high, and were built by the French.

"On the opposite, or southerly side of the stores, is the artillery yard, or ordnance depot.

"Opposite to this, on the very bank of the river, is the market house, which is usually furnished with beef, pork, some mullard and veal; fish of several sorts in abundance, and cheap; wild ducks and other game in season; tame turkies, fowls, ducks, and geese; and vegetables of all kinds during the whole year.

"The Spaniards had the advantage of a free school, in which boys were instructed in the rudiments of their language. The two teachers attached to it were paid by the crown.

"The grand powder magazine of the French and Spaniards is situated over against the government house, on the opposite side of the river, where a guard was always stationed, and generally relieved weekly.

"During the administration of the baron Carondelet, between 1791 and 1796, a ditch was extended round the city, of about eighteen feet in width, with ramparts of earth, and palisades nearly six feet high along the interior or inner side of them. Five large bastions were erected at proper distances, and likewise five intervening redoubts. The bastions were regularly constructed. Each of them was furnished with a banquette, rampart, parapet, ditch, covered way, and glacis. The curtains were wholly formed of palisades, planted at a small distance from each other, and therefore not capable of much defence even against musket balls; they had a banquette within, and a ditch and glacis without. A small redoubt or ravelin was placed in the centre of each bastion; and all the latter were of sufficient size to admit of sixteen embrasures, four in each face, three in each flank, and two in the gorge facing the city.

"These works of defence were badly supplied with ordnance. Few of the bastions were furnished with more than four or five pieces of cannon. That on the east, or lower end of the city, had its full complement; and the covered way was likewise pretty well supplied. This arrangement or distribution of the ordnance was rather singular; it seemed to be mounted on those places the most invulnerable, and the least liable to be attacked. An assault by way of the sea was hardly to be expected, especially as the river was well defended eighteen miles below, and as a fleet, wholly unobstructed by land batteries, would find it extremely difficult to ascend against the rapidity of the current. The south-west bastion, with a counterguard and traverses, and a small redoubt on the back of the river, constituted the whole defence on the upper side of the city. The first was usually supplied with ten or twelve, and the second with five pieces of cannon. Not more than ten pieces, however, could be brought to bear on any body of men descending the river. As soon as an enemy landed on the open banks, which was by no means difficult, the bastions became totally useless. A skillful officer at the head of disciplined troops, in any degree acquainted with the country, would have experienced no great trouble from these works, especially as they were mostly defended by raw militia, among whom regular duty was irksome, and considered as a grievance.

"The inhabitants and others passed in and out of the city by means of four gates. The two next the river were the most considerable, and they were situated sixteen hundred and twenty yards from each other. The two in the rear, or on the back part of the city, were of much less note; one of them was placed on the road leading to lake Pontchartraine: They were defended by a breast-work of no great strength or utility. All the gates were of wood, formed of palisades ten or twelve feet long. They were shut every night at nine o'clock, and after that hour no one was permitted to walk the streets without leave from the governor; those who transgressed this regulation were seized by the guards and detained till morning. House servants, by particular indulgence, were sometimes allowed to pass the streets, on business for their masters or mistresses, till eleven o'clock.

"Exclusive of the fire in 1794, already mentioned,

New-Orleans suffered by a prior one in 1788, when about nine hundred wooden buildings of all descriptions, mostly old, were reduced to ashes. Those built on their ruins have contributed to the beauty of the city.

"Such in some degree were the features of New-Orleans at the time it fell into the hands of the United States. Since that period it has been greatly improved; population has increased, new springs are given to commerce, property immensely augmented in value, the works repaired and strengthened, and much additional security afforded to the capital of Louisiana."

Since 1812, however, New-Orleans has improved with a rapidity which would indeed have staggered the ideas of its primitive settlers; its old French dwellings are to be sure more plenty than the Knickerbocker edifices in our own city, but still the modern buildings have so hemmed them in on every side, that they seem to stand more as monuments of the past than as dwellings of the present time; but more of this at another time; our ship sails to-morrow, and heaven grant that Æolus may favor us with prosperous breezes to waft our vessel over the broad bosom of Neptune's watery realm.

Excuse both the length and material of this epistle, and console yourself with the reflection that it is the last. I hope soon to meet you, till then accept the good wishes of

Your obliged friend
and humble servant.

APPENDIX.

TO A BROTHER;

EVER DEARLY BELOVED,

BUT STILL MORE TENDERLY ENDEARED BY LONG SEPARATION,

The following Pages are inscribed,

BY ONE WHO HAS LEARNED, BY EXPERIENCE,

TO SYMPATHIZE WITH THE OPPRESSED:

WHICH,

AS A FEEBLE EXPRESSION OF FRATERNAL FEELING,

HE WILL BE PLEASED TO ACCEPT FROM

THE AUTHOR.

PREFACE TO THE APPENDIX.

Having taken some pains to select from a large series of letters the portions which compose the foregoing pages of this work, the author thought it advisable to affix an appendix, in which he might throw together a few more items relative to the soldier's life, as well as a few incidents derived from communications received by him from several of his old companions. Many months have glided by since he took leave of the youthful band to whom he has taken the liberty of dedicating this volume, but still their remembrance is fresh in his memory, and the hope of again meeting with many of them in the social walks of life a source of anticipated enjoyment.

There is one sad thought that casts a gloom over his reflections; the grave hath claimed its victims. Many, alas! very many of those with whom he once exchanged the friendly salutation are no more, a soldier's requiem hath tolled their knell, and a soldier's tear moistened their ashes; their journey through life was short—peace, peace to their souls.

APPENDIX.

CHAPTER I.

"Every man," according to Shakspeare, "hath business and desires such as they are," and through the seven scenes of life's great drama plays various parts. The world is one great compound from which every man may cull his simples, a great mart where all may traffic, a stage where each may fret away his hour ere he retires behind the curtain of life for ever.

What boots it when the clod of the valley shall press upon his bosom, whether his pathway had been rugged or smooth? What boots it whether he had been monarch or peasant, so that it might be said of him

"He gave to misery all he had—a tear;
"He gain'd from heaven, 'twas all he wish'd—a friend!"

Even as the waters close over the lifeless form committed to their bosom and all again is tranquil and serene, so the lapse of a few short years obliterates the remembrance of man. The marble monument may transmit through a period of time the names of some whose dust hath mingled with their kindred earth within the proud inclosure of the abbey walls, but time shall crumble even the chiseled urn and waste its fragments upon the breeze.

How true were the reflections of our countryman, who stood amid the splendid tombs which stud the solemn aisles of Westminster, and asked, "What then is to insure this pile which now towers above me, from sharing the fate of mightier mausoleums? The time must come when her guilded vaults, which now spring so loftily, shall lie in rubbish beneath the feet; when, instead of the sound of melody and praise, the wind shall whistle through the broken arches, and the owl hoot from the shattered tower; when the glarish sunbeam shall break into the gloomy mansions of death, and the ivy twine round the fallen columns, and the foxglove hang its blossoms about the nameless urn, as if in mockery of the dead. Thus man passes away; his name perishes from record and recollection; his history is a tale that is told, and his very monument becomes a ruin."

Byron continued the same reflection, when he asked,

" What is the end of man? Old Egypt's king
" Cheops, erected the first pyramid
" And largest, thinking it was just the thing
" To keep his memory whole, and mummery hid;
" But somebody or other rummaging
" Burglariously, broke his coffin lid.
" Let not a monument give you or me hopes,
" Since not a pinch of dust remains of Cheops."

The page of history, however, may serve to lengthen out the memoirs and the record of man, and snatch from the revolving millions of earth's sons, some few, whose names to transmit to posterity, and thus may the pen of the biographer indite a more enduring tablet than even the loftiest of Egypt's towering pyramids.

How pregnant is the mind of man with a longing after immortality! and how various the changes through which he strives to attain it! and so sanguine is each votary of success, that every scribbler who sends forth a volume to the world, imagines his name embalmed in the embrace of future ages.

Early in life I had what I imagined to be a literary turn of mind, and even when quite young, I would pore over the delightful stories of the Arabian Nights, or the Seven Champions, and in all my rambles I delighted to keep companionship with Gulliver or Maunchausen, and I loved to call forth the applause of my school companions by copious extracts from these productions. The history of Sinbad was a great favorite with me, and the renowned achievements of that celebrated knight, St. George, filled me with profound respect for that most valorous champion. Don Quixotte, too, formed a conspicuous part of my library; and I even degenerated so far from the line of my studies as to admit into my little collection the History of Richard Turpin, and the Life and Adventures of Captain Kidd. With a profound knowledge of these illustrious works, it will readily be perceived that I had sufficient ground for my literary opinions. I imagined that authors of such justly admired and celebrated productions must be men of the most profound erudition, and moreover, that the reward of such labors must be little less than a kingdom.

My resolve was made—I too would be an author. I would ransack other worlds and create new demons and deities to eclipse all that had gone before. Already did I see my name blazoned forth, embalmed in the caresses of the universe; in my mind's eye I could see wealth pouring in at every avenue, and the homage and adoration of the world continually sounded in my ears. With contempt I looked upon the plodding tradesman, and despised the very name of traffic.

One day, shortly after my resolution, I retired to my

study, to embody [into form some marvelous idea that I had conceived, already impatient to see the result of my labor. I sat down, mended my pen—all was still, and I looked upon the snowy surface of the foolscap paper before me—I dipt my pen in the inkstand, then turned over the paper, and sat for a long time wondering why I didn't commence. I wiped my pen—again I mended it, although I had not yet touched the paper. Again I held the weapon over the devoted sheet, still no traces of the ink soiled its whiteness. I threw down the pen, seized my hat, and angrily left the house. I crossed fences and walked over fields, without any knowledge of what I was doing, and my course was only stopped by the appearance of a rather formidable barrier crossing my path, and I had already made some progress through the waters before I recollected that with every step I was leaving terra firma farther in the back ground. This plan that I had inadvertently chosen to cool my disturbed brain succeeded. I turned, and, enfeebled by my exertion, fell in a reclining posture on the rich moss-covered banks of this beautiful stream. 'Twas indeed beautiful; the water, clear as crystal, glided over a white pebbled bed, and meandered through a rich grove of woodland. Here I reclined, and soon forgot my troubles in the sound sleep that overcame me—and my wakeful visions were succeeded by still more romantic dreams. I thought that I was in my study reveling in the brightest anticipations of future wealth and renown, when suddenly the door opened and the aged figure of a man beckoned me to follow him. I rose, obeyed the summons, and he led me to a little hill that appeared but a short distance, and seating himself, bade me follow his example,—then turning to me, he said,

"Son, I am the magician Omar, and have power over all the spirits in the world; I have summoned thee to instruct; follow my instructions and be wise."

I started and gazed upon him; his long white beard reached almost to his knees, and a few silver locks were scattered over his head.

"Speak," continued Omar, "tell me what wish is uppermost in thy mind, and it shall be gratified."

"Father," cried I, "show me the wise and illustrious men whose productions have astonished the world."

He smote the earth, and the little hill changed into an enormous mountain, and the whole world lay beneath it.

"There," said he, "there is the puny world, whose honors and renown men covet. Look around," he continued, "and see in the millions of bright and sparkling luminaries above us, worlds like this.

I looked, and the world was but a speck, and seemed but as one of the twinkling stars above us.

"But stop," said Omar, "thou hast not yet had thy wish."

Again he smote the earth, the mountain vanished, and we were in the midst of a great city.

"Follow me," said the magician, and he led the way up a lone dark staircase, to a sorry garret. By a small table, with a dull twinkling lamp, that threw its feeble light but dimly over the dreary apartment, sat the wasted and enfeebled form of a solitary inmate, pensively gazing on a work before him.

"Look," said Omar, "tell me who thou thinkest sits in that lone chamber."

I looked—the emaciated form sat motionless before me, save that his bony hand trembled as he held a blotted scroll before him, and seemed to be lost in the depth of his research.

"That," cried I, "is the attenuated form of poverty or crime—one reduced to the last stage of adversity, and perhaps even now poring over his time-worn and rejected appeal to the humanity of the affluent."

"Hold," cried Omar, "that man has bewildered the world by the profoundness of his knowledge, and shed a lustre over his memory by the sublimity of his intellect. He is an author, and the productions of his pen have called forth the homage of princes."

"Father," cried I, "dwell no longer on this dark and gloomy abode of knowledge; turn to the bright scenes of glory, where authors revel in luxury and wealth."

"Wealth," cried Omar, "satiates a thirst for knowledge—luxury deadens the intellect; men look not," he continued, "in the rich and fertile places of the earth for mines of gold and diamonds, but in the barren and sandy desert—where vegetation finds no root. Men," continued Omar, "are often unknown till they have been long forgotten, and that glory is shed on their memories that was denied to them whilst living. Look at that lone student,—poverty is his lot, and the cravings of his enfeebled appetite call forth no pity from those that revel in the luxury of his intellect. Learn and be wise; the path that leads to glory often leaves in abject poverty its brightest votaries."

I looked. The magician had vanished. The student's lamp was flickering; its last gleam expired, and I awoke.

The sun had just set, and its last rays were gilding

the edges of the silver cloud. I rose and returned home; my bright visions of wealth and glory were gone,—and I was contented to walk in the beaten track of life, and leave the rich imaginations of romance to minds more suited to the task.

To this laudable resolution I remained a firm adherent for many a plodding year, while the excellent gentleman in whose employ I spent this juvenile portion of my life, endeavored to teach me how to dispose of laces and bobbins to the best possible advantage; but at length the troubled spirit burst its narrow confines, the latent spark which had been lit in youthful days now began to kindle, and ere long burst forth into a blaze upon the pages of an annual.

Again the dancing images of wealth and glory flitted before my eyes, and the remembrance of the magician's words no longer haunted me with scenes of poverty; all again became light and cheering, and again I resolved to become an author. The counter was speedily transformed into a desk, and the vender of merchandises became a chronicler of the sayings and doings in the land of Gotham; thus, for a while, to practice in the nursery of the art before I blazed forth upon the world, transfused upon the pages of a ponderous tome.

O tempora! who can anticipate my misfortunes? Who can ever forget the ravages of that worst of epidemics, that swept like a withering blast over our land, carrying terror and death in its train? Who that watched by the bedside of the dying victim, can ever forget his agony! his distorted features! his ghastly visage! his convulsive gasps! as the destroyer pierced his fangs into his vitals? Who that saw towns and cities lifeless and deserted; church-yards strewn with the unburied dead that mourned over the sudden loss of brother! husband! friend! can ever forget the gloom and blackness that hung like a pall upon that desolating season! At such a time was the advent of my editorial career: ask me not the issue.

" The engineer,
" Who lays the last stone of the sea-built tower,
" It cost him years and years of toil to build,
" But in a night he see's the tempest
" Sporting in its place, may look aghast as I did."

'Twas then that the first bugle-note disturbed the ears of that youthful band whose horses hoofs have since clattered over the prairies and mountains of the west. To one unacquainted with the world, its tinsel has a glittering appearance. The showy trappings of a light dragoon mounted upon his prancing charger, the burnished blade of his scymetar glancing in the sun beams, and his drooping plume gaily fluttering upon the breeze, was too dazzling a sight not to captivate the hearts of many a votary at the warlike shrine: but let the aspiring youth but spend a single month amid the monotonous and dreary duties of the camp; let him wake with the bugle sounding in his ears, and again retire at its bidding; let his every movement and duty be regulated by its sound, and it will soon lose much of its melody.

For a week or two the soldier's life may appear pleasant enough: every thing is new, and seems calculated to give token of continuance of pleasure; but a speedy reverse robs it of its novelty, and changes its excitement into gloom.

I can now remember the first time that I ever was posted as a sentinel; with a heart swelling well nigh to bursting with pride did I pace the sentry walk, and although no other duty of the soldier is more tedious, I cared not to be relieved from a situation so fraught with every ambitious feeling of the soul; like Banquo's, spirits flitted before me, the vision of every hero whose deeds I had ever listened to; but how changed in a few weeks! none was more willing to be excused from the tedious and toilsome duty of a sentinel than I was; and I was not alone in the misfortune, around me on every side were my companions groaning under the weight of their disappointments.

Life in every situation has its sorrows, but, in addition to its every-day cares and troubles, the soldier has to endure the reflection that he chose his own course, and his reproaches fall mostly upon himself.

I will here insert two or three extracts from letters that I have received from the dragoons since I left the army. One writes thus:

"Winter is now over; the snow has entirely disappeared, and the ice is fast dissolving in its own element; every thing begins to assume a more cheerful appearance; our men are all engaged in making extensive preparations for gardening; every thing is bustle and life; discontent now no longer openly displays itself among the regiment, but a consciousness of their situation seems to show them the necessity of paving the way as smoothly as possible until the fulfillment of their engagement gives them back their liberty. But as for me, I am unchanged—the seasons bring no new sensations to my bosom, save that each in turn, as it passes, shortens my bondage. I appear to be shut up in a dark and gloomy cavern, with only one outlet, the certainty of at length arriving at which alone supports me amid the conflict of my feelings. I know of no class of men so entirely destitute of all means of enjoyment as soldiers; it is like entering a convent, to enlist in the service; one dissolves all connection with the world, its enjoyments and its prospects, and ties himself down to a line of life which, whether agreeable or not, he must submit to."

From the tenor of the above extract one may readily imagine the state of feeling existent in a regiment where each individual entertains such sentiments, and especially in the regiment of dragoons, where a combination of young men may be found of superior caste.

Perhaps better than I can convey them may the feelings of the soldier be deduced from their own words. The following extract is dated in May last:

"I write in a hurry. You may think it strange that a soldier can be so pressed with business as not to have time to write to his friends; but it is even so. I fear you may think that I have neglected you too long, and indeed I have longer than I should, but you know that *I am not my own master.* My business is so divided into days, weeks, months, and quarters, that the very dread of it seems to make the time pass quicker than it would; but on the other hand, reflection, anticipation, and anxiety lengthen it. I have yet to see the broad Mississippi twice shrouded in ice before I can expect to return to my once happy home. The leaves have twice to wither and twice to put forth— the earth to be mantled alternately with the winter's snow and the summer's verdure; and the seasons, with all their varied changes, are each twice to reign solely and absolutely over earth and its creatures before I can feel any kindred sympathy with the world. I often ask myself, where is that energy, that ambition, that pride, hope, all the feelings of joyousness that once incited me to strive for a place among the beings with whom I once associated? they have withered 'like the leaves of the forest when the autumn wind hath blown;' but like them, I hope, only for a season."

But I know the ardor of youth often overleaps admonition and advice, and leads at once headlong into the world to learn the sweet and the bitter things of life by actual experience. Fain would I speak to every youth upon the continent of America, and tell them, as they value every thing dear to them on earth, as they look forward to preferment and respect among men, and almost, might I say, happiness hereafter, choose any other occupation than that of a despised ill-treated, self-abhorred soldier.

CHAPTER II.

The gorgeous twilight of a western climate began to gather about the valleys, though the mountain tops still reflected back the last rays of the setting sun; the season of harvest had gone by, and autumn, the lovliest quarter of our western year, had seared the leaves in the forests, and tinged the lingering verdure with its thousand varied hues; chirping amid the half naked branches of the trees, the squirrels sported as they skipped from limb to limb, the woods were enlivened by the evening song of the cricket, and the fawn and its dam might be seen quietly grazing upon the plains around. The scenery of this region was bold, wild, and romantic; a mountain ridge extended along the borders of an undulating prairie, skirted on the farther side by a grove of towering oaks: in the distance, gently meandering through the grass, might be seen a little stream which was fed by the various rivulets that murmured down the mountain side, dashing from rock to rock, and sprinkling the neighboring herbage with their spray.

Such was the scene through which a small party of dragoons were strolling toward the Camp Des Moines, from a visit to the ruins of Fort Madison, the dilapidated remains of a former military station long since abandoned to the ravages of the elements. Around it may be seen a few miserable log-huts, the dwellings of an indolent race of half-breeds and squatters, but the whole scene is one wearing the inhospitable garb of poverty, wretchedness, and decay. The rude hamlets of these miserable beings are barely sufficient to keep off the chilling blasts of the wintry winds, which, in that dreary season of the year, whistle through the fissures and crevices of the walls.

But, strange as it may seem, this region was the home of a little family, whose only aim seemed to be to promote the comfort and happiness of each other. It consisted of an old revolutionary soldier, his wife, and grand-daughter, a girl of about seventeen, who, though cheerful and contented, seemed but illy to accord with the uncongenial spirits around her. High-minded and intelligent, graceful in form, and lovely in feature, she seemed indeed the guardian naiad of the land.

> " And ne'er did Grecian chisel trace
> " A nymph, a naiad, or a grace,
> " Of finer form, or lovlier face."

Living upon a stipend but scantily apportioned to their necessities, this revolutionary pair and their lovely grand-daughter had passed several years amid the rude scene that surrounds the ruins of Fort Madison; but content, smiling content, seemed stamped upon their visages. Bending under the weight of years, this aged pair had out-lived the pleasures to be derived from the groveling enjoyments of time, and in the full assurance of a joyful acceptance, kept their eyes bent forward to the dawning of a brighter day beyond the confines of the grave.

The sylph-like form of her upon whom all their earthly ties were concentred, scarce ever glided from before them; but with an assiduity prompted by the holiest impulses of affection she ministered to their happiness, and strove to render the declining hours of their lives unburdened with a single sorrow. She was indeed an angel hovering over their pillow, or gently ministering support to their tottering steps. But, alas! 'tis sad to see so lovely a flower rearing its tender stem alone, amid a wilderness of rank exuberance; for she seemed to have no more affinity to the rude throng around her, than "the lovely exotic, transplanted from some eden-like clime, has with the carved and gilded conservatory that rears and shelters its luxuriant beauty." Still, I know not why we should indulge in sorrowful reflections. She was contented— she knew not the world, but she was happy in her ignorance—aye, far more happy than they who thread the devious mazes of life's giddy whirl amid its throng and tumult; then why transplant the fragile flower from its parent soil, perchance only to wither and to die in a strange clime.

There seemed a holy calm diffused around this

dwelling—a sacredness, rendered more joyous by the fearful contrast with the scene around. Let the mind wander for a moment to some distant spot, wild, rude, and inhospitable—thorns and thistles covering the land—decay and misery resting upon the dwellings; then picture this little group to your imagination, when the twilight of evening had gathered over the land thus disposed; the aged patriot, dressed in the long waistcoat and breeches of the olden time, seated in a rustic chair, one shoulder supported by a crutch, and in the other hand a huge ivory-headed cane—and opposite him, his still more enfeebled partner supported upon a cushioned easy-chair—her hands clasped together—her eyes now turned toward heaven—now resting upon the placid features of "the flower of the wilderness," as from the black-letter pages of a huge silver-clasped family Bible she read a portion with a tender pathos, rendered the more solemn by the reverence of her manner. When she had ended the chapter, and closed the book, the old soldier said, in a solemn tone of voice, "Let us thank God for all his mercies." They all knelt down—the young dragoons knelt too—O had the infidel been there, his stubborn knee would have bent, and his heart would have softened as the old man poured forth his soul's most inmost prayer. I have heard the prayer ascend from the pulpit, from the social group, from the family altar, but never did the supplication of a mortal fall upon the ear more laden with the burden of the soul, than the tremulous thanksgiving of this aged man. For a moment after he had pronounced the solemn amen, the silence was unbroken, and the tottering old man was the first to rise from the posture of supplication.

The youthful party of dragoons took leave of this

happy, holy family, and wended their way along, through the moss-covered relics of this cluster of mouldering habitations, and passing the ruins of Fort Madison, continued their walk to the Des Moines.

Well may it be imagined what was their thoughts and conversation during their homeward journey—the sweet simplicity of the lovely girl—the animated hospitality of the old soldier—the calm piety of the aged mother—together composed a group that reminded them of those who were dear to them at home.

Between the fort and the encampment lay a strip of wood skirting from a deep forest, that extended for many a mile along the margin of the river. As the party were following the foot-path that winded amid the trees, they discovered, a little in advance of them, a group of Indians around a camp-fire preparing their evening meal. Upon a near approach they proved to be a small party of the Sac and Fox tribe, whose wigwams were about six miles distant from the camp.

Not caring to disturb the group, the dragoons were passing by without noticing them, when one of the Indians perceiving them, exclaimed, " How-ee, how-ee, so-ger, so-ger!"—whereupon the dragoons approached them, and were somewhat surprised to recognize in the speaker the well remembered features of Black-Hawk. To meet with this chief in his native wilderness, and wrapped in his blanket, one would hardly imagine that he had ever been the lion of the day, amid the fashionable circles of the metropolis—" the observed of all observers" in the east; as here he sat with the Prophet, and a few other Indians, occupied in preparing an evening meal. The old warrior recognized in one of the dragoons the countenance of a friend who had shown him much kindness and attention when journeying through the cities of the east, and his expressions of joy were vehement and almost extravagant.

After partaking of a mouthful of the Indian fare, the dragoons shook hands with the party, obtaining the promise of a visit from them next day, and again journeyed toward camp. Ascending a little eminence, they could overlook the broad river as it hurried on its course, and stretch the eye over a dense wood bordering the prairie—the moonbeams were glancing over the white tents, the horses quietly grazed around, and just as they entered within the inclosure of the sentry-walk the swelling notes of tattoo broke upon the stillness of the scene.

The night was too pleasant to waste in sleep, and the return party from Fort Madison were joined by several more of their companions, who determined to hold a social sitting, and after the roll-call, adjourned to an elm grove, where the events of the day—the visit to the fort—the revolutionary pair—the lovely granddaughter, and the meeting with Black-Hawk, afforded plenty of matter for a pleasant gossip. Among this company was Corporal Tim, whose fund of anecdote seemed as prolific as the widow's cruse. He had been the life of the regiment from the first enlistment, and his store of information seemed as fresh and plenty as ever. I never heard a man tell a story better than Corporal Tim could, and it may not be wondered at that he was called upon on the present occasion to enliven the party with what a sailor scruples not to denominate a yarn, but which the corporal always declared to be "real matter of fact."

"This fact," said he, clearing his throat, "I know to be true, because I've heard the old gentleman tell it more than twenty times without altering a single word. Down there in Kentucky," said Tim, " when the country was all wild and unsettled, Daniel Boon began to feel that the state that he was living in was getting to be too much crowded, and so he and his brother that used to be called the squire, and a nigger boy, thought that they'd come over and take a hunt through Powell's Valley. You see Dan had been down there the year before, and had taken a terrible liking to the country thereabouts, because, as he used to say, there was plenty of elbow-room. The people down through Virginia and North Carolina were coming in too thick, and a man had not a place to breathe in. Dan was brought up in Culpepper county, and did nothing when a boy but fire at targets, until he got so that he could bring down a squirrel only by taking away his breath without touching him."

Some of the party looked a little incredulous at this, but Tim assured them that it was a fact, which was enough to establish it beyond a doubt, so he went on again.

" The story that I am going to tell you, is just as Dan used to tell it himself. He said that he was hunting one day along side of the Cumberland mountain, and discovered a gap or low place in the mountain, which he ascended to the top, and thence he imagined he could see to the Ohio river. He thought in his own mind that it was the most beautiful country in the world. He returned to the camp, and informed his brother what he had seen, telling him that they must up and go across the mountain. They did so, and traveled on to Scragg's Creek, where the deer were so plenty that they soon loaded their seven horses with shaved skins, and he started his brother and the servant boy back with them to North Carolina. He told his brother to bring back to him as many horses as he could get, and he would have their loads ready against his return. He staid and hunted there, and never saw the face of man for eight months to a day. He declared that he never enjoyed himself better in his life; he had three dogs that kept his camp while he was hunting, and at night he would lie by his fire and sing every song he could think of, while the dogs would sit round him and give as much attention as if they understood every word he was saying.

"At the end of eight months his brother and servant boy came to him with fourteen horses. His brother informed him, that when he got into North Carolina with his peltry, the Indians had fallen upon the frontiers, and that he had to go with others against them. Boon had the packs nearly all ready, and in a day or two they loaded the horses and started for home. They traveled the first day, and until about ten o'clock the next day, when he saw four Indians, with as many horses loaded with beaver fur. They were crossing each other; and seeing plainly that they must meet, he cautioned his brother and the servant boy not to let the Indians have the guns out of their hands, for they would be sure to make an attempt to get them, under the pretence of wanting to examine them. The Indians endeavored to get their guns, but they would not let them get possession of them. The Indians then went round Dan's horses and drove them off with their own. Dan said he looked hard after them awhile, and then (not thinking it prudent to attack four men on their guard with but one man and a boy to back him) he put off for home. They went on that day and till nine or ten o'clock of the next: he then observed to his brother and the boy, that if they would stick to him he would turn about and follow the Indians even to their towns but he would have his skins and horses back. They agreed to it, and immediately pursued hard after them, and came in sight of them the fourth day. 'Now,' said Boon, 'we must trail them on till they stop to eat.'

The Indians at length halted, hoppled their horses, cooked and ate, Boon and his companions watching them all the while. He well knew that having eaten they would all lie down to sleep, except one. They did so, and the one who was on guard sat on a log at the head of the others, and Boon and his boys had to creep on all fours for a hundred yards, to get near enough to shoot. Boon then told his brother that he would take for his own mark the one on the log—that he (the brother) must aim at the one on the right, and the boy at the one on the left, and that when he gave the signal they must fire, and keep loading and shooting, making as much noise and using as many different tones as they could. They fired, and he *tilted his man over the log*, but the others bore him off. The Indians fled, and they followed for three quarters of a mile, shooting and yelling; then came back, gathered their own horses and those of the Indians, put on their packs and the packs of beaver fur, and drove them safe to his own house in North Carolina."

The report of a gun, followed by a loud command of "Turn out the guard!" here broke Tim's story off, and warned the party that "something was to pay" in camp, and taking different routes, they cautiously slipped by the sentinels and gained the quarters unobserved.

The camp by this time had become alarmed; the

prisoners' roll was called, and one was missing. This fellow had contrived to slip off his handcuffs, and by cutting through the back of the guard tent, watched the opportunity when the sentinel's back was toward him to give him the slip, but making somewhat of a rustling noise as he scampered over the dry leaves and brush, he failed to elude the quick eye of the soldier on the second guard-post, who levelled his carbine, but fired without effect. This vigilant sentinel was none other than our quondam friend Turpin, (a sketch of whose character is given in another portion of this volume,) whose celebrity as a speculator had long ere this become a proverb throughout the regiment, but who, before this signal act of promptness, had evinced but few traces of either courage or decision.

A detachment of the guard was immediately ordered in pursuit of the fugitive, but returned after several hours search without success. The next morning two detachments more, each under the command of a lieutenant, were sent in quest of the deserter, but in like manner returned from a fruitless search, after spending three entire days in scouring the woods and hiding-places in every direction. Weeks passed on, but no tidings of the fugitive; he had probably steered his course down the Mississippi and sought a retreat from observation and pursuit in some retired part of the country.

After all, the deserter must be an unhappy being, however pressing the ills which drove him to the event. He carries with him the burden of an unquiet conscience, and must ever be haunted with the dread of apprehension. He knows the story of his wrongs, but finds no sympathy; for truly, in the language of the bard, "The thief doth fear each bush an officer."

CHAPTER III.

Like the crusaders returning from the wars of Palestine, and wending their way toward their native land after their weary pilgrimage; turning to take a last look at the holy city ere they depart from it for ever; bending forward in fond anxiety toward the destined goal, still casting one long lingering look behind; so may now be seen here and there a solitary dragoon, returning from his toilsome campaigns, to once more mingle in the scenes and with the friends of home and childhood, happy in his deliverance, as the bird rescued from the cage, or the convict liberated from his cell.

Freed from the monotonous bustle of the camp, the world wears to him a brighter and more lovely aspect; he can now revel in its enjoyments without the heavy clank of his chains tracking his footsteps; no longer the bugle note echoes in his ear, or the harsh command claim his pliant obedience; he now can breathe free air and feel a right to mingle with his fellow-beings, and mould his pleasures to the dictates of his will, regardless of the tyrannical displeasure of "a little brief authority."

Experience is the best, but the most severe of masters; if its lessons are severe, they are at all events lasting; did the pathway of life lead us ever amid its sweets, we would lose half of its enjoyments; it is the thorny path and severer trials that makes our happiness the richer for the contrast. The dragoons have read a lesson from its pages that death only can obliterate.

Liberty! happy, thrice happy sound! he only can

taste thy sweets in full, who has drank of the bitter cup of thy bereavement! What were the enjoyments of Damocles when surrounded by the profusion of an eastern court, while the glittering sword impended over his head hung by a single hair? Prize liberty, ye who enjoy it, as the jewel of your existence; and when ye envy the glitter of this world's trappings, remember that too often it is only the gilded harness of slavery and oppression.

* * * * *
* * * * *

It was on the afternoon of a lovely day toward the close of summer, when the approach of a new detachment was announced to the dragoons stationed at Camp Jackson. There is a certain indescribable feeling of excitement caused by the arrival of new recruits at a military station which can only be appreciated by those who have been long accustomed to look upon the same faces, and engage day after day in the same dull routine of duty. New faces often wear familiar features, and new companions often prove to be old friends; their coming always serves to enliven the camp, and never fails to impart a tone of cheerfulness to almost every soldier.

The new detachment came nearer and nearer, and their bright blades and trappings glimmered in the sunbeams as they defiled over the rich green prairie extending eastward from the encampment. The dragoons flocked from their quarters to greet their new companions, each eager to trace among them the features of some familiar face. Now the deep notes of the bugle rang across the plain and every minute shortened the space between them and the camp—every countenance seemed to speak some pleasurable anticipation as their eyes eagerly sought to catch a first glimpse at the new comers.

In double column the detachment approached the scene of their new habitation, and at the word of command, the horses, as if instinctively, obeyed at the check of their riders, and martialled themselves in line before the encampment. Among this youthful band was one whose quick eyes glanced hurriedly over the features of the assembled throng; his ruddy cheeks glowing with the freshness and energy of youth, and his light curling hair escaping in ringlets from beneath his forage cap. Again and again did his large blue eyes search with an eager and inquiring glance every visage in the crowd, as if he would read there some well known features.

The captain of the new troop now dashed the rowels in his horse's sides, and rode furiously from one flank to the other, surveying the ranks with an apparent solicitude that they should sustain, by their deportment, his reputation as a tactician; then taking his station in front, he gave the command,

"Attention! prepare to dismount. Dismount!" which last command was obeyed by the troop with an alacrity that evinced the eagerness with which they complied with it.

"Lead off by the left flank!" cried the captain, and each young trooper hastened to conduct his charger to the inclosure appropriated for their reception.

Having performed the duties of the stable and unburdened themselves of their accoutrements, the newly recruited dragoons began to mingle with their somewhat more experienced companions, and many a hearty salutation was exchanged as friend met friend with eager joyousness.

But the young blue-eyed soldier, with his curling locks, stopped not to listen to their friendly salutations, but with an anxious face that told of " hope deferred," hurriedly searched every tent throughout the encampment.

"I thought," said he to himself, "that he would have been the first to meet me, but in vain has my eye wandered over every countenance, and still I cannot see him—he could not have wantonly hid from me—no, no, he must have read my anxiety in my look. Perhaps he is sick!" continued the young soldier, as at length he had searched the last tent in vain to meet the embrace of a brother!

His eye glanced toward the hospital, and his countenance once more became lit up with a smile of anticipation, though tinged with the tenderness of anxiety. Hurriedly he bent his steps toward the habitation of the sick—but even there he found not him he sought. His countenance fell—the big tear started to his eye, and for a moment he stood the picture of disappointed hope.

In the anticipation of meeting with a long absent brother had this youthful votary at the shrine of Mars mingled in the revelry and hardships of the camp; from one station to another had he journeyed in this expectation; but still they met not each other; he came but a few hours too late; at noon that very day the brother whom he sought had bade farewell to his companions and commenced the journey of his homeward route. Thus did they unconsciously avoid each other. Still not here did their sorrows end; the same disappointment that the young soldier now experienced in not finding a brother at the camp, awaited that brother upon his return to the home where he anticipated a like meeting.

Ye who read these pages without appreciating the fullness of sorrow centered in the first moments of blighted anticipation—who have been cradled in the lap of luxury, and are strangers to disappointments and sorrows, traverse back with me in imagination through the simple detail of this narrative. Have ye followed beloved parents to the grave? Have ye been called to mourn over the decay of early hopes and blasted prospects? Have ye struggled with the ills of adversity, and become familiar with its attendant evils? If ye have, then may ye anticipate something of the feelings of a youth who had left the precincts of a home rendered alternately bright and clouded by the chequered pathway of life, to enter upon the dull and dreary duties of a soldier's life, willing to endure its hardships, and withstand its trials and privations, that he might meet with a brother, and share with him his toilsome and heavy hours.

Anticipation may serve to keep up a forced excitement, which must soon become the more deeply disappointed, when, after months of fruitless search, the desired object eludes our grasp at the moment when we had fancied its attainment most certain.

O how altered the prospect! how blank the future! how lustreless every scene, that but the moment before had glowed with buoyancy and life! how nerveless every spring of action! how cold and callous to every thing around it, becomes the heart, when sunk under the pressure of the disappointment of a long cherished hope.

Such, if indeed from this picture you may appreciate them, were the feelings of the young dragoon, whose large blue eyes had in vain searched amid the throng of the camp to rest upon the features of a brother—through their long lashes now glistened the tear-drop, but in a moment it was dashed aside, and forbidden to return—his high soul yielded but for a season to sorrow, then assumed its wonted temperament—happy indeed is he, who can look upon sorrows and trials with the eye of a philosopher, nor yet forget the tenderer sympathies of our nature.

But time is the grand panacea for all our afflictions—the seasons rolled around—again the cold blast swept over the prairie—the broad Mississippi was sealed with a covering of ice, and nature betook herself to repose. There is something delightful in the appearance of a winter in the far-off regions of the west—prairies—trees—mountains—cabins all covered with their mantle of snow—and through the cloudless night the pale moon, casting her mild beams almost shadowless upon the broad expanse, seems striving to lengthen out the departing day.

With the returning spring again came the usual accompaniments to the soldier's duty—new recruits were enlisted to fill up the many vacancies in the corps; the horses were got in readiness, and all things about the camp put in requisition for another campaign. The following extract is from one of the dragoons:

"I am of opinion that this summer's campaign will be attended with all the trials and privations of the last, without any of the exciting scenes that yielded interest to that. I would much rather remain where I am, than again tramp through the savage regions, beyond the last traces of a civilized foot-step, under the heat of a burning sun, over shadowless prairies, and all for the sake of looking at a few painted Indians: to be subjected to every hardship—suffer for want of water, and deprived not only of all the comforts, but even destitute at times of the necessaries of life—let him who likes, be a soldier!"

At the end of the same letter was the following postscript:

"I have broken open my letter, after having once sealed, to inform you of the unfortunate circumstance which occurred last evening. Your Byron is no more; he expired, after a short illness, upon the prairie, from whence, this morning, his lifeless body was removed to the water side. He fell into the hands of Bugler Goodrich after your departure, and received from him all the kindness and attention which it would have been possible for you to have bestowed yourself."

I was led to exclaim, upon reading the above postscript, Alas, poor Byron!

It would be cruel in the extreme were I to forget in this history to pay a due tribute of respect to thy memory, thou kindest and most amiable of horses. Yes, indeed, "thou partner of my toil," many a pleasant day have we had together; and although the wolves of the prairie, and the buzzards, that oft cast an envious glance at thee ere thy gentle spirit fled from its exhausted frame, have fed their ravenous appetites upon thy flesh; yet, Byron, will I not forget thee; thou wast a faithful horse to me, and I will be thy faithful chronicler; thy character shall not suffer at my hands; the world shall hear of thee, Byron, and wherever these pages shall transmit the story of the trials wherein thou didst bear a conspicuous share of the glory, there shall thy name be heard. Farewell, Byron! thou wast but a horse, yet thou wast the most amiable of thy race.

At Jefferson Barracks, at the time of drawing our

horses by lot, I had previously fancied a dark sorrel that I had picked out at the pasture ground at St. Louis. One of my companions who stood next in line to me while the drawing was going on, held this horse by the halter, and it chanced that I had hold of the very one that his eye had rested upon; and as strange as it may appear, every other horse and man in the company had been drawn except him and myself and our respective horses. He then drew, and my horse fell to his lot. I of course, being the last, had no need to draw, and accordingly, we agreeing to "swap," each got the horse that he had chosen. I named mine Byron, after his illustrious namesake, and bearing such a title, he soon became well known through the regiment.

CHAPTER IV.

Conclusion.

Reader,

I know not to whom I address myself, but I will imagine you a father of a family—a man who has seen his children grow up around him and go forth into the world. Have you a son a soldier? If perchance you have, practice resignation and hope for his return. If you have not, tell your sons, when they go forth, to shun the recruiting officer as they would avoid the upas tree; tell them that his gold is dross, his promises lies!

Are you a mother? as you rock the cradle of your infant boy, sing to him no warlike ditty; and when he shall listen to your never-to-be-forgotten admonitions, tell him never to be a soldier.

Do I speak to a young man entering fresh upon the pathway of life? learn by the experience of others, and heed not the visionary fables of glory at the cannon's mouth; flee away from the rendezvous, for fear of being entrapped into misery.

But perhaps this volume may be in the hand of one, who, as his eye rests upon page after page of its contents, can say AMEN to my injunctions and advice. Cheer up, despairing soldier, the longest day of sorrow has an end. The bright sun will penetrate through the darkest clouds. Your season of sorrow is almost over; learn a lesson from the past; go to your home and your friends and tell them to profit by your experience.

Have I in this volume unconsciously aroused the spirit of military glory in a youthful mind? If so, friend, alter thy determination; rather would I blot out the passage with my tears than be the cause of your misery. Here again I warn you, enlist not, as you value your own happiness; if you would not, for a term of years, willingly deprive yourself of liberty, enjoyment, self-respect, society, friends, the opinion of the world, all, all that serves to make life worth living for, then, I repeat it, do not enlist.

At the time that I am now writing I have lost much of that bitterness of feeling that I ever experienced during my service in the army, yet I now unhesitatingly say, that were I reduced to the last extremity, and starvation stared me in the face, the army would be my last resort.

Perhaps throughout this volume I have spoken in such terms as to be misunderstood in regard to the scenes of pleasure and various diverting occupations that I was engaged in; I would now do away every impression that any such recital was calculated to make, by stating that such scenes were "like angel's visits, few and far between," and like a drowning man catching at straws, one clings to them in hope of diverting his mind for a season from the real wretchedness of his situation.

Of all the blessings which serve to add happiness to our existence, liberty is the dearest; without it, all others lose their charm. The poor man, who labors for his daily bread, and gains an honest livelihood by the sweat of his brow, feels, even amid the toils and labors of his occupation, the satisfaction that his will is, at least, his own; no task-master watches his movements, no jealous eye of little brief authority rests like an incubus upon his every action. Tell me, is not he far happier than could be the man, even though surrounded with all the luxuries of life, still subject to the nod of a tyrant?

If I have spoken boldly on this point, I have also spoken feelingly—and it has been my hope, while writing these pages, that they might be the means of warning many an unwary youth to be on his guard, and take care how he gives too credent an ear to the artful stories of the recruiting officer.

There is an indescribable feeling of excitement aroused by the martial tones of the spirit-stirring drum, and the swelling echoes of the bugle note, that the mind, once enraptured with their sound, can never entirely divest itself of—'tis this that casts around the unwary youth the first web of that enchantment, which, like the fabled spell of the magician, lures with delicious poison, and lures only to deceive—'tis this that, amid the tumult and horror of the battle-field, inspires the warrior with an ardor that prompts him to the scene of fiercest conflict, and endues him with a more than human bravery—'tis this that melts the soul of the same blood-stained warrior, when, stretched upon his couch, he listens to the milder strains of music, when some fairy hand sweeps o'er the magic notes.

I have seen the group of infant soldiers swarming like the gathering hive, after the discordant, but soul-inspiring noise of the kettle-drum—and I have seen the aged veteran with his hoary locks, transfixed with mute and breathless ecstacy at the music of the martial band. I have seen the tawny savage of the wilderness forget the elk that led him in the chase, as the bugle note vibrated on his ear—and the dying soldier seem to lengthen out his last breath, to catch the echo of its tones.

O there is a thrill that music gives the soul, unlike the power of all other earthly things—it can rouse the gentlest into fury, or chain the monster with a silken thread. Beware then, you who may enjoy the blessings of home and friends, the comforts of the domestic circle, and the cheerful fireside—beware, I say, lest the tones of martial melody shall call you from your happy homes, to be the pliant slaves of a few favorite children of a privileged monopoly.

A soldier's life is, indeed, the life of a slave: slavery rendered the more galling by the reflection that he riveted his own chains. The citizen can but little appreciate the feelings of a youthful mind thus trammeled, made to bow in subjection to those whom he heartily despises—whose feelings are blunted to all the finer sensibilities of our natures, and whose ears are shut to every consideration of pity or compassion—who are clothed in an authority which they know not how to exercise, save in gratification of a selfish and misjudged pride. In speaking thus, I do not speak of all the officers; no, there are some, who, despite the situations they occupy, still retain the feelings of men, of husbands, and of fathers. But enough of this—I have already, I hope, said sufficient to satisfy the most ambitious aspirant after military fame, that the American army holds out to him but slender hopes of promotion and glory; and should any enlist in the service, after having given these pages a candid perusal, he can afterward, when he would weep over his folly, blame only himself.

In drawing this volume to a conclusion, many, very many reflections crowd upon my mind. I can wander in memory back through all the scenes that are here recorded, and dwell fondly and delightfully upon many a recollection. Time has passed away—and having been withdrawn from the every-day duties of the camp, I can now cull from the crowd of my reflections, many upon which memory loves to pause.

To the reader who has borne with me through these pages, I now must say farewell—indulging the hope that their perusal may be instrumental in turning the feet of many an unsuspecting youth from the paths of military thraldom. Life is too precious and too short to be thrown away in empty and fruitless searches after the bubble reputation; and least of all should the young enthusiast seek it at the cannon's mouth.

THE END.

The Far Western Frontier

An Arno Press Collection

[Angel, Myron, editor]. **History of Nevada.** 1881.

Barnes, Demas. **From the Atlantic to the Pacific, Overland.** 1866.

Beadle, J[ohn] H[anson]. **The Undeveloped West; Or, Five Years in the Territories.** [1873].

Bidwell, John. **Echoes of the Past:** An Account of the First Emigrant Train to California. [1914].

Bowles, Samuel. **Our New West.** 1869.

Browne, J[ohn] Ross. **Adventures in the Apache Country.** 1871.

Browne, J[ohn] Ross. **Report of the Debates in the Convention of California, on the Formation of the State Constitution.** 1850.

Byers, W[illiam] N. and J[ohn] H. Kellom. **Hand Book to the Gold Fields of Nebraska and Kansas.** 1859.

Carvalho, S[olomon] N. **Incidents of Travel and Adventure in the Far West; with Col. Fremont's Last Expedition Across the Rocky Mountains.** 1857.

Clayton, William. **William Clayton's Journal.** 1921.

Cooke, P[hilip] St. G[eorge]. **Scenes and Adventures in the Army.** 1857.

Cornwallis, Kinahan. **The New El Dorado; Or, British Columbia.** 1858.

Davis, W[illiam] W. H. **El Gringo; Or, New Mexico and Her People.** 1857.

De Quille, Dan. (William Wright). **A History of the Comstock Silver Lode & Mines.** 1889.

Delano, A[lonzo]. **Life on the Plains and Among the Diggings;** Being Scenes and Adventures of an Overland Journey to California. 1854.

Ferguson, Charles D. **The Experiences of a Forty-niner in California.** (Originally published as *The Experiences of a Forty-niner During Thirty-four Years' Residence in California and Australia*). 1888.

Forbes, Alexander. **California:** A History of Upper and Lower California. 1839.

Fossett, Frank. **Colorado:** Its Gold and Silver Mines, Farms and Stock Ranges, and Health and Pleasure Resorts. 1879.

The Gold Mines of California: Two Guidebooks. 1973.

Gray, W[illiam] H[enry]. **A History of Oregon, 1792–1849.** 1870.

Green, Thomas J. **Journal of the Texian Expedition Against Mier.** 1845.

Henry, W[illiam] S[eaton]. **Campaign Sketches of the War with Mexico.** 1847.

[Hildreth, James]. **Dragoon Campaigns to the Rocky Mountains.** 1836.

Hines, Gustavus. **Oregon:** Its History, Condition and Prospects. 1851.

Holley, Mary Austin. **Texas:** Observations, Historical, Geographical and Descriptive. 1833.

Hollister, Ovando J[ames]. **The Mines of Colorado.** 1867.

Hughes, John T. **Doniphan's Expedition.** 1847.

Johnston, W[illiam] G. **Experiences of a Forty-niner.** 1892.

Jones, Anson. **Memoranda and Official Correspondence Relating to the Republic of Texas, Its History and Annexation.** 1859.

Kelly, William. **An Excursion to California Over the Prairie, Rocky Mountains, and Great Sierra Nevada.** 1851. 2 Volumes in 1.

Lee, D[aniel] and J[oseph] H. Frost. **Ten Years in Oregon.** 1844.

Macfie, Matthew. **Vancouver Island and British Columbia.** 1865.

Marsh, James B. **Four Years in the Rockies; Or, the Adventures of Isaac P. Rose.** 1884.

Mowry, Sylvester. **Arizona and Sonora:** The Geography, History, and Resources of the Silver Region of North America. 1864.

Mullan, John. **Miners and Travelers' Guide to Oregon, Washington, Idaho, Montana, Wyoming, and Colorado.** 1865.

Newell, C[hester]. **History of the Revolution in Texas.** 1838.

Parker, A[mos] A[ndrew]. **Trip to the West and Texas.** 1835.

Pattie, James O[hio]. **The Personal Narrative of James O. Pattie, of Kentucky.** 1831.

Rae, W[illiam] F[raser]. **Westward by Rail:** The New Route to the East. 1871.

Ryan, William Redmond. **Personal Adventures in Upper and Lower California, in 1848-9.** 1850/1851. 2 Volumes in 1.

Shaw, William. **Golden Dreams and Waking Realities:** Being the Adventures of a Gold-Seeker in California and the Pacific Islands. 1851.

Stuart, Granville. **Montana As It Is:** Being a General Description of its Resources. 1865.

Texas in 1840, Or the Emigrant's Guide to the New Republic. 1840.

Thornton, J. Quinn. **Oregon and California in 1848.** 1849. 2 Volumes in 1.

Upham, Samuel C. **Notes of a Voyage to California via Cape Horn, Together with Scenes in El Dorado, in the Years 1849–'50.** 1878.

Woods, Daniel B. **Sixteen Months at the Gold Diggings.** 1851.

Young, F[rank] G., editor. **The Correspondence and Journals of Captain Nathaniel J. Wyeth, 1831–6.** 1899.

Library
Sampson Technical Institute